VĀSTUSŪTRA UPANIṢAD

Vāstusūtra Upaniṣad

THE ESSENCE OF FORM IN SACRED ART

Sanskrit Text, English Translation and Notes by
ALICE BONER
SADASIVA RATH SARMA
BETTINA BÄUMER

MOTILAL BANARSIDASS PUBLISHERS
PRIVATE LIMITED • DELHI

First Edition: Delhi, 1982
Reprint: Delhi, 1986
Third Revised Edition: Delhi, 1996
Fourth Revised Edition: Delhi, 2000

ISBN: 81-208-0090-7 (Cloth)
ISBN: 81-208-1455-x (Paper)

Also available at:

MOTILAL BANARSIDASS
236, 9th Main III Block, Jayanagar, Bangalore 560 001
41 U.A. Bungalow Road, Jawahar Nagar, Delhi 110 007
8 Mahalaxmi Chamber, Warden Road, Mumbai 400 026
120 Royapettah High Road, Mylapore, Chennai 600 004
Sanas Plaza, 1302, Baji Rao Road, Pune 411 002
8 Camac Street, Calcutta 700 017
Ashok Rajpath, Patna 800 004
Chowk, Varanasi 221 001

Printed in India
BY JAINENDRA PRAKASH JAIN AT SHRI JAINENDRA PRESS,
A-45 NARAINA, PHASE I, NEW DELHI 110 028
AND PUBLISHED BY NARENDRA PRAKASH JAIN FOR
MOTILAL BANARSIDASS PUBLISHERS PRIVATE LIMITED,
BUNGALOW ROAD, DELHI 110 007

CONTENTS

PREFACE TO THE FIRST EDITION

After long studies and meditations before the sculptures in the cave temples of Ellora, Alice Boner discovered on her own what she called *Principles of Composition in Hindu Sculpture.*[1] For many years she had tried to find in the Śilpaśāstras, the authoritative texts on temple architecture and sculpture, confirmation of her insight. First she came across the *Śilpa Prakāśa*, also published by E.J. Brill, Leiden (1966). Thereupon she struck on the *Vāstusūtra Upaniṣad* which at the same time confirmed and substantiated her proper intuition. It was her deep perception of the archetypal language of Form[2] which helped her to understand this important text even in the corrupt form of the manuscripts which had at first come to light. When finally a better manuscript was found by Pandit Sadasiva Rath Sarma, a Devanāgarī transcript had to be prepared and the critical work on the text had to start again. But Alice Boner soon fell ill and had to leave India in 1978, never to return again. At that time, she entrusted me with the revision of the text and translation, including the critical and exegetical notes. Even during her illness, Alice Boner and I worked together on the text, and till the last weeks of her life she gave me precious advice. It was her great desire to see this text published – the culmination of her work and thought on fundamental principles of Indian art. In April 1981, I could only convey to her the news that the manuscript had been completed and handed over to the publisher. A few days later she passed away.

Pandit Sadasiva Rath Sarma has given us invaluable assistance in deciphering the meaning of the text in the light of his traditional knowledge. He has also provided the line drawings as illustrations.

Varanasi
December 1981 Bettina Bäumer

---

[1]Originally published by E.J. Brill, Leiden, 1962; new Indian edition: Delhi, Motilal Banarsidass, 1990.

[2]Cf. her early article "The Symbolic Aspect of Form", in J.I.S.O.A. XVII, 1949.

PREFACE

TO THE THIRD REVISED EDITION

by
BETTINA BÄUMER

After the first publication of this text in 1982 and its reprint in 1986, general interest in the principles and practice of form in the Indian traditions of architecture, sculpture and other visual arts has increased tremendously. Not only art-historians and indologists, but also modern architects and artists, as well as the general public, are now keenly aware of the need to go back to the origins and insights of this almost unbroken tradition, so that we don't lose our roots and fall prey to the superficial imitation endemic in modern culture. Therefore the texts describing the principles and practice of form, namely the so-called Śilpa- and Vāstuśāstras, are no longer of merely historical and scholarly interest, they also concern our daily lives; it may be the way we deal with the environment, the space in which we live and the objects of use and beauty, not to mention the sacred which has been mostly governed by the rules of tradition.

Due to this interest and research in the field of Śilpa- and Vāstuśāstra, some additional texts have been published in the last 14 years.[3] Unfortunately, the market has also been flooded with a lot of cheap literature on Vāstu/Śilpa, promising success in all worldly and superworldly matters if one adheres to the principles of Vāstu described therein. Hence the need is that much greater for authentic texts and translations.

In light of all the hitherto known Śilpaśāstras, the *Vāstusūtra Upaniṣad* still stands out as an extraordinary text. This has been recognized by eminent art-historians like Dr R.N. Misra: "The *Vāstusūtra Upaniṣad* is important for many reasons, but most significantly in that it uncovers a lost tradition even as it offers the śāstric basis of compositional diagrams of sculpture as well as their artisanal

[3]For example, *Mayamatam*, Treatise of Housing, Architecture and Iconography, ed. and transl. by Bruno Dagens, 2 vols., IGNCA and Motilal Banarsidass, Delhi 1994; *Śilparatnakośa*, A Glossary of Orissan Temple Architecture, ed. and transl. by Bettina Bäumer and Rajendra Prasad Das, IGNCA and Motilal Banarsidass, Delhi 1994.

connections as were in practice ..."[4] He also relates the text to the larger context of Indian literature, aesthetics and art traditions. The uniqueness of the text lies in the fact that it is concerned with fundamental (and therefore universal) principles of form (*rūpa*) in the larger context of a tradition in harmony with cosmic and divine forces (*adhibhūta* and *adhidaiva*), and their relation to the human body and mind (*adhyātma*).

In her Introduction to the first edition of the *Vāstusūtra Upaniṣad*, Alice Boner elaborates on the content and special significance of this text. However, while revising the text, I was struck by some interesting points which were not clearly noticed in the first edition.

One point worth noting, which has also been discussed by Alice Boner, is that this text which has *vāstu* in its title actually speaks more of *rūpa* and *śilpa*, in the sense of sculpture. It frequently refers to the discipline of art as *vāstuveda* (e.g. III.12), with a great sense of authority. The term *rūpa-vāstu-ṣaḍaṅgaṃ śilpam* (I.8) explains the relationship of these terms: the text deals with the six limbs of art (*śilpa*), their form and layout (*rūpa-vāstu*). Here the meaning of the term *vāstu* is more associated with the ground plan, the dwelling-place and abode of the gods in an image-panel, and not with a temple. In fact, the entire text does not contain any of the common words for 'temple' – *prāsāda, devālaya, mandira, devagṛha* etc. *Vāstu* then refers in a more general sense to the structural principles and to the basic form-language, of which both, architecture and sculpture, are but the expression.

Instead of speaking of structural temples, the VSU mentions cave temples and image halls for meditation of ascetics. The terms used are *pratimāśālā* (I.9, *rūpaśālā* in the Ṭippaṇī), *rūpaśaile rūpaśālā* (IV.10) and *śailaguhā* (VI.6). Could the term *mahāśaila* used by the Ṭippaṇī (on I.9) also be referring to monolithic architecture/sculpture ? There are not many examples in Orissa, but in any case the text goes much beyond the boundaries of its place of origin.

Secular architecture (*lokavāstu, gṛhaśālā*, III.6) is only hinted at, and throughout the text the Vedic origins of the various forms and structures which cannot even be classified under the terms 'architecture' or 'sculpture', are stressed. The parallelism between the science of Śulva and Śilpa is constantly demonstrated, as in the case of the

[4] R.N. Misra, "Traditional Indian Art: Alice Boner and After", Lalit Kala Akademi, Alice Boner Memorial Lecture, Bhubaneswar, 27.1.1995, p. 6 (unpublished).

Yūpa, or sacrificial post, and its anthropomorphic transformation in the image of the Puruṣa.

Again, the common element which justifies the title *Vāstusūtra-Upaniṣad* is the sacred geometry underlying sacrificial altars and so on (Śulva), anthropomorphic images and image-panels (Śilpa) and sacred or secular architecture (Vāstu). But here geometry is not merely a technical device, it is the very means by which to infuse inner meaning (*bhāva*) into the work of art (V.1).

In the case of image-making, the basic geometrical diagram is called *pañjara*, 'cage' or 'skeleton', and it consists of lines, points, circles, squares, triangles and diagonals. More than mere geometry, all these basic forms are part of an organic view of the universe and the human body. It is here where the originality of the VSU lies, for these conceptions are not found in any other Vāstuśāstra currently known. As Dr R.N. Misra remarked: "The making of a *pañjara* by the *sthāpaka* was supposed to be a ritual act simulating the process of creation, a creation which had a macrocosmic reference point. In this entire setting the circle (*vṛtta*) was not merely a spherical shape but the symbol of the Universe as well as of Time, thus constituting the dimensions of time and space (*sa vṛttaḥ kālaḥ, vṛttam iti viśvam*) ... In that manner a *pañjara* purposely and consciously integrated the *adhibhūta* with the *adhidaiva*, the fundamental elements with the gods." (R.N. Misra, art. cit., p. 7).

The term *pañjara*, in place of which other texts such as the *Śilpa Prakāśa*[5] use *yantra*, has been found in different contexts which confirm its technical meaning in Śilpa. Since translators of such texts were often unfamiliar with Śilpa traditions, the term has generally been translated literally as 'cage'. Examples from different sources may be given: The first occurs in the *Nārada Śilpa Śāstra*, of which V. Raghavan has edited and translated the chapters on painting.[6] The text describes various motifs painted on the floor (*bhaumike*) which are either enclosed in a *pañjara*, or the *pañjara* is treated as a separate motif: *caturaśrāṃ madhyarekhikāṃ pañjarākṛtiṃ... kalpayeyuḥ*

[5]Rāmacandra Kaula, *Śilpa Prakāśa*, ed. and transl. by Alice Boner and S.R. Sarma, E.J. Brill, Leiden, 1966. A new revised edition of this text is under preparation.

[6]V. Raghavan, "Two Chapters on Painting in the Nārada Śilpa Śāstra", in: *Journal of the Indian Society of Oriental Art*, 3 (1), June 1935. The VSU also refers to Nārada as one of the propounders of the Sthāpakavidyā or Śilpavidyā (I.6).

(Pāṭha 71). Dr V. Raghavan translates it as "of square design, or with lines inside, of a shape of a *pañjara*" (p. 24), and gives the following note on *pañjara*: "*Pañjara* may simply mean cage-like design or the architectural motif of that meaning niche." (p. 31).[7] Yet, in the light of the Śilpa meaning, the passage should be translated as follows: "(Various forms) should be imagined-and-created (*kḷp-*) in the form of a compositional diagram (*pañjara*) within a square consisting of central lines (etc.)." In the previous paragraph, the text describes drawing the lines "in accordance with general measurements, in even lines and in conformity to (the rules regarding) pose-lines." (Transl. V. Raghavan, p. 24.) In his note, V. Raghavan also relates the term *aviruddha sūtrapāta* to the lines called *brahmasūtra*, etc. (p. 31). It is therefore clear that even in a different tradition of Śilpa, one ascribed to Nārada and of South Indian origin, the term *pañjara* is used, in the context of painting, in the same technical meaning of 'compositional diagram consisting of fundamental lines'.

Another confirmation comes from a completely different source, namely the Sirpur stone inscription from the time of Mahāśivagupta (8th cent. A.D.).[8] It is worth quoting it entirely:

> *divyādeḥ sakalasya jantunivahasyoccāvacaiḥ karmaṇāṃ vaicitryādayamadbhuto bahuvidhāvasthairvapuḥ pañjaraiḥ. [yaḥ] prasāda bṛ[ha]cchalena kathitaḥ saṃsāra eva sphuṭaṃ paśyantastadidaṃ manaḥ kuruta bho pāpeṣu mā bhūmipāḥ.* 21[9]

R. B. Hira Lal's translation of *pañjaraiḥ* etc. by "with cage-like bodies" is obviously besides the point. The following revised translation by Prof. R.P. Das is more in accordance with the technical meaning:

> Oh kings! do not turn your minds to sins seeing what has been clearly depicted of this world under the guise of the temple in the diversity of acts/conditions of all creatures at [different] levels high and low – from celestial beings downwards – with their bodies [sculpted/carved] in (accordance) with (diverse) *pañjaras* (compositional diagrams).

---

[7] V. Raghavan cites Dubreuil, *Dravidian Architecture*, pp. 13–14.

[8] I am grateful to Prof. R.P. Das for drawing my attention to this interesting source.

[9] *Epigraphia Indica* XI, pp. 184–201, ed. by R.B. Hira Lal.

Another confirmation of the technical meaning of the term *pañjara* comes from a text which has been frequently quoted by the Ṭippaṇī of Somabhaṭṭa on the VSU, and which has in the meantime been critically edited and translated: The *Śilparatnakośa*[10] gives the following brief definition of *pañjara*:

> The *vyakta mūrti* (manifest image) should always be based on a *pañjara*.
> On the stone (surface) a diagram should be drawn with various lines.
> The centre-point (*marman*) of the image should be ascertained in order to position the limbs. (vv. 453b–454)

In the section on image-making (Pratimālakṣaṇa) the drawing of a *pañjara* is said to be the first work of the sculptor after dressing the stone (v. 7).

In fact, in most of the early temples in Orissa and elsewhere, we find unfinished relief carvings where only the outlines have been engraved but not executed.

The architectural meaning of *pañjara*, especially in South-Indian terminology, is different in that it refers to a decorative motif which has a cage-like structure.[11]

The meaning and description of the term *pañjara* in the VSU is therefore not isolated, rather it clarifies the use of the term in other contexts in which it had not been properly understood.

As one comes to the historical question of placing the text, attention should be drawn to a few important facts which have not been noticed earlier. As mentioned before, the fact that the text does not refer to structural temples, and mentions only 'image-halls' and cave-temples, points to an early stage of development. It is difficult to relate the images described in the VSU to any particular site in Orissa, such as the Udayagiri–Khandagiri caves which are Jaina, though they do conform more to Western India Caves such as Elura. However, the reference to such image-halls and caves as places for the meditation of ascetics would apply even to Jaina and Buddhist sites as well.

---

[10] *Śilparatnakośa*, A Glossary of Orissan Temple Architecture, by Sthāpaka Nirañjana Mahāpātra, ed. and transl. by Bettina Bäumer and Rajendra Prasad Das, IGNCA and Motilal Banarsidass, Delhi 1994.

[11] Cf. *Encyclopedia of Indian Temple Architecture*, Vol. I. Part 2, Glossary, and other volumes.

The meditational purpose of images is stressed at least as much as their use in worship (*arcā, saparyā, pūjana*; the word *pūjā* as such is not used). In a text dealing with image-making and the connected rituals it is surprising not to find any reference to temples and temple worship (*pūjā*). The socio-religious implication is indicated by its remark that the aniconic Vedic sacrifice is for *brāhmaṇas*, but the other castes and women need a visible representation of the Divine in order to focus their worship in the right way (cf. I.7). The different religious traditions (here called *mārga*) arise from the worship of different deities (cf. V.24), and their names also point to an early stage, such as: Raudras worship Rudra (= Śiva), Sauras worship Sūrya, Ambinas worship Ambā, and Aiḷas worship Iḷā (comm. on V.24). Whatever may have been changed or added in the course of copying and transmission of the text in the 'semi-literate' circles of *śilpīs* and *sthapatis*, there are sufficient traces of its early origin. But this is not the place for a detailed historical discussion. I have only introduced some further points for reflection. A satisfactory solution regarding the date of origin or composition of the text cannot be found easily.

* * *

The text has been revised on the basis of the five manuscripts. At every stage of this work of comparing the edited text and manuscripts and making the necessary revisions in the text, translation and notes, Professor Rajendra Prasad Das and Sri Sadananda Das have offered me their full assistance. On the whole not many changes were made, but an added precision and faithfulness to the MSS was introduced. This includes some readings as *lectio difficilior*, where the Pandits engaged in the first edition had chosen an easier reading. The placement and identification of Sūtras was sometimes found to be different in the edited text and MS क. The new arrangement hopefully adds to the clarity.

Accordingly, some improvements could be made in the translation. For example, in Sūtra II.6, instead of the earlier translation "First a circle (is made)", the new translation reads: "In the beginning is a circle. The circle is the All." The two purposes of images, namely for meditation (*dhyāna*) and for worship (*arcā*), are mentioned in III.16 with commentary. This meaning is brought out more clearly in the new translation. Similarly, the term *rūpaśaila* in Sūtra IV.10 has been more appropriately rendered by 'cave-temple' (instead of 'rock'). Thus, without changing the overall meaning of the text and translation, as far as possible clarity and precision have been improved. Inspite of our attempts to find any other MSS, we have not been successful and have had to rely on the five previously extant MSS.

The notes of the Ṭippaṇī of MS क have been given as footnotes to the translation. In addition, a few notes have been taken from other MSS, as indicated. The critical and exegetical notes by the editors have to be read alongside the text.

ABBREVIATIONS

AB	Aitareya Brāhmaṇa
AV	Atharvaveda
AVP	Atharva Veda Paippalāda Saṃhitā
AVŚ	Atharva Veda Śaunaka Saṃhitā
Br.	Brāhmaṇa
Bṛhad. Up.	Bṛhadāraṇyaka Upaniṣad
Chānd. Up.	Chāndogya Upaniṣad
Comm.	Commentary: explanatory text of VSU following the Sūtras
Jaiminīya Up. Br.	Jaiminīya Upaniṣad Brāhmaṇa
Kauṣ. Br.	Kauṣītaki Brāhmaṇa
Muṇḍ. Up.	Muṇḍaka Upaniṣad
ṚV	Ṛgveda
ŚB	Śatapatha Brāhmaṇa
TS	Taittirīya Saṃhitā
Up.	Upaniṣad
VS	Vājasaneyi Saṃhitā
VSU	Vāstusūtra Upaniṣad

LIST OF ILLUSTRATIONS

LIST OF MANUSCRIPTS

क palmleaf, in good condition
size: 38 by 3, 5 cm.
33 leaves, 4 to 5 lines per page, broad margin
script: Oriya
Sūtras clearly marked, list of Sūtras after each Prapāṭhaka, with notes Pariśuddhi Ṭippaṇī of Somabhaṭṭa
found in 1976 at Kurumachaini village, courtesy of Sri Kalicharan Mishra of Banki
time of copying: 15th year of king Rāmacandra Deva, either Rāmacandra I, whose 15th aṅka was between 2.9.1579 and 22.8.1580, or most probably Rāmacandra III of the Khurda Bhoi dynasty, whose 15th aṅka was ca. A.D. 1829, for a ruler Rājā Haricandana.
Name of the copyist: Kāmadeva Udgātā. Probably copied by the same as the Nigama Diṇḍima Ṭippaṇī, copied in A.D. 1826–27.

Beginning: *OṂ Vāstusūtropaniṣad*
Śāntipāṭha: *bhadraṃ karṇebhiḥ...*

Colophon: *paramarṣibhyo namaḥ*
saṃpūrṇeyaṃ vāstukarmāvatāra-pippalādasya ātharvaṇīyavāstusūtropaniṣat ।
uḍradeśikena ātharvaṇodgātrā somabhaṭṭena kṛtā pariśuddhiṭippaṇī samāptā ।
idam ātharvaṇīya vāstusūtropaniṣad ātharvaṇācārya somabhaṭṭena kṛta viṣayabodhani ṭippaṇī sameta likhitaṃ mayā bāṅkī kurumacaini grāmavāsinā vāstuśāstrikāmadeva udgāthā śri Rāmacandradeva bhūpālasya pañcadaśāṅke rājā Haricandana nṛpārtha
Oṃ namo mahādevyai ।

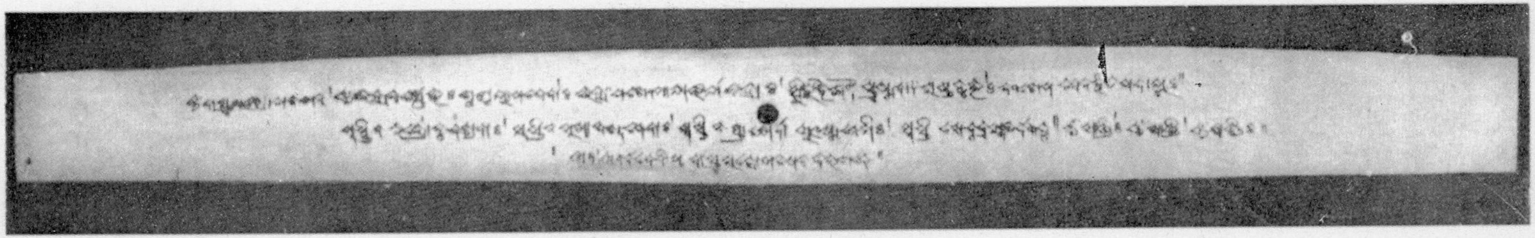

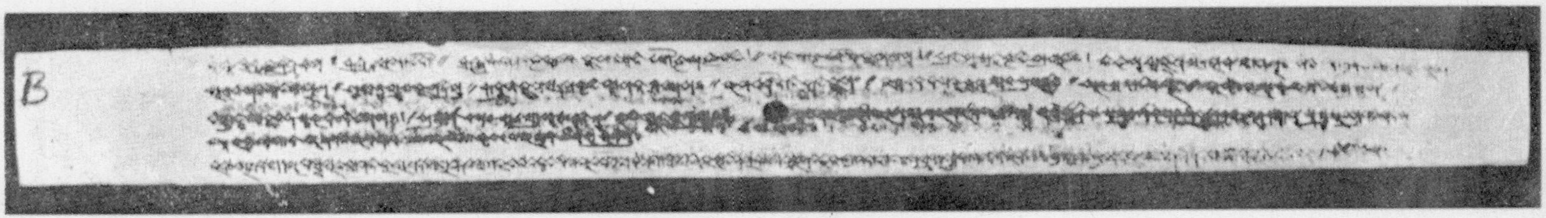

Ms क

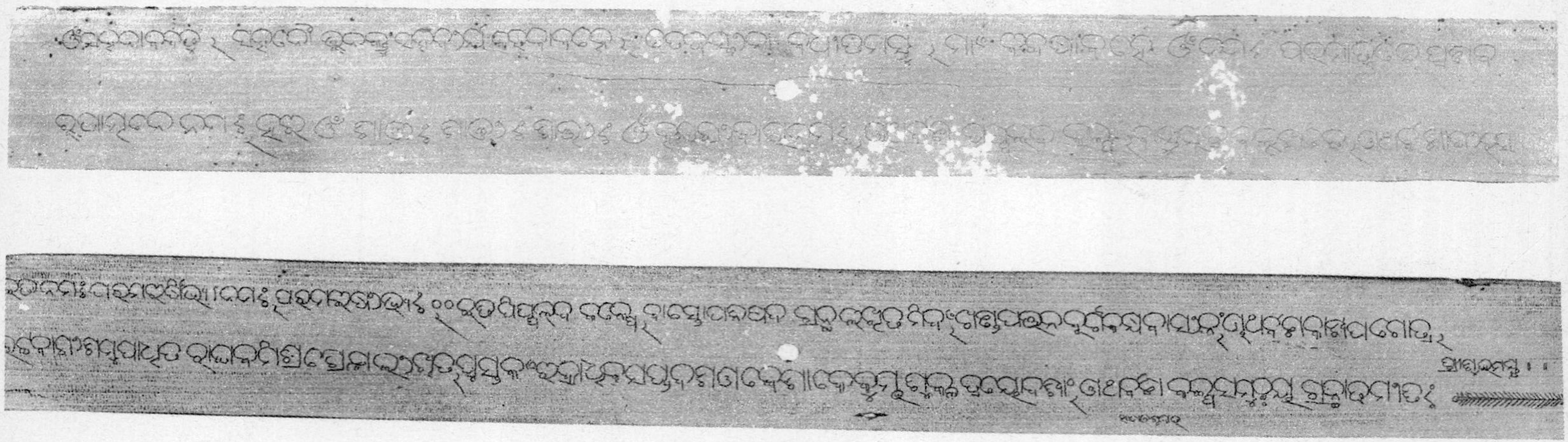

Ms ख

ख palmleaf, in good condition
size: 30 by 3, 5 cm.
65 leaves, 2 lines per page
script: Oriya (circular)
Sūtras not clearly marked, some Sūtras missing, sometimes different order, faulty Sanskrit
Date of copying: 26 February 1790
Obtained from the late Rājā of Khandapara Garh, District Puri, first discovered in 1973

Beginning: Śāntipāṭha: *sahanāvavatu...*
Oṃ namaḥ paramātmane praṇavarūpātmane namaḥ ।
OṂ hariḥ, śāntiḥ śāntiḥ śāntiḥ ।
OṂ hayagrīvāya namaḥ ।
Ātharvaṇa Pippalādakalpa Vāstusūtra vilikhyate । (p. 1)
p.2: Śāntipāṭha: *bhadraṃ karṇebhiḥ...*

Colophon: p. 64: *paramarṣibhyo namaḥ. iti brahmavedīya paṅka-kalpe divyapuruṣa bhagavantaḥ Pippalādasya vyākhyānam* ।
OṂ śāntiḥ OṂ śāntiḥ OṂ śāntiḥ ।
p. 65: *paramarṣibhyo namaḥ paramarṣibhyo. iti Pippalāda-kalpe Vāstūpaniṣadaḥ grantha likhitam idaṃ Khaṇḍapaṭṭana Durgākakṣāvāsinā Ātharva-Kāśyapagotra Bhaṭṭavāgīśa upādhita Rāghavamiśreṇa likhitam pustakaṃ Rudrādhika saptadaśa abde śāke kumbha śukla trayodaśyāṃ Ātharvaṇa-Kalpasamuccaya-granthāt iti* ।
Śrī śubham astu ।

ग palmleaf, in good condition
size: 37 by 3, 5 cm.
29 leaves, 5 lines per page, on both sides double lines with numbers within flowers
script: Devanāgarī
Sūtras not distinguished, some Sūtras missing, faulty Sanskrit, without notes, mantrakhaṇḍa in appendix (5 pages)
found at Govardhana Maṭha or Śaṅkarācārya Maṭha, Puri, courtesy of His Holiness Śaṅkarācārya Nirañjanadeva Tīrtha
time of copying: 17th aṅka of Vīrakeśarī I of Khurda Bhoi dynasty, on Vijayā Daśamī, Tuesday = October 10, 1749 A.D.

Beginning: *OṂ yadantarikṣaṃ pṛthivīmuta dyāṃ...*
Ātharvaṇīya vāstusūtropaniṣad prārabhyate
namo Pippalādagurave

Colophon: p. 29: From *Viśvakarmā mā* ... up to ... *ha saḥ svāhā* ।
likhitaṃ Vāstuvedākhyapustakaṃ sumanoharam ।
prītaye Śaṅkarācārya Govardhanamaṭheśvaraḥ ।
Vīrakeśarī bhūpālaḥ guṇeṣu cāṅkake śubhe māsāśvine kujadine vijayādaśamyā śrīrāja Kautsasagotrā Bhaṭṭavaṃśadvija mayā Caṇḍeśvarākhyaviduṣā vareṇa likhitam idam ।

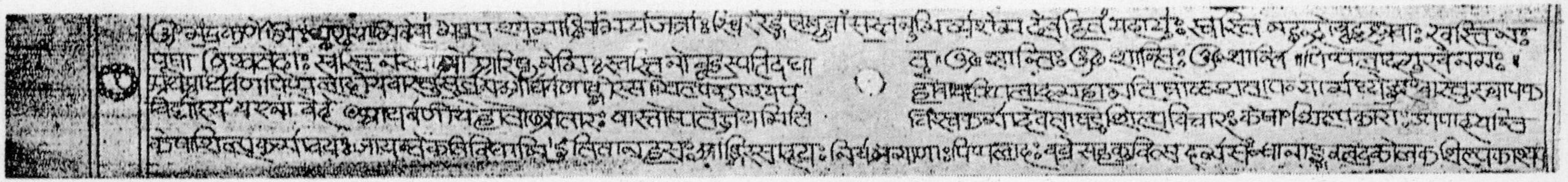

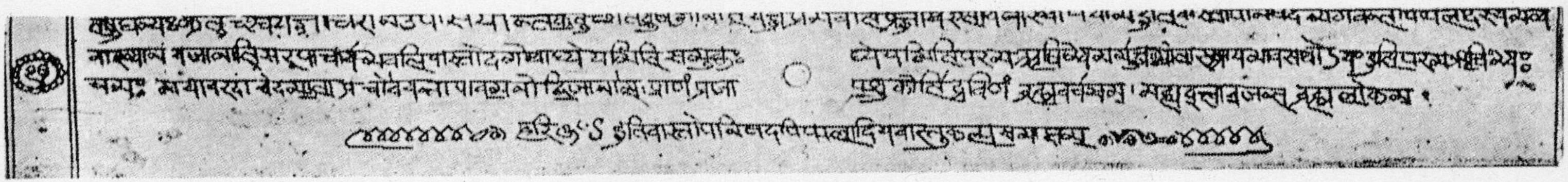

Ms ग

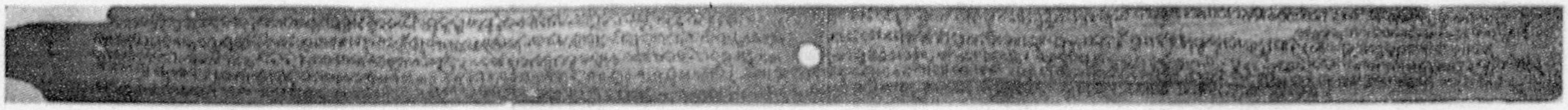

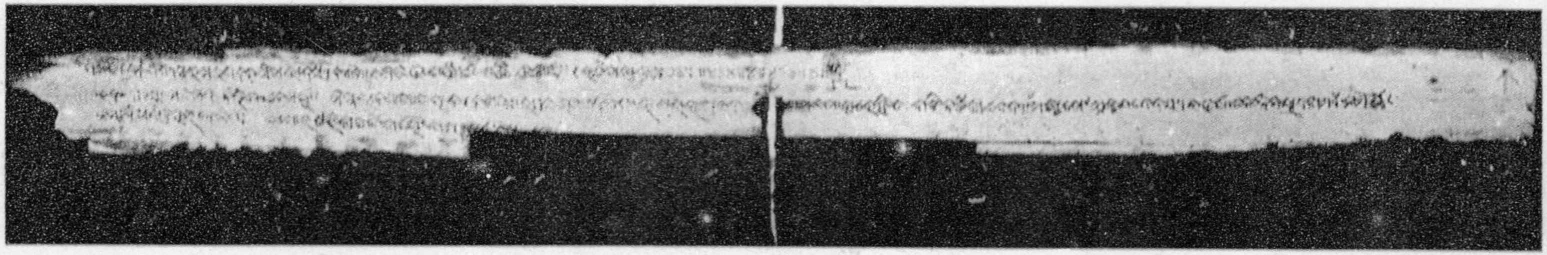

Ms घ

घ palmleaf, old, partly worm-eaten, some leaves broken (pages 10, 14, 15, 17 ruined)
size: 37 by 3 cm.
17 leaves, 5 to 6 lines per page
script: Oriya
Sūtras sometimes marked, with short notes between the lines
courtesy Pandit Raghunath Dasa of Banki, District – Cuttack
date: 4th aṅka of Mukundadeva (I from 1657–1688, 4th aṅka Vijayādaśamī would be 15 September 1659, II from 1798–1817, 4th aṅka would be 27 September 1800 A.D.

Beginning: *bhadraṃ karṇebhiḥ...* (Śāntipāṭha)
svasti no indraḥ ... (Śāntipāṭha)
Pippalāda gurave namaḥ । *Ātharvaṇa Pippalādakalpa Vāstusūtra vilikhyate* ।

Colophon: *iti saṃkalpakalpe divyapuruṣaḥ bhagavantaḥ Pippalādasya vyākhyāna* । *OṂ śāntiḥ śāntiḥ śāntiḥ* ।
iti ṣaṣṭhaprapāṭhakaḥ. idaṃ Vāstūpaniṣad vilikhyate mayā Pippalāda śākhāśākhinaḥ deśādhyāyinaḥ Ātharvavedīya Nārāyaṇa Udgāthā nāma purohitaḥ Bāṅkī carcikādevyā maṇḍape Mukundadevasya caturthāṅke vijayadaśamyāṃ saṃpūrṇā ।
namaḥ Pippalāda-gurave, namo carcikāyai ।

ङ palmleaf, in good condition, not so old
size: 31 by 3, 5 cm.
49 leaves, 4 lines per page
script: Oriya
with few notes above the lines, Sūtras not distinguished, without date
found in Nirakarapura

Beginning: *Śri gaṇeśāya namaḥ, avighnam astu* ।
Śāntipāṭha: *bhadraṃ karṇebhiḥ...*

Colophon: *iti Pippalādīya Vāstusūtropaniṣad samāptā* ।

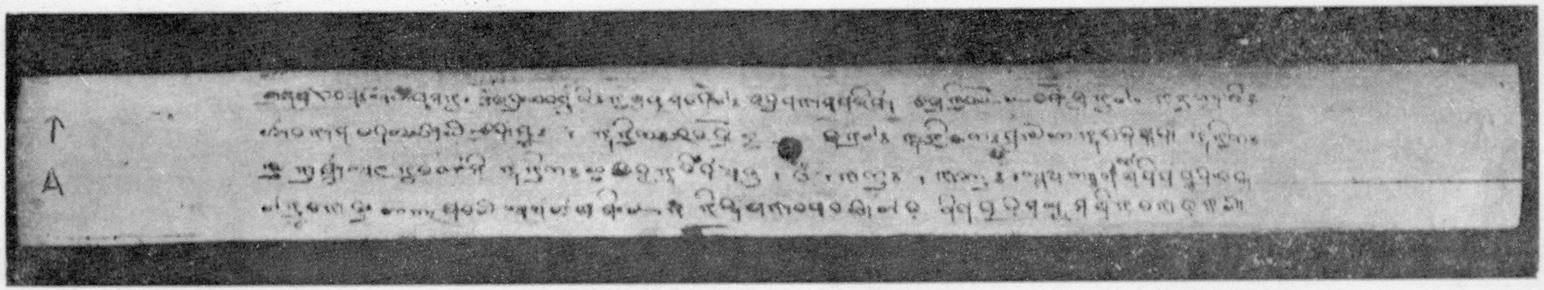

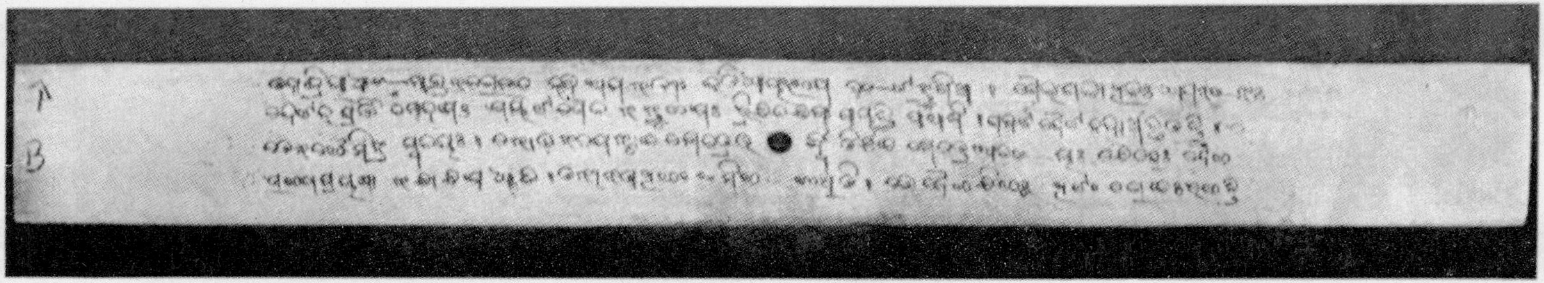

Ms ङ

INTRODUCTION

by
ALICE BONER

The Vāstusūtra Upaniṣad (VSU) attributed to the Paippalāda Kalpa of the Atharvaveda presents a challenge to various disciplines: to the indologist, because it is the first text on Śilpa or Vāstu called an Upaniṣad; to the historian, because it reveals a situation in which image-worship had still to defend itself against the predominance of Vedic ritual, and therefore its dating and historical position is very difficult to ascertain; to the linguist, because the text contains archaic and popular elements and the Sanskrit is rather poor, so as to leave many ambiguities; and ultimately to the research scholar in Śilpa, who will find in it an approach to the study of Indian figurative art quite different from that of the known Śilpaśāstras, since it does not contain rules for producing particular forms of art, but analyses the very principles and processes of form-figuration.

The VSU, which we present herewith in an English translation, is known in five different copies on palm-leaf, four being written in Oriya characters and one in Devanāgarī. These manuscripts were found in remote villages of Orissa by Pandit Sadasiva Rath Sarma during his extensive survey of eight Atharvavedic villages: Goruala, Basudevpur, Dharakote, Nirakarapur, Banki, Kurumachaini, Khandapara and some villages in Mayurbhanj District, in the years 1973, 1974 and 1976. In 1975 another text related to these was found, called the Vaiśravaṇa Śilpācāra which gives more details about the ritual accompanying the process of image-making. In 1976 Pandit Sadasiva Rath Sarma discovered one commentary on the VSU, written from the Tantra-Yoga point of view by Nigama Ḍiṇḍima. The fifth manuscript was found in 1976. It is in the form of Sūtras with commentaries and marginal notes by Somabhaṭṭa, giving some of the references of quotations in the text. This last manuscript appears to represent the most original version of the VSU and therefore we have taken it as the basis of our translation. The Sanskrit text edition has been based on this MS. The text has been studied together with Pandit Sadasiva Rath Sarma, a traditional scholar of Śilpāgama of Orissa. The aim of the translation offered herewith is not only to make accessible to a wider public the fundamental principles governing the art of image-making in ancient India, but also to show the universal relevance of form-language.

Śilpa or Vāstu[12], here meaning sculpture, is the subject of this extraordinary text. The language of Śilpa has, like any other professional language, its own particular concepts and terminology, which is not accessible to philosophical analysis alone, and as most Śilpa texts, the VSU is also written in very defective Sanskrit.[13] In order to understand the texts on Śilpa, one has to be familiar with the traditional way of thinking, work processes and terminology of the practicing artist. This translation may not be the last word in the interpretation of this difficult text, but it is hoped that it will clear the ground and facilitate the proper understanding of its symbolism and artistic principles.

The Vāstusūtra is divided into six Prapāṭhakas, just like the Praśna Upaniṣad of the Atharvaveda, attributed to the same sage Pippalāda. Here also Pippalāda replies to questions put to him by disciples, which in the VSU are the following three: Ātharvaṇāṅgirasa, Śilpakāśyapa and Kuvitsa (Kośala). While in the Praśna Upaniṣad there are six disciples who ask very different questions about the mysteries of Being and Becoming, of Prāṇa and Praṇava, in the VSU the questions of all three disciples are centered around the sole argument of Śilpa or Vāstu, its various aspects, its origin, its purpose, its principles and methods of creation, its very secrets and its

[12] In India, unlike as in Europe, no principal distinction is made between Fine Arts and Practical Crafts. All handiwork (manufacture) is Śilpa, from painting, sculpture, and architecture to pottery, weaving, engineering, mechanics, metal-casting, leather work, perfumery etc. and the term is also applicable in a certain sense to dance, music, poetry, drama, medicine etc. In this text, quite exceptionally, the word Śilpa only means sculpture, and so does Vāstu, which as a rule is particularly applied to architecture. Since in our text both these terms are used in the sense of form-figuration, we feel justified in employing, besides the original terms, the word Art, in the sense of Fine Arts, wherever more convenient.

[13] This is not surprising, according to the remark made by A.B. Keith, *A History of Sanskrit Literature*, Oxford, 1928, p. 464: "Architecture, Śilpa or Śilpiśāstra, Vāstuvidyā is represented by various anonymous works... many of the texts are written in a pretence of Sanskrit and their verses are extremely rude."

function and use in human society. The reason why this treatise is called Vāstusūtra and not Śilpasūtra, although it exclusively deals with sculpture and not with Vāstu, generally understood as architecture, may be because it deals with the lay-out, the composition of sculptures, and not so much with their modelling. As in architecture no building can be erected without a geometrical ground-plan and a mathematical plan of the elevation, such a fundamental principle is here postulated for images. No image destined for worship should ever be made without first tracing a geometrical plan of its essential configuration, called *pañjara* or *khila-pañjara*, giving its fundamental disposition and movements in space, which are responsible for its character.

Moreover, this treatise is not called a Śāstra but a Sūtra because it does not deal with rules and regulations for all types of art-production as Śilpaśāstras generally do, but it is a profound study of fundamental principles of the origin, of the how and why of form-figuration and of its ultimate necessity and purpose. Its character as a kind of an Upaniṣad is brought out by the fact that it contains an esoteric doctrine, in which the production of Śilpa is considered as a sacrificial act and is throughout based on philosophical and metaphysical conceptions. In answering every question Pippalāda goes back to first principles with numerous references, implicit and explicit, to the Vedas, Brāhmaṇas and Upaniṣads. In Pippalāda's conception the language of form is equivalent to the spoken or written word, giving expression to a vision of divine Truth and touching the deepest mysteries of Existence.

So even if this text were not to claim the rank of an Upaniṣad, it would by its very content reveal a marked precedence over the hitherto published Śilpaśāstras. These Śilpa texts, of which many are known, cover a period of approximately one thousand years, from chapters on Śilpa in the Matsya Purāṇa in the 4th Cent. A.D. to the Viṣṇu Dharmottara and the Bṛhat Saṁhitā in the 6th Cent., followed by the the Viśvakarmā Prakāśa, Śukranīti, Śilparatna and many others. Parts of the Agni Purāṇa and other Purāṇas also deal with Śilpa, and so do almost all the Āgamas down to the 13th and 14th Century.

Judging by their contents, all these texts belong to a subsequent stage in the development of Śilpa, because they take Śilpa for granted as an existing phenomenon. They describe Śilpa in its outer manifestations and give directions and prescriptions for its various disciplines and functions. None of these texts questions the phenomenon of Śilpa itself. None questions or explains its origin, except by adducing some fantastic genealogy in order to prove its descent from the Creator of the universe and thus to sanction the sacredness of its teachings. But as far as our knowledge goes, nowhere is the elemental nature of form itself investigated, nor its connection with basic cosmic laws and its dependence on them, nor its function in this phenomenal world and its action on the spirit of man. None of the Śilpa texts suspects that form in itself constitutes an independent language and could have a meaning, quite apart and transcending the object represented. None of these texts therefore would deem it necessary to study the nature or constitutive elements of form, as none would deem it indispensable to study the constitutive elements of words to understand their meaning, or grammar and syntax to understand the sentences they form.

A further consequence of this is that, ignoring the intrinsic nature and character of form apart from the object represented, these texts also did not recognize its constitutive function in the composition of images. Composition invariably came to mean, not any significant pattern of forms, but a system of measurements and proportions, called the Tālamāna. The Tālamāna system is quite appropriate and necessary for achieving a harmonious build-up of single figures in the round, but has not much meaning in a relief composition carved on panel or wall, where figures with multifarious intricate actions are represented. Neither has it any ritualistic or philosophical foundation and hence no further significance for the interpretation of images, except when differentiating between images of Devas, heroes, humans and subhuman creatures, setting certain standards of height and proportions for each of them.

Not having gone back to first principles of form-creation, as does the Vāstusūtra, the Śilpaśāstras evidently could only deal with contingent laws and rules concerning image-making as well as temple-building, which belonged to existing practice and experience of their own time.

A further reason why the Śilpaśāstras are silent about principles of composition and deal only with iconographical details may be that they were written by scholars, not initiated in the practical experience of art-production, but who only described theoretically the already existing works of art. In India as elsewhere traditional artists and craftsmen formed closed communities, who transmitted the secrets and rules of their art only orally from master to disciple or from father to son. They were rarely confided to writing, and if ever they were, it was always under strict injunction not to divulge the secrets of their science outside their own community. The Vaiśravaṇa Śilpācāra text even goes as far as to forbid transmission to a disciple and only admits transmission to one's own son.

For the VSU, however, the science of composition, the *pañjara-vidyā* or *nyāsa*, is the most important subject. It represents the profoundest professional secret and thus the highest degree of initiation. It was accessible only to masters, who had acquired it through a life-long practice and single-minded devotion.

The essential concern of this text is to demonstrate that the use and language of form, far from being invented for the simple delight of the senses and for extolling the beauties of the world, has a far deeper significance. It is considered an autonomous, direct reflection of cosmic laws and expression of religious and metaphysical conceptions. Pippalāda deals with the elementary questions about form-figuration asked by his three disciples, who, as Vedic sacrificial priests, are unfamiliar with this subject: How and why Śilpa came into being? What is form? How is it created? How does it operate? He impresses upon them that Form is like Vāk, the creative Word, and its means of expression equivalent to the written or spoken word. Although working in a different medium it has equal power of evoking a vision of ultimate Reality, of the eternal divine Law governing the universe, of penetrating into the essence and truth of Being. It acquires a metaphysical dimension, which one does not sense in the Śilpaśāstras.

Pippalāda substantiates his arguments by a deep spiritual vision and by numerous references to the sacred scriptures, the Vedas, Brāhmaṇas and Upaniṣads. He is insistent on the value and importance of figurative art as a vehicle for transcendental knowledge. Since, without disparaging sacrificial ritualism, he makes such a strong case for image-worship, it looks as if he were speaking under the stress of a controversial situation, where priesthood may have been divided over the question of accepting or rejecting worship of divine images. Such a situation may have arisen at a time when, in Orissa and in South India at least, the Aryan invaders with their aniconic sacrificial ritual were confronted with the indigenous, long standing and profoundly rooted tradition of image-worship, and a mutual accomodation had to be found.[14] It is significant in this respect, that they are Vedic Ṛṣis who are questioning Pippalāda, eager to learn what is the background, meaning and purpose of image-making. The Pippalāda of our text, although fully imbued with Vedic tradition and Upaniṣadic doctrine, appears to be the representative of the indigenous traditions, because he stoutly maintains that the power of images to elevate the soul and guide it towards final emancipation is as strong as that of sacrificial practices. He attributes to the Sthāpaka the same merit and rank as to the sacrificial priest and calls him Śilpodgātṛ, Śilpahotṛ or Vāstuhotṛ. Conversely the Vedic priests who question Pippalāda, very respectfully address him not only as Master, but as Vāstukarmāṅgāvatāra (incarnation of the art of form-figuration), and also as Ṣoḍaśakala Puruṣa (Puruṣa of sixteen parts, i.e. perfect Man) or Dharmapuruṣa.

Thus, even if we have to assume that the VSU has been strongly influenced by local traditions, and that in its present form it cannot be much older than the known Śilpaśāstras, its substance is certainly more fundamental than those texts.

This text which is a formidable vindication of the power of form-language has a message also for us late-comers. The understanding of the language of form, left inoperative in a society dominated by purely literary education and almost exclusive dependence on verbal and written communication, has nowadays almost vanished. The VSU, however, was addressed to a people who lived a natural life, with no printing presses to dull their vision. They depended on the faculty of reading the language of form and figure as much as on oral communication.

Writing was a rare art and printing was unknown. The ancient myths and legends, sung by the bards and evoked by the mantras of the Udgātaras at Vedic sacrifices were transmitted to them also by the images created by the artists. These images had a life of their own and a forceful reality which sunk their message into the heart of the devotee through the eyes instead of the ear.

It is a psychophysical fact that sense-impressions through the eyes and ears have a more compelling, a more direct action on the subconscious strata of the soul than discursive arguments. The subconscious obeys and is directly dependent on universal cosmic laws. When art-forms take their being from fundamental cosmic princi-

---

[14] Interpretation suggested by Dr G.C. Tripathi.

ples, they participate in the essential structure of the universe and contain a natural symbolism to which unsophisticated human beings respond instinctively, unconsciously. Take an obvious example such as the meaning of space-directions and their inescapable influence on human consciousness, which can never be inverted by any acrobacy of imagination. The upward direction towards the zenith, for earthly beings the highest point of the heaveny vault from where the sun sheds its vivifying light, will always be felt as the world beyond our earthbound existence to which our aspirations and yearnings tend as to a lost homeland. Our conception of the divine powers which mysteriously govern our life, to which we aspire to be united at the end of our pilgrimage, will always be felt as being above and not below the plane of the earth.

On the other hand, the nadir below our feet has a pull in the opposite direction. It attaches us to the earth which, together with our life-substance, nourishes our physical appetites. It enmeshes us in inextricable bonds of worldly ties. When we aspire to break away in an upward movement, the gaping abyss below our feet sometimes manifests an uncanny attraction, into which the unwary may sink at any moment, never to return. These two opposite pulls can never be inverted.

The East is the region from where the sun rises every day of our lives, and therefore represents the quintessence of all beginnings, of all that is young and strong, beautiful, whole, fresh, full of hope and promise. The West means decline, the end of the journey, of life, of hope, of activity, but also the end of worldly attachment, of joyful and painful bonds. It faces night, the darkness of the great Unknown, beyond which perchance a new day, a resurrection may be awaiting. At any rate it is the region of rest, of retrospect and peace.

The North and the South, in our northern hemisphere are connected with the feeling of cold and heat, of darkness and light, of stability and volubility. In India the opposite is the case: the South is the region of death, whereas the North represents the region of the Divine, of immortality. The Polestar, which never moves from its place is the fixed centre around which our stellar world is revolving. In India the Polestar (*dhruva*) has acquired symbol-value for everything stable, fixed, immoveable. The equinoxial and solsticial points mark the ever recurring phases of this eternal revolution.

It is impossible to escape these elemental cosmic contingencies. We are born with them, we are part of them and they live as compelling necessities in our subconscious. All arts are in some way or other determined in their expression by laws beyond human making. But perhaps none of the arts is so strictly bound up with earthly contingencies as are the visual arts, working as they do with the grossest elements and most heavily governed by the physical laws of the cosmos.

What to moderns may appear as a severe limitation and frustrating restriction on individual expression in art, a hampering of inspiration, had a deep meaning for the ancients. They were whole and one with cosmic forces. They felt themselves as integrated parts of the universe, of one and the same substance. Their vision therefore was not blocked up within the narrow limits of their own individuality and their own small ambiance, but transcending them went to explore the tremendous mystery of creation. There man discovered the fundamental relationship and connexion of all elements and recognize their correspondence within himself. The Earth was his body, the rocks his bones, the waters his blood, the Sun his eyes, the quarters his ears, the trees and plants his hair, and so at death he knew that he returned his own body to the elements of which it was composed, and his soul merged into the supreme Ātman. He drew all his inspiration and his strength from the contemplation of the divine powers, by which he himself and the whole cosmos were created and sustained.

In Pippalāda's doctrine the space-directions and also the symbolic forms of the elements are considered to be the rock-bottom of all form-figuration, the very ground on which art-creation stands. In the hands of the architect or the sculptor North-South becomes the vertical or Fire-line (*agni-rekhā*) with an upward direction. East-West becomes the Water-line (*ap-rekhā*) with a horizontal, even, restful position or at times with a powerful expansion to both sides. The diagonals South-West to North-East, or South-East to North-West are the Wind-lines (*māruta-rekhā*) which engender dynamic movements. These lines all cross or converge at a central point, which is called the *brahmabindu* or *marman*, the matrix of the entire display of forms.

If Śilpa or Vāstu, the visual arts, are thus inextricably bound to material contingencies in space, they are, on the other hand, free and unconditioned by time. This is to say: they are not, like the vocal arts, bound to a time-sequence or to intellectual operations for transmitting their message. Visual representation gives a synthetic all-embracing total view which transcends time. By the simultaneous presentation of all its parts, a painted or sculptured object acquires the power of directly penetrating the vital centres of the beholder. It is apprehended at one and the same time by all his organic and intellectual faculties without having to be mentally connected through a sequence of impressions. Especially the symbolic representation which transcends space-time-conceptions, in which all dimensions coalesce into a single entity, can thus be brought in their totality into a formula, which can directly be apprehended by the inner vision. That is how a graph or an image or an object can become a powerful instrument for transmitting a metaphysical vision, for kindling a speculative imagination. Thus many things which mere words cannot express can be told in the language of form with the help of images.

The myths and legends of all ancient religions used symbols for their metaphysical esoteric conceptions, represented visually and simultaneously by objects like the Omphalos or the Cosmic Egg, the Stone of the Kaaba, the World-pillar, the Śivaliṅgam, or by abstract signs and line-diagrams called Yantras. Anthropomorphic figures of divinities came later for expliciting the recondite meaning of symbols when these were no longer obvious and accessible.

Fritjof Schuon, in his book: *The Transcendent Unity of All Religions* (*De l'Unité transcendente des Religions*, Gallimard, 1948) says that the sensible form is what corresponds most directly to the intellect, by reason of the inverted analogy which plays between the principle and the manifested (order of things), so that the highest realities manifest themselves in the most striking manner in their most distant reflection, which is the sensible or "material" order.[15]

The VSU constantly extols the extraordinary power inherent in figurative art for communicating a vision of supreme truth, for giving a taste of the infinite that lies beyond the material world and ultimately leading the devotee to liberation. Because of its efficiency in operation figurative art is considered as the best of all arts, having its source in the mind of Prajāpati, the Creator Himself.

The VSU doctrine of art-production is based on the Vedic conception of the origin and evolution of the universe from the One Supreme undivided Principle. In a short introduction to the 4th

[15](My translation). See the entire ch. IV: La question des formes d'art, pp. 76–90.

Prapāṭhaka Pippalāda says: In the beginning Brahman was the only Existent (Sat). He potentially holds in Himself the entire creation. He is without qualities (*nirguṇa*), but in order to bring forth creation He assumes qualities and becomes *saguṇa.* The first concretization produces Mind, this may be the mind-determination of the Creator, but may equally be the seed of the human mind. Brahman, the Cosmic Creator lives in the human heart as a flame, or, as said in other texts, as the Puruṣa of the size of a thumb. He is the Life-force (*prāṇa*) of all that exists which is expanding into the infinite forms of manifestation, yet in itself remains forever One and the same.

In the Ṛgveda (VI.47.18) it is said:

> *Rūpaṃ rūpaṃ pratirūpo babhūva...*
>
> He became corresponding in form to every form,
> This all is to be looked upon as a form of Him.
> Indra by his magic powers (*māyā*) goes about in many forms,
> Yoked are his ten hundred steeds. (Tr. Griffith)

The original Form expands into forms of infinite varieties.

The *Bṛhadāraṇyaka Upaniṣad* (II.5.19) specifies further:

> He (Ātman), verily, is the steeds. He, verily, is tens and thousands, many and endless. This Brahman is without an earlier and without a later, without an inside and without an outside. This soul (Ātman) is Brahman, the all-perceiving. (Tr. R.E. Hume)

Slowly and by degrees Pippalāda reveals the origin of images, the process by which they are brought forth and the influence they exert on the devotee. He does not do it in a systematic order, but begins by extolling the end in view: the inspiring, elevating and purifying influence of the image on the beholder. From the contemplation of images grows delight, from delight faith, from faith steadfast devotion, through such devotion arises that higher understanding (*parāvidyā*) that is the royal road to liberation (*mokṣa*). Pippalāda goes to the extent of saying that without the guidance of images the mind of the devotee may go astray and form wrong imaginations. Images dispel false imaginations and point out the right way of worshipping the divinity.

But where are the spiritual sources of such images to be found? He replies: It is in the mind of the Ṛṣis, who see and have the power of discerning the essence of all created things of manifested forms. They see their different characters, the divine and the demoniac, the creative and destructive forces, revealed as they are in their interplay in the eternal round of *saṃsāra*. From understanding the diverse characters and qualities of all manifested phenomena a distinct and particular vision of the laws of the universe is formed. This is what finds expression in sacred myths and songs, such as the hymns of the Ṛgveda. These hymns reflect the deep-rooted conceptions of a people, developed through centuries of inner experience and contemplation and metaphysical speculation. The vision the Ṛṣis and bards had of this gigantic drama of cosmic powers in eternal conflict was the life-substance of a people still intimately aware of the structural and dynamic complementarism of those powers. Today it is called mythology, but in ancient times these myths were a living reality, from which the Sthāpakas drew the subject-matter for their work. It is here that they found the source of their inspiration. This is true not only of India, but of all ancient traditional cultures which were still in intimate contact with cosmic forces.

With this question, from where the artist drew the subject-matter and inspiration for his work, Pippalāda deals in a single sentence. For him this matter was self-evident and he could not envisage any other possibility. As long as man could draw from the accumulated life and religious traditions from experience of centuries and millennia, he was amply nourished by an inexhaustible flow of images for his own creative work.

But when this source dries up, or for reasons undetermined it loses its meaning for him, his imagination is inevitably diverted towards the outer world, the material existence, where he must find his fulfilment and his satisfaction. He then applies the entire power of his mind to the phenomenal existence which he tries to investigate and to penetrate and then to use for his pleasure and comfort. Instead of adding and enriching the experience transmitted to him by his ancestors in the life of the spirit, he rejects their inheritance and uses all his energies in an attempt to penetrate and master the forces of nature, analysing, dissecting, subduing the outer world, in order to make it more comfortable for his material existence. His creative imagination, launched into the outer world, including the stellar dimensions of the universe, has no doubt fathomed depths and heights of the manifested world never dreamt of before and has achieved miracles of investigation, inventions, constructions. But it is also responsible for the lack of direction, for the confusion and restlessness of the present times. Having lost its cosmic and human bearings, modern mind is floating between heaven and earth, between spirit and matter, not knowing where to attach itself. The attitude of man embedded in a tradition is governed by a centre, from which he draws his strength, while when detached from tradition it becomes centrifugal, scattered in all directions. The more the technical achievements are engulfing existence, the more the human soul becomes alienated from the great world-soul, the Ātman.

The chaos prevailing in our modern art-production is nothing but the consequence of this dissipation and alienation. The Vāstusūtra is not the personal opinion of a master of art, but the expression of the spiritual situation of a people firmly settled in a living tradition. They did not consider anything as an alien outer phenomenon, but felt themselves in active conjunction with all elements of the cosmos, and through this with the great unknown divinity on whom this All depends. This has to be remembered for truly appreciating the words attributed to the great sage Pippalāda.

In the first Prapāṭhaka Pippalāda gives a short outline of the six fundamental disciplines which have to be mastered by the Sthāpaka: the knowledge of stones (*śailam*), the compositional diagram (*khilapañjara*), the carving of stones (*śaila-bhedanam*), the disposition of limbs or parts (*aṅgaprayoga*), the determination of character (*bhāvanānyāsa*), the final integration of all forms (*sambandha-prabodhana*). These are treated in detail in the six Prapāṭhakas of the Vāstusūtra. He starts with the cryptic assertion that the principal and fundamental knowledge the Sthāpaka must have, is the knowledge of the LINE and the CIRCLE. This axiom is symbolically illustrated in the form of the YŪPA. The Yūpa is originally the sacrificial post erected to the East of the sacrificial hall for tying the victim of the sacrifice. In its simplest form it consists of a straight wooden post, either cylindrical, octagonal or sixteen-angled, crowned by a spherical or hemispherical head. In the VSU this form is interpreted as a grand symbol: The spherical head is the Earth or the Universe (*viśva*), the straight post represents action or creation (*karma*). The joining of the two produces Viśvakarman, the creator of the Universe, the supreme divinity of Śilpa. At the same time it incorporates and illustrates the fundamental principles of LINE and CIRCLE, which, as constituents of all visible forms in the Universe are the particular and essential knowledge of the Śilpin or Sthāpaka. It is called

Śilpavidyā or Vāstuvidyā. Mediating between the sensible and the suprasensible order of things, it gives access to the subtle essence of all phenomena, to the world of the spirit, to the world of the gods. Since this knowledge has the power of leading from outer reality to the apprehension of transcendent reality behind all phenomena, it is called divine.

Pippalāda who stands on the ground of Upaniṣadic doctrines, which postulate the fundamental unity of all creation, originating from a common divine source, almost verbally repeats the words addressed by Yājñavalkya to Maitreyī in the Bṛhadāraṇyaka Upaniṣad (II.4.14), but interprets them in the opposite sense: because without duality, and thus without sense-perception, there would be no art.

The general principles of form-creation are graphically illustrated and demonstrated in the lay-out of compositional diagrams for images, described in the second Prapāṭhaka. These diagrams are called *pañjara*, which word has two meanings. It is either "skeleton" or "cage".[16] They are eminent and clear symbolic representations of the Upaniṣadic conception of world-creation. In the *pañjara* it is represented by the central point, the *brahmabindu*, from where a circle is traced encompassing the main elements of the image. The central hole made by the compass is called *sthiti*, the firm position of the circle, pregnant with the multiform elements of manifestation. It is the one unitary principle, the support and the soul of the circle. This circle represents the full but undifferentiated whole of the universe. It is the womb wherein single beings are formed by separating lines. These lines are straight and are compared to the rays of the Sun on the physical plane. In the metaphysical sense the sun's rays are considered the forces creating all manifested life. In the *pañjara* they direct movements of the figures within the ambit of the circle and the square encompassing the circle marking the limits of the manifest existence.

The most important straight lines traced across these diagrams are the vertical middle-line, the horizontal middle-line, the obliques connecting the ends of the middle-lines and the diagonals from cor-

[16]In the text both meanings occur: they are "skeletons" when their lines determine movements of figures inside the composition. Although not visible they are, like the bones in the human body, the indispensable support of all forms. When on the other hand they divide the composition into regular compartments controlling the disposition of the single figures, it becomes a "cage" and is called *koṣṭhaka*.

ner to corner, which all have their particular significance, explained further on.

When in the outlay of the compositional diagram Pippalāda mentions a double circle to the right and the left of the middle line, intersected in the middle, and considers them to represent Puruṣa-Prakṛti, this may be understood as a reference to the dual principle of the Sāṃkhya doctrine and to its theistic application, where Puruṣa is the God and Prakṛti his Śakti. But the text refers also to the doctrine of Prāṇa and Rayi (Energy and Matter) attributed to the same Pippalāda, expounded in the Praśna Upaniṣad. Prāṇa is the Life-breath, the Life-force-principle, the mysterious Energy which animates all creation. It is something beyond all what in modern science is explained in various ways, as chemical elements, molecules, atoms, waves, vibrations, electrons etc. underlying all cosmic phenomena. It is something formless, immaterial, although all-pervading. It cannot be apprehended by any sense-perception; yet it is the unscrutable ground and moving principle of all existence. Rayi is the crystallization of this life-force into sensible elements, primordial materialization, the first product having form, in which the working of Prāṇa is apprehended, realized and reflected. Prajāpati in the Praśna Upaniṣad I.4 says: "These two will make creatures for me in manifold ways." This means unity in duality, as of Śiva and Śakti, the Father-principle and the Mother-principle, which are in many ways a universal symbol.

Without entering here in detail into the complex cosmic symbolism of the lines of the *pañjara* as it is given in the second chapter, let us consider the general background of these conceptions. Not only the temple but also the image panel is considered to be a representation of the universe, a complete microcosm. The great elements in the macrocosm – usually five i.e. earth, water, fire, air and space or ether – correspond in the *pañjara* to the different types of lines (with the exception of the element *ākāśa* which, being invisible, cannot be represented). The spaces created by these line divisions represent the Earth (rhombus), the Sun (circle) and the four great continents of the earth created by the two essential dividing lines, the central vertical and horizontal. The upright triangle symbolises fire and the downward directed one, water. These micro-macro-cosmic correspondences are again another way of equating image-making and hence image-worship with the Vedic sacrifice. For the sacrifice in all its elements and actions re-creates the cosmos and thus ensures the continuity of life. It is the means par excellence to permit the interaction between the gods, men and the cosmos (*ādhidaivika, ādhyātmika, ādhibhautika*). This same interaction is going to be produced by the divine image, whose "essence" is the underlying *pañjara*. It is therefore not surprising that the lines constituting the *pañjara* are called *huta*, sacrificial offerings or oblations.

Sacrificial, cosmic and human elements have to be combined in order to achieve the object of sacred art: bringing man in harmony with the cosmos and with the gods and thus making him attain his goal, which is ultimately *mokṣa*, liberation.

Only an insight into this basic conception can help us to understand the subtle and often apparently abstruse play of correspondences and symbolic allusions of the text which is so characteristic of Upaniṣadic thinking. It is quite possible that the meaning of many a symbol has been lost or forgotten even in the course of the development of the same tradition, and that, therefore, mistakes have crept in the copying of the text, confusing the clear symbolism. This is the only possible explanation for some obscure statements, as for example, the identification of the square as the outer frame of the panel with water in Sūtra II.11, which has no equivalent in any known Vedic or Purāṇic symbolism. The comparison with a water tank only shows that it is not an original symbol but a secondary conception. But even such mistakes cannot blur the fundamental vision of the panel as a microcosm.

Giving some examples of these correspondences we can observe the following symbolism: The element Air or Wind is represented by corner-ears inside the square, formed by lines corresponding to the ends of the central enclosing vertical and horizontal border-lines. Their nature is represented in the only visible form of air, that is to say in water-bubbles or air-bubbles caused by the action of wind upon water. The corner-ears very likely also signify the four quarters of space in the surrounding atmosphere. They enclose a central rhombus. These first three figures, namely the circle, the square and the rhombus, have all a concentrating, collecting function in the constitution of the *pañjara*.

The interior dividing lines initiate the differentiation within the whole. The first two mentioned are the central vertical and central horizontal lines which divide the circle into four parts. According to Hindu conceptions they demarcate the four continents of the earth. These two lines, the vertical and horizontal, converge at the centre, in the *marma-bindu*, which is the essence of life, the life-principle or Brahman, as mentioned before, from where everything takes its origin. The vertical middle-line is the back-bone or support of the universe, the "*axis mundi*", represented sensibly in the figure of Mount Meru or the Tree of Life. Here, along the vertical middle-line also begins a differentiation in the hierarchy of values. The horizontal middle-line and all its parallels are so to say adjuncts of the vertical middle-line in that they mark these different levels and stages of being. Thus in the order of the *guṇas tamas* will be below, *rajas* in the middle and *sattva* the upper layer.

The course of the Sun is considered to be diagonal, and therefore is compared to the wind-lines, the diagonals crossing the square from corner to corner. These are lines of great power and stress, on the sensible material plane as well as metaphorically, when they symbolize the vivifying power of the Sun. In a plastic representation they give dynamic movement, speed and energy to all forms.[17]

The element Fire is said to be emerging from the body of the earth in the fire of sacrifice. This earthly fire is represented as an upright triangle with its base on the groundline and its point on the upper end of the central vertical line, or else it is inscribed in the circle. The three lines by which it is composed are called *trihuta*, that is: three offerings of the sacrifice, since the line is compared to a sacrificial oblation. Most divine forms reposing in themselves are enclosed within an upright triangle, as representing the harmony of the heavenly world. It conveys a feeling of peace as well as an upward aspiration.

An inverted triangle traced across the fire-triangle from the upper corners of the square to the lower end of the vertical middle-line, or again inside the circle, is called the waters (in Tāntric symbolism it is the Yoni). It suggests downward penetration and absorption. By their interaction these two triangles form the *yantra* of mutual attraction, the *mithuna-yantra*, which is the basic diagram for numerous divinities with their Śaktis.

All these forms contained in the *pañjaras* have to be understood on the cosmic as well as on the metaphysical plane. The text develops arguments on these two corresponding lines, and they have always to be interpreted in their ambivalent significance. A striking example in

[17]See Dante, Paradiso, Canto X: *Vedi come da indi si dirama/L'obliquo cerchio che i pianeti porta, /Per sodisfare al mondo che gli chiama:...*

point in the description of the elements is the statement that when Agni (Fire) is joined to Āpas (Water), the divine state arises, which is the Great Delight (*mahacchandas*, which can mean both, metre and delight). On the cosmic plane Fire and Water stand at opposite ends. They are eternally conflicting, irreconcilable, mutually destructive elements. They are the only two elements of whom conjunction is inconceivable. And yet it is precisely the union of these opposites which makes man transcend the limitations of earthly life.

This evidently can only be understood on the metaphysical plane, where both these conflicting elements are seen in their higher, complementary function. Pitting their energies against one another, they are responsible for keeping the life of the cosmos in balance and for securing its eternal motion. The fiery and the liquid element are here reconciled by the necessity of creation. They are the upper and the lower arch forming the great world-egg, the matrix of all that is, that was and is to be. The *yantra* expressing this concept is in the form of two intersecting triangles, which is called *ākarṣaṇīyantra*, the attraction of opposite principles, and the science and power of the Ṛṣis to use it for conjuring is the *ākarṣaṇī vidyā*.

In this way the image of the universe and the powers that govern it are projected on the panel in pure, yet significant lines by means of the *pañjara*. These lines are no abstractions, but living forces which become operative in determining the essential character and movements of the figures and their most relevant expressions. By the symbol-value of such lines and diagrams the Sthāpaka was enabled to bring out the subtle essence (*rūpatattva*) of divine figures, and in this sense the sculpture becomes a reflection of the work of the supreme Creator.

As a general principle it is said that forms predominantly in the vertical are in the nature of fire. They stand for divine aspiration and illumination and are proper for *sāttvic* divinities. Like a flame they rise from below upwards, raising the spirit of the beholder towards a vision of divine truth, like for instance the image of the standing Viṣṇu with arms along the body in the same vertical direction.

Forms predominantly in the horizontal are in the nature of water, like a flowing river. They either express a sense of expansion towards the infinite or convey a feeling of restful balance, of stillness in complete withdrawal from action. Viṣṇu lying on Śeṣanāga in the world-ocean comprehends both these conceptions. Sometimes horizontal sideway movements may express a powerful assertive mood, as that shown by Viṣṇu Trivikrama with outstretched arm and leg. Forms in the diagonal are mostly in a fighting attitude, dynamic and aggressive. They show divinities struggling to subdue āsuric inimical forces.

If the Sthāpaka was not dissimilar to the Hotā by his power of evoking divinities, he was not dissimilar to him either in his manner of operation. The entire process of carving was guided by an elaborate ritual: Every act connected with the creation of images, every tracing of line and circle was an *āhuti*, a sacrificial offering, performed with the appropriate mantras. As described in the Vaiśravaṇa Śilpācāra these acts are: selecting the propitious moment for initiating the work, setting the stone on *darbha*-grass and purifying it with milk and curds, taking bath, doing *japa*, entering the workshop, appointing the Ācārya, doing *pūjā*, breaking a coconut (*arghya*), laying the measuring thread, setting the *marman*, tracing the circle and the lines. These operations are described in the Vāstusūtra as religious operations. The actual carving begins with an invocation to the goddess of the chisels and a sort of mental or oral Agnihotra sacrifice incumbent on the Sthāpaka, by which Agni Vaiśvānara is propitiated and accidents to the chisels are prevented. The respect for the stone from which the image is born was so great that even the stone-chips cut off in the process of carving were ceremoniously disposed off with the proper mantras.

In this intensely religious attitude, by correctly tracing the compositional diagrams (*rekhāṅkana*) and setting their lines in conformity with their character, the Sthāpaka could, no less than the Hotā, call forth all the thirty-three gods, the Ādityas, the Rudras and the Vasus and place the devotees under their protection.

The primary condition, however, for obtaining such a grace was, that the form-structure be absolutely perfect, which means in conformity with the essential character of the divinity. The perfection of form here did not mean the display of physical beauty, but the adequacy of the compositional outplay to the significance and inner meaning of the image. Just as in Vedic sacrifices the laudatory hymns had to be composed in different metres according to the specific character of the various divinities, thus also the compositional diagrams for their visual representation had to have their appropriate specific connotations. In both cases the injunctions are very strict. The Gāyatrī metre, the Triṣṭup, the Uṣṇik, the Anuṣṭup, the Bṛhatī, the Jagatī etc. are all destined to different divinities and therefore have each its particular rhythm and number of syllables. Their singing is governed by strict rules in respect to the number of repetitions, rhythm, intonation, strength of voice, including the Stomas and Pṛṣṭhas, all in combination with the libations to be offered. Similar principles are valid, or rather imperative in the system of Rāgas in Indian music. Each Rāga has its own particular, strictly limited range of notes, its upward and downward movements and variations, within which it finds expression for the particular ideas and feelings that have to be expressed. Departing from these rules would destroy the whole meaning of the melody. In the sacrificial operations any, even the slightest mistake made in the ritual would have fatal consequences for the priest as well as for the sacrificer and had to be atoned for. In the same way the composition of divine images had to be strictly in accordance with certain lines of the *pañjara* appropriate to the character and aspect of every divinity. Such discrimination alone would enable the Sthāpaka to find the proper form-context capable of invoking the divinity and calling forth a response. Here also the slightest deviation from the correct lines and proportions would miss the aim, render the image ineffective and send the artist to perdition. As sacrificial rituals, mantras, metres, songs and melodies were instruments for moral and spiritual support, thus were images of divinities.

The profound knowledge of form-structures, which could bring out the transcendent and esoteric value of images is presented as the exclusive secret of the master-sculptors. But for a proper understanding of the meaning of lines and forms it required also people sensitive to their language and subtle influence, so that meditation of images properly composed could touch and lead them to visions of higher truths. When cave-temples, called Mūrtiśālās, with sequences of sacred images on their walls were excavated in the mountain-sides as abodes and also for the purpose of the meditation of *tapasvins*, this certainly could happen only at a time when the power of images, the very language of form was taken for granted and perhaps possessed even higher eloquence than the spoken word.[18]

---

[18]In the Mūrtiśālā-vidhāna of the Kukkuṭṭikāgama (unpublished) there are elaborate descriptions of cave-temples of various kinds, which were made as abodes and places of meditation for hermits and *tapasvins*. Some were plain and some with images. Three of the Cave-temples of Elura (Cave 14, 15 and 21) are described with their ground-plans and the sequence of their images. They have different appellations according to their underlying *yantras*.

In the fourth Prapāṭhaka Pippalāda describes a division of the panel to be sculptured, which is superimposed on the *khila-pañjara*, but does not interfere with it. It only serves to circumscribe the single parts of a composite image by a net-work of vertical and horizontal lines (a kind of a 'cage'). It is like the groundplan in architecture which gives the position and dimension of the various parts of a building. The panel is divided into sixteen equal squares or rectangles called *koṣṭhakas*. The four central divisions are reserved for the main divinity, and the two vertical compartments on each side are for secondary divinities. The two central compartments in the uppermost region contain the head and the aureole of the main divinity, while the two corner-squares are for adoring Yakṣas, Gandharvas and Apsarases. In the lowest region the two central squares are for the seat or the vehicle of the main divinity or for defeated adversaries. The two outer squares are for human worshippers.

Here the hierarchies of values outlined in the *pañjaras* are demarcated with precision. The main divinity has to occupy the centre, the place of Brahmā, secondary divinities such as consorts are by its sides. Subordinate divine beings are in the upper two corners which are heavenly regions. Human worshippers are on the earth-plane in the lower corners, vehicles are supporting the divinity in the two lowest central squares, where also sometimes defeated adversaries are placed. In principle all these various component figures should be kept in their proper places, and for the main divinity this is axiomatic. It always occupies the centre, sometimes from bottom to top. For accessory figures there is a certain latitude, especially with regard to their dimensions, as seen in many sculptures. But in general they also keep their prescribed positions.

While the lines of the *pañjara* give life and movement to the figures and can therefore be compared to a skeleton being invisible in the body, the lines of the *koṣṭhaka* denote a static timeless outlay of the image and therefore can be called a 'cage'.

Yūpa

One of the links between Vedic symbolism and image-making is the Yūpa, the Pillar or Pole, leading to the representation of the Puruṣa, the archetypal Man. Therefore descriptions of Yūpas are interspersed between those of composed images which are the principal subject of this text.

In the first Prapāṭhaka, as will be remembered, a simple Yūpa was described, consisting of a straight post and a spherical head, as the symbol for Viśvakarman. In the second Prapāṭhaka some Yūpas are described with either eight or sixteen angles, which serve to fulfill various desires of the devotees. In the fourth Prapāṭhaka Pippalāda deals with a Yūpa of an entirely different form, which is not meant either to tie sacrificial animals, nor to fulfil special desires. As the first Yūpa was a symbol for Viśvakarman, this appears as a solemn symbol for the universal Puruṣa in his cosmic and human manifestation. It is in the form of an upright stone-pillar, quadrangular and not quite as high as a human figure. The post is divided in height in six equal parts, in which the stratifications of elements in the material world are represented in four sections, from the lowest and grossest, the earth, to the highest and subtlest, the region of light, each one having its presiding deity and being consecrated with an appropriate mantra. The earth-part with Bhūmi Devatā occupies the lowest section. The *mithuna*-part above that occupies two sections with Rudra Devatā, the part of the life-breath occupies two further sections with Prajāpati Devatā and the light-part with Savitṛ Devatā is in the uppermost section. In the same way the human form is built up according to these four elements: The earth-part contains the feet and legs up to the knees and is in the region of material activity. The procreative part reaches from the knee up to the navel. Over this arises the seat of the life-breath in chest and heart up to the neck, and the whole is crowned by the uppermost part, the head, the seat of divine light. Man here grows out of the elemental structure of the cosmos and is connatural to it. He is not the measure of all things, the "*Homo universalis*" as he is commonly assumed to be in the classical traditions of the West. The cosmos is not seen in the image of man, but man is seen in the image of the cosmos.

The primeval Puruṣa in the famous Puruṣa Sūkta (ṚV X.90) is sacrificed and dismembered by the gods to become the substance of the universe. The gods, who may stand for the elemental natures, out of his various parts fashioned the creatures of earth and air, of mid-air and heaven, the sun and the moon, Indra and Agni, the hymns of the Vedas and human beings: Brāhmaṇas, Kṣatriyas, Vaiśyas and Śūdras. He is dissolved into all elements of creation, and only when by sacrifice he is reintegrated as the totality of Being, he recovers his identity. In the form of the sacrifice he stands for all the gods, Rudra, Prajāpati, Vāstoṣpati... and becomes the "Pillar of the universe", the

"*Axis mundi*".

After Pippalāda has dealt with the technicalities of composition and the fundamental form-structures he comes to the content of the images. The variations in the aspects of divinities he explains in analogy to the sentiments perceptible in human beings, shown in their forms, attitudes and expressions. In the Nāṭyaśāstra dealing with dance and dramaturgy and allied arts, the eight principal sentiments or essences (*bhāva* or *rasa*) that occur in human behaviour are described in four groups of two, related to each other as cause and effect. But in the Vāstusūtra they are presented in a complete psychological order, where every sentiment is the consequence of the previous one and the cause of the following one: The basic emotion of all living beings is LOVE (*śṛṅgāra*). Love creates MIRTH and LAUGHTER (*hāsya*), but often also leads to SORROW and PAIN (*karuṇa*). Pain degenerates into ANGER (*raudra*), but Anger can be sublimated into HEROISM (*vīra*), which leads to fight. Fight motivated by anger creates FEAR (*bhayaṅkara*). One party is defeated and feels DISGUST (*bībhatsa*), and so gives up the fight. Who thus relinquishes everything finally finds PEACE (*śānta*). In the representation of sentiments fundamental space-direction is vital. Serene, peaceful images are substantially on vertical lines, sorrowful or inert images are on the horizontal, angry moods are on mixed lines, the heroic and aggressive figures are mostly on the diagonals.

This can be called the cosmic aspect and motivation of sentiments. But the question is how are they related to Brahma-knowledge which is said to be the root of all form-figuration? When Pippalāda says that the mind is the cause of various human dispositions and that these give rise to various conceptions of divinities, it could be taken to mean that divinities were mere creations of human fancy. But what he means to say and explains further on is, that divinities respond to and satisfy human needs. Their conceptions however take place in the mind of the Ṛṣis, the mediators between the world of men and the world of the gods. It is here, in the world of Brahman, in its primary concretization and differentiation, that elemental powers assume character and form of divinities. Ṛṣis have a penetrating vision of the divine world beyond the reach of ordinary human beings. In their deep meditation they visualize the powers of the universe in their essence and substance. *Brāhmaṇas* with their sacrifices may also participate in such realizations. When offering oblations in the fire the sound of the mantra supporting the offering contains the very essence of the divinity which is invoked. The mantra reveals the intrinsic nature, the elemental powers, the quality and mood, the actions and emanations of the divinity. This the Ṛṣis and *brāhmaṇas* strive to approach by worship, *tapasyā* and constant effort of contemplation, till their whole being becomes imbued with this divine essence and its form appears before their inner eye. The image, extolled in word and song, is reflected in the carved figure. This realization is not attained at once, it is reached by a gradual approach. As in the Purāṇas the structure of the cosmos is described as consisting of fourteen worlds (*bhuvana*), thus also the birth of an image is evolved through fourteen stages called here *bhuvanakoṣa*. In the Bṛhad. Upaniṣad II.15 not only the elements constituting the cosmos, but also the elements constituting human nature are described as fourteen. They are: *śarīra, retas, vāc, prāṇa, cakṣu, śrotram, manas, tejas, śabda* (or *svara*), *hṛdayākāśa, dharma, satya, mānuṣa, ātman*. All are pervaded and held together by the *tejomaya amṛtamaya*, the Soul and immortal Life-principle. These categories of creation are enumerated as beginning with the grossest and culminating in the subtlest and most spiritual element. But when the Ṛṣis meditate to realize their manifested form, the development takes place in the reverse order. Since it is the mirrored reflection of the ontological process, it will necessarily begin with the apprehension of the subtlest essence, with the mantra-sound, and finally reached concretization in form.

In Nigama Ḍiṇḍima's commentary[19] the doctrine of the origin of Devas from cosmic forces or their relation with them is cogently and vividly illustrated, as will be seen by the two examples of Viṣṇu and Rudra: "Viṣṇu is Brahman, this is said in the Veda. He is famous for having three steps in the form of Trivikrama, (pervading) the worlds of Bhūḥ, Bhuvaḥ and Svar. This is the *bhāvarūpa* of Trivikrama: "He whose steps are all the beings and whose third step is immortality in heaven." ... He who is the goal of men, he is Nārāyaṇa, the supreme Puruṣa. "Men" means waters, the waters are the ocean, the ocean is endless, its colour is like the clouds – this is the conception of the Sthāpakas. Viṣṇu is verily the life-breath, what is life-breath is wind. The nature of the wind is the life-breath of the serpents. The serpents eat wind, their life depends

[19]The text of the Nigama Ḍiṇḍima Ṭippaṇī has not been included because on the whole it does not contribute to the understanding of the VSU and is at places rather confusing. Therefore some significant passages have been quoted in full.

on wind. Viṣṇu is the Lord of Life, lying on the serpent, he is the Lord of the universe, being mounted on the life-breath. "Viṣṇu is the all". Time is turning like a wheel, that (wheel of) time is his weapon. Viṣṇu is mounted on the life-breath whose characteristic is sound, sound is the manifestation of life-breath, this is the conch, his other attribute, it is the sound of the cavity of the *ājñācakra*. The sound of life-breath is the mantra. Viṣṇu is Virāṭ. By his mace the evils are removed and the enemies are destroyed. Viṣṇu is the Lord of nectar, he holds a lotus symbolizing nectar... His Śakti which is born from the ocean is Candrā. All (Śaktis) belong to Nature, Nature is the seed (origin) of form. Similarly the vehicles: the carrier of Viṣṇu consisting of life-breath is the Haṃsa who is carrying the nectar, this is the knowledge of the *paramahaṃsa*, it is the object of meditation of the *paramahaṃsas*. From the nature of the Haṃsa comes the heavenly bird who carries the life-breath, whose head is the immortal, whose two wings are sacrifice, the sounds *haṃ* and *saḥ*, he is Garutmān, the carrier of nectar (immortality)... According to this Vedic conception from Viṣṇu's nature arises his image...

Similarly also the character of Rudra (is described): He is born from the mountain and his form comes from the conception of white snow. He is Āśutoṣa, i.e. free from unsatisfied desires. He is the ideal of the Yogis who are dwelling in caves, he is the Lord of all, Paśupati, he has three eyes, these three eyes are the sun, the moon and fire, just as the *bilva*-leaf has three petals, which is the medicine of the sages. The work of the sages is sacrifice, the sacrifice is verily *dharma*. Paśupati mounts the sacred Bull. Rudra dwells in the wilderness of the snowy mountain and sports with Pārvatī. She is Ambā, the forest-dwelling Pārvatī. By wearing snakes which are a form of death, he is the conquerer of death (Mṛtyuñjaya). His weapon is the spear which has three light-points corresponding to the three *guṇas*, it pierces the ignorant and kills the enemies. As the Yogis discern the matter by means of body, speech and mind, so is Rudra's weapon. Rudra has two sons, one is Skanda who has the power of arms, the other is Gaṇadaivata who has the power of knowledge. Where the physical power and the power of knowledge are joined together by the essential nature, this one is most powerful, such is Rudra. Rudra is shining by the strength of these two powers. Rudra devours all evils, therefore he has a blue throat (*nīlagrīvā*). He is OṂ, the embodiment of the exclamation *vaṣaṭ*. In the Atharvaveda (XIII.4.25–26) his glory is praised: "He, verily, is death, he is immortality, he is the monster, he is the fiend. He is Rudra, winner of wealth in the giving of wealth; in uttering homage he is the sacrificial exclamation Vaṣaṭ duly employed." (Griffith).

Rudra is the nature of the Yogis dwelling in the mountains. Rudra's *bhāvarūpa* is born from Nature, from which the *tattvarūpa* of all the gods originates. From the *tattvarūpa* (essential form) come the images (*pratirūpāṇi*)."

Considering this kind of creative process in analogy to that of the Ṛṣi taking place in the mind of the Sthāpaka it will be clear that his vision was safely based on metaphysical conceptions, supported by continuous references to sacred scriptures and the effort to understand their esoteric meaning. This was not a simple intellectual acceptance or adherence. The ancient artist had a deep feeling of being himself an integrating part of the cosmos and of participating in all its categories and elements, a feeling acquired by innumerable generations in uncounted centuries of meditative experience.

The consciousness of the fundamental unity of the sensible and the suprasensible world is further evidenced when space-directions themselves are said to be creating the forms of Devatās, which express their character and determine their influence on human beings. The East is connected with Āditya (Sun-god), the divinity awakening all life, the South is associated with Yama (god of Death), the destroyer and transformer of life, the West is connected with Varuṇa (upholder of universal Law and god of the Sea), where the sun sets and life finds rest. The North gives birth to Soma, the spiritual elixir fertilizing the human mind, the Earth or Dhruvā brings forth Agni, the fire that establishes a direct, so-to-say vertical, connection between the human world and the divine. The different character of Devas calls for different ways of worship, which are all accepted as valid with remarkable tolerance and none is condemned.

In the sixth and concluding Prapāṭhaka Pippalāda once more reminds his disciples that the work of the Sthāpaka is a creation similar to that of Prajāpati, who had to do severe *tapas* (penance) in order to bring forth the universe. Therefore the human creator of form also has to undergo a severe discipline in order to adequately fulfil his mission and vocation.

As a help and guidance to this end he describes the nine form-elements which are indispensable for creating and completing a sacred image: setting of compositional lines, ornamentation, gestures, weapons, postures, vehicles, secondary divinities, adversaries and adorers. Of these the first, the composition of directing lines has already been dealt with in previous chapters, both in respect to *pañjaras* as to *koṣṭhakas*. But of the *koṣṭhakas* he gives now further details. The reason why the panel should be divided into sixteen *koṣṭhakas*, he says, is because the Puruṣa (the universal Being) is composed of sixteen parts. These sixteen parts are enumerated in the Praśna Upaniṣad VI.2 as: *prāṇa, śraddhā* or *buddhi, ākāśa* or *kha, vāyu, jyoti, ap, pṛthivī, indriyas, annam, vīryam, tapas, mantra, yajña, lokāḥ, nāma* and *rūpa*. Of these some are cosmic and some are psychic elements. Since in Upaniṣadic doctrines both are equated there is no principal distinction between the two. But, in what way they should be distributed within the sixteen divisions of the square (or rectangle) is not evidenced otherwise, except in the sense that the Puruṣa, as the symbol of universal creation, is pervading the entire composition.[20]

In the commentary of Nigama Ḍiṇḍima the three horizontal layers are distinguished as being ruled by the three *guṇas*. The lowest layer of four compartments is called the *tamas* region, the middle region of eight compartments belongs to *rajas*, to the Life-force, and the uppermost layer of four compartments is divine light, the *sāttvic* region. Compare also the build-up of the human body in form of the Yūpa.

In the Praśna Upaniṣad I Pippalāda discourses at great length upon the two fundamental and complementary constituents of the universe, determined by the conception of Rayi and Prāṇa, as well as of human nature, the mortal and the immortal, the formed and the formless. All that is endowed with form, material, dense, dark, undergoing continuous change belongs to Rayi, the mortal part. All that is formless, luminous, unchanging belongs to Prāṇa. The moon with its changing phases is mortal. It is the region of the Fathers, from where the souls of those who did not aspire to ultimate release return to earth. The sun with its unchanging power and its all-animating rays is immortal, the region of light from where there is no return to earth for those who by their life and practice have aspired to Brahmahood.

In the *Śatapatha Brāhmaṇa* IV.1 it is said: "Now, in the begin-

---

[20]Compare the Vāstupuruṣa, in S. Kramrisch, *The Hindu Temple*, Vol. I, pp. 67f.

ning, Prajāpati was (composed) of both these, the mortal and the immortal. His vital airs alone were immortal, his body mortal: by this sacrificial performance and by this order of proceeding he made his body uniformly undecaying and immortal." (Tr. J. Eggeling).

Whereas the whole panel has three layers, the main figure has four parts, from below upwards, which correspond to the parts of the Puruṣa derived from the Yūpa. This is also compared to the Yogic division of the human body into two essential parts: the physical (hence mortal) part, which according to the Advayatāraka Upaniṣad reaches up to the eyebrows, and the spiritual (hence immortal) part which partakes of the divine light in the head, including the aureole which makes visible the light of immortality.

What gives life and warmth to Indian images is not display of physical strength, but the Prāṇa, the unscrutable inner breath of life which determines the entire conception of the universe.

Ornamentation (*Alaṅkaraṇa*)

When in the 5th Prapāṭhaka it is said that the limbs of Devatās should correspond to human forms, this does not mean that they should be represented in a naturalistic way with all anatomical details. From other Śilpa texts and from the evidence of Indian art in general it becomes clear that likeness only means likeness in function and expression. It is even enjoined that limbs should not be shown with their bones, joints, muscles and veins, but in a simplified, synthetic form: The head is likened to an egg, the neck to a conch-shell, the arms to elephants' trunks, the legs to inverted banana-stems. These are vivid images not only of their configuration, but more so still of their function.[21]

Ornaments are not simple embellishments to enhance the attractiveness of divine figures. They do that, of course, but have at the same time a more important function by shifting emphasis from anatomic form to geometrical or decorative patterns. They help transfiguring human forms into something beyond. Adherent draperies enclosing human forms, floating scarves surrounding them, girdles, necklaces, armlets, wristlets, anklerings and garlands encircling limbs create an independent pattern of lines that plays along

---

[21] See Abanindra Nath Tagore: *Indian Artistic Anatomy*, republished by the Indian Society of Oriental Art. 17. Park Street, Calcutta-16.

and across their movements, partly concealing their physical appearance. Resolved into abstract ornamental patterns, human figures are divested of their material character and transferred, as it were, into a subtler state of being. They lose their earthiness and weight, and by the very contrast with the artificial quality of the ornaments, begin to breathe and to radiate with a stronger plastic expression. The crowns, headdresses and aureoles finally show the transmundane light which irradiates from their heads. They are the supreme signs of their divinity. In this way ornaments assume a great importance, since they are efficient means for creating the feeling of a divine presence. If one would try to divest any of the sacred images of their ornamentation, only a plain human creature, however beautiful, would remain.

Postures and Gestures (*āsana* and *mudrā*)

In the representation of divinities two different kinds of symbolism are observed: One is the connatural symbolism inherent in their postures and gestures, their features and expressions. The other is an attributive, auxiliary symbolism shown by the weapons and emblems in their hands, by their seats, vehicles and attendant divinities. Both kinds of symbolism are used in sacred images. The postures and gestures are derived from those used by the priests performing sacrifices, and the text describes in detail a number of them with the significance they have in the act of sacrifice. Their exact significance in the image however is not explained in the Vāstusūtra.[22] But these poses and gestures are to be used only for the figures of the main divinities, for no other figure.

Whether this exclusive use of sacrificial gestures for figures of divinities was meant to emphasize the sacrality of the image, or its ritual character, or to operate as a sort of compromise and understanding between the practice of sacrificial ritual and image-worship, it will be difficult to say. Perhaps this measure fulfilled all the purposes at once. For answering the question one has to examine the inner meaning of the gestures in the ritual.

[22] Cf. Nigama Ḍiṇḍima Ṭippaṇī on VI: "The ornaments are there for attracting the people, the gestures have the purpose of showing the *sāttvika bhāva* (subtle expression of feelings) and others of the image, the weapons have the purpose of showing the rājasic *bhāva* (active, energetic mood) of the image, which is of the nature of their power, the vehicles have the purpose of showing the special quality of the image (is the tāmasic *bhāva* implied?). The worshippers are to show the relationship of the soul and Brahman."

Weapons (*āyudha*)

The weapons wielded and the emblems held in the hands of Devatās, although secondary in importance, are eloquent determinants of their character and function. Some are permanent features in the hands of certain divinities. Some are changed whenever the divinity assumes a different aspect. Twelve such weapons are described with their seed-words (*bījamantras*), by which they have to be consecrated and used. In the *bījamantra* alone lies their essence and power. Without it they are ineffective. Thus also the sculptor, while handling the chisels is enjoined to constantly repeat the *bījamantra* of the divinity he is carving.

Seats and Vehicles (*vāhanas*)

The basic nature of the various divinities is further illustrated by the seats or vehicles on which they are placed. They reveal their fundamental character and say whether a divinity is sāttvic and its worship would lead to liberation (*mokṣa*), or is rājasic and its adoration would grant worldly satisfactions, or it is tāmasic and would be helpful in overcoming and destroying enemies. In the latter case, at the place of the seat or vehicle, such fiendish powers are represented, in the form of Rākṣasa or demons, crushed under the destructive and liberating onslaught of the divinity.

Secondary Divinities (*upadaivata*)

The secondary divinities, placed by the side of the main divinity are all female and are called Śaktis. Here Vedic and Tāntric conceptions seem to be overlapping. The main divinities are all Vedic who as a rule are not so closely associated with female divinities as are Tāntric divinities. In the Vedas most female divinities are independent powers. They are not, or only loosely connected with any male divinity, and are not called Śaktis. In Tāntric conceptions only, apart from the great Mother-Goddess, who rules supreme in many forms, the Śaktis are not independent powers, but incorporate the Energy of the various male divinities whom they accompany. They are mostly represented as their consorts. In this text the Śaktis are basically divided into two categories: the powers of the Devas who lead to worldly attainment and satisfaction (*bhoga*) and the powers who lead to purification, spiritual knowledge and liberation (*mokṣa*).

Each divinity is accompanied by one or the other Śakti with a different significance and the devotee will choose according to the way he has decided to take in life. Pippalāda once more reminds his hearers of the two basic ends of human life. He says: When Prajāpati had brought forth Time, which means the changing ephemeral world, he created the South and the North. From the South the Pitṛs (Fathers), the Night, the Moon, the Darkness and the way of constant return. From the North the Devas, Savitṛ, the Day and the Light, the way of final liberation or immortality. The Śaktis are differentiated according to the way (*mārga*) they are meant to incorporate and lead. To give a few examples: Indra's Śakti of renunciation is Yajña (sacrifice), his procreative Śakti is Indrāṇī. Vaiśvānara, the sacrificial Fire, has a burning Śakti Svāhā and a maturing Śakti Svadhā. Viṣṇu has a supporting Śakti Bhū-Pṛthivī (Earth), and a liberating Śakti Lakṣmī or the golden Hariṇī. Yama has two Śaktis, one Ākūti for protection, and one Mṛtyu for giving death. Hiraṇyagarbha as a personified divinity has three Śaktis: Gāyatrī, Sāvitrī and Sarasvatī, Knowledge, Intelligence and Supreme Wisdom.[23] Śruti is similarly personified and is represented with her Śaktis Bhāratī and Sarasvatī.

While the conception of Śakti is Tāntric, many of the Śaktis together with their presiding deities retain their Vedic character. The Śaktis of Rudra are Ambā and Ambālikā, Ambā for spiritual liberation, Ambālikā for fruition and enjoyment. These two represent the transcendent and the worldly aspect of this divinity, but they resemble very little the Śaktis connected with Rudra, when he has taken the name of Śiva, such as Gaurī, Pārvatī, Umā.

In the sculptured panel the Śaktis are placed to the right and left of the main divinity.

Adversaries and Adorers (*arinaḥ* and *stuvakāḥ*)

It is the mission of the Devas to uphold the order of the Universe and to fight the adversaries who are constantly intent on destroying it. The eternal tragic dichotomy of opposite forces splitting the world of manifestation is traced back by Pippalāda to the origin of creation.

[23]These three Śaktis are those for whom the three parts of the Mahāgāyatrī Temple in Koṇārka were built, and who there are based on their particular proper *yantras*: Gāyatrī in the Garbhgṛha, Sāvitrī in the Mukhaśālā, Sarasvatī with Gaṇeśa in the porch. See: A. Boner, S. R. Sarma, R.P. Das, *New Light on the Sun-Temple of Koṇārka*, Varanasi, Chowkhamba Sanskrit Samsthan, 1972.

He says: "Prajāpati first brought forth Mind, from which arose Life and Action." Action however is inconceivable in a void, it has to have an object on which it can be exercised, a resistance, a counterpart, by which alone it assumes reality. Therefore he distributed two kinds of knowledge, *parāvidyā* and *aparāvidyā*, real and unreal, spiritual, and material, transcendent and earth-bound knowledge. The Asuras choose unreal knowledge (*aparāvidyā*) and eternally obstruct those who search the divine Order of things (*parāvidyā*). In the images they are sometimes represented as standing up and contesting the supremacy of the Devas, sometimes as demons and goblins crushed under their feet. To counter and neutralize their tāmasic powers Ṛṣis have to meditate, priests have to offer sacrifices and people have to worship. For helping the gods, the protectors of holy Order, with praises and prayers, the image shows Yakṣas, Gandharvas and Apsarases in the two uppermost corners, and human worshippers in the two lowermost corners. This completes the composition, which in each case presents a condensed, abridged reflection of the eternal conflict of cosmic forces inherent in worldly existence and the resolution of the same, the salvation of created beings in the heart and with the help of the Devas.

The Vāstusūtra concludes by stressing again that the knowledge of art, the sacred Vāstuvidyā, is not an end itself, but that it leads to that supreme spiritual knowledge which results in liberation.

After Pippalāda has made a circumstantial and penetrating analysis of the spiritual, intellectual and technical processes involved in the creation of cult-images, a question still remains to be cleared.

What exactly does Pippalāda mean when he insists on the fact that the knowledge of LINE and CIRCLE is the quintessence of Śilpavidyā? Why does he say that it is this knowledge alone which makes the Sthāpaka a master of his art and nothing else? How is this to be understood?

This cryptic, axiomatic assertion obviously cannot refer to the simple technical process of tracing a line with the thread or the measuring rod or drawing a circle by means of a compass. For such achievements there was no need to write a Vāstusūtra. This evidently refers to some other, cosmic and spiritual dimensions of these two elements of form-creation.

What Pippalāda has in mind can only refer to the fundamental form-principles, which in their subtle relationship constitute the entire cosmic manifestation. The CIRCLE and the LINE, with their developments into second and third dimensions, such as plane, cube and sphere, actually embrace the whole display of visible forms in the universe.

The line and the circle have opposite, yet complementary functions inherent in their intrinsic nature. The circle collects, circumscribes and encompasses form. It gathers substance concentrically and thus creates volume. It determines a limit and is thus essentially static and finitizing. The only movement which it may have is in itself. It may be contracting or expanding, or when rotating, participating in the element Time. The curve as a segment of a circle necessarily participates in its nature and functions.

The straight line, on the other hand, is not formative in itself. It is essentially active, dynamic. It penetrates, cuts, divides, disrupts the uniform whole. While the curve unifies and retracts everything towards a centre, the movement of the straight line runs out into infinite space. It is bodyless, limitless. Only when crossed by other straight lines or broken into angles it becomes formative and thus responsible for all fundamental geometrical figures and bodies in the universe, triangle, quadrangle, octagon, hexagon, pentagon and their correlatives in the third dimension.

This spatial order of things displayed in three dimensions is not dead matter, but a living organism with movement as a fourth dimension. Movement is Time. Time is movement in which circle and line participate in different ways. The circle has a recurring, cyclic movement and time, with measure and rhythm as its inherent essential quality. The straight line has a non-recurring, limitless movement without measure, except that given by deviations or by extraneous elements, such as collision with other lines.

These elementary factors constituting the physical world are captured symbolically in the *pañjara*, all elements compressed in two-dimensional space. As line and circle determine the forms and functions of nature, they equally have to determine the structure of the *pañjara* and the entire vocabulary of form-language used by the human creator. Every *pañjara*, the geometrical diagram of every image of divinity is like a universe in miniature, the totality and quintessence of a universe, where all powers are potentially present. The fundamental pattern of the image is created by the intimate interaction of Space and Time, of static and dynamic elements incorporated in its lines. The diversity of images is obtained by a selective use of these lines. Some lines are stressed, some overemphasized, some subdued and some completely suppressed, according as to which are the forces, the tendencies, the *guṇas* that are to be shown, in order to bring out the character of the image. The artist will never deviate substantially from the fundamental lines which carry the symbol-significance of the image, but within their ambit he is free to unfold his personal vision, exploring the infinite possibility of these patterns, experimenting with various combinations and alternatives, with whatever his intellect and understanding, his religious feeling or speculative imagination may inspire him. His creativity is not impaired, but greatly stimulated and enriched by the underlying cosmic pattern, which opens to him vast and profound visions of the spiritual aspects of the cosmic web, and at the same time provides him with an unerring guidance in his search for the revelation of this ultimate mystery.

The expression of eternal Law, not of individual fancy, is the purpose of this art. That is why Pippalāda says that for achieving a significant, valid form-creation the human artisan has to realize in his intimate self the interplay of these two opposite yet complementary structural elements of the manifested world – the line and the circle – and their final compact and harmony. On these should be established all work that comes from his hands.

That these principles were not simple theory, but were realized in general practice is confirmed by Nigama Ḍiṇḍima's Commentary on the Vāstusūtra Upaniṣad. He says that the principles of composing images as explaining the *pañjaras* were valid throughout the country, from the Vaitaraṇī to the Cauveri, that means throughout the southern part of India. If he mentions only the east-coast it may be because he was living in Orissa, but factual evidence shows that these principles were followed also in the western provinces of the country. Not only the sculptures of Mahābalipuram and Kanchipuram, but also those of Elephanta, Deogarh, Elura, Badāmī bear ample testimony to this fact.

Evidence of their application is found in the book: *Principles of Composition in Hindu Sculpture* (Cave-temple Period) by Alice Boner.[24]

In this book numerous sculptures in the cave-temples of southern and western India are analysed for their compositional structure, and these are demonstrated with detailed drawings of their static and

[24]Second edition, Delhi, Motilal Banarsidass, 1990.

dynamic elements. Although these analyses were done by mere study of compositional contexts without knowledge of any text or theory, they show a remarkable resemblance to the *pañjaras* propounded in the Vāstusūtra, even to their symbolical implications. This goes to prove that in those sculptures, dating back from the 6th to the 9th Cent. A.D., the theories expressed in the Vāstusūtra were in full evidence and were applied with full knowledge of their meaning, so as to be recognizable even to untutored contemplation.

An old Sthapati of Sambalpur, when asked what was a *pañjara*, laughed and said: "The *pañjara*! Yes, that is a thing which was known in the Dvāpara Yuga, but in the Kali Yuga, who knows about it?" Such an utterance also indicates that the *pañjara* was no simple technical device for producing good and harmonious compositions, but a secret and sacred knowledge which enabled the sculptor to produce images that not only were of perfect form, but could convey a spiritual message to the devotee.

Medieval sculpture too was essentially informed by the same principles, but they were less rigorously applied, and often over-grown by the florid and exuberant modelling of living form and of ornamentation hiding the fundamental pattern.

If Sthapatis of to-day no longer know what is a *pañjara*, still the general principle of concentric composition, transmitted by tradition, seems to be rooted in their subconscious. Much of their work follows such principles as a matter of course, by the force of habit, probably unaware of their meaning and their implications. While preserving the forms, this, of course, deprives their work of much of its inner life and significance, and may account for some of the mechanical character and unexpressiveness of later sculpture.

But in many Indian miniature paintings, preferably of the Pahari schools from the 16th to the 18th Century, unaffected by Mogul influence, such laws of composition can be detected. They are at times so striking that one is inclined to think that two-to-three-hundred years ago a certain conscious knowledge and practice of such compositional patterns was still alive among painters, although applied in a different medium and form. This would show how principles solidly based on cosmic laws and inspired by a metaphysical vision are not easily upset. They hold good through centuries as long as they are not disrupted by extraneous, uncongenial influences. It would also prove that an infinite variety of forms can grow from one single root, when it is established on solid ground and universally valid principles.

THE POSITION OF THE VĀSTUSŪTROPANIṢAD IN THE ATHARVAVEDIC LITERATURE

by
DIPAK BHATTACHARYA

1. The Atharvaveda and the Vāstusūtra

The Vāstusūtropaniṣad (VSU) claims to be an Upaniṣad attached to the Atharvaveda (AV). This Veda deals with magico-religious matter while the VSU is a treatise on the Vāstusūtra and Śilpaśāstra dealing with architecture and sculpture. Naturally one may ask whether the claim of the VSU is justified.

There are evidences of the existence of a Śilpa-Vāstu-Śāstra based on the AV. The Bhāgavata Purāṇa[1] (ca. 9th Cent. A.D.) mentions architecture as an Upaveda of the AV, i.e. as one of the secular sciences derived from the AV. Śrīdharasvāmin (14th Century) further explains that this means the science of Viśvakarman. Mahidāsa, a 16th Century scholiast also knew the Śilpaśāstra as an Upaveda of the AV. Also a perusal of the AV and its ancillary literature (all earlier than the 4th Cent. B.C.) convinces one that this Veda has enough material for being regarded as the original source of the science of architecture. Vāstoṣpati, the lord of the house is raised to a position of particular importance in the AV and a group of hymns are named after him. These hymns are used in later times in building houses. Exact terms for the house, the establishment, building material and a lot of related material appear for the first time in the AV. The importance of the building is a characteristic feature of the AV literature and the majority of the mantras which the Gṛhyasūtras prescribed for house-building are taken from the AV.

But we had nothing to bridge the long gap between the ancient AV literature with the potentiality of giving rise to a science of building (architecture/sculpture) and the actual emergence of such a science as evidenced by the said information from the Bhāgavata in ca. 9th Cent. A.D. Hence when Dr A. Boner approached me through Dr B. Bäumer to write a foreword to the Vāstusūtropaniṣad it was

[1] Bhāgavata 3.12.37–39.

a pleasant surprise for me that an AV-Śilpaśāstra has at last been found. This Upaniṣad claims itself to be based on the AV and also to have originated from Viśvakarman. In these respects it tallies with the traditional accounts of the Atharvavedic Śilpaśāstra.

2. The date of the VSU

In spite of the great expectations the VSU can naturally raise in the minds of Vedic scholars it remains a problem text.

There are a lot of ancient and modern lists of the Upaniṣads of the AV. None of these known to me mentions the VSU. It is also different from all other Upaniṣads in its subject matter and presentation.

The recognised listed Upaniṣads came into being in two major stages. 13 or 14 major Upaniṣads belong to the latest phase of the Vedic age and most of them are pre-Buddhistic. Another set of about 200 minor Upaniṣads came into being (mostly) in the 1st millennium A.D. The VSU is different from all these. The said Upaniṣads are of theological nature, primarily dealing with religious theory and practice. The VSU on the other hand is primarily a Śilpaśāstra – a treatise on sculpture and architecture. Thus its subject matter falls outside the general scope of Upaniṣadic discussion.

The absence of the VSU in the prevalent inventories of Upaniṣads as well as the peculiar nature of its contents might be explained by the currency of the treatise among artisans as a secret treatise. But then it will be impossible to connect this particular text with the said Bhāgavata tradition about AV-Śilpaśāstras, which indicates public awareness about the currency of AV Śilpaśāstra.

In fact there are internal evidences in the VSU to show that in its present form it is much later than the Bhāgavata Purāṇa. Some of the geometrical terms used in the VSU are of very late origin. The words *sarala rekhā* (II.9)[2], *samāntarāla* (II.16) etc. occurring in the VSU are technical terms of Rekhāgaṇita (Linear Mathematics Euclidean Geometry) introduced in India through the Arabs. The Arabs came to India in the eighth century. But even during the time of Bhāskarācārya II (12th Cent. A.D.) Indian mathematics was not at all influenced by the Arabs. In fact the main credit of the introduction of Rekhāgaṇita and the above mentioned geometrical

[2]Note by the Editor: the term *sarala rekhā* for a straight line occurs in Saṅgīta Ratnākara VI.29, also III.145.425 etc., where there is no influence of Arab geometry. The text is dated to the first half of the 13th Cent.

terms goes to Jagannātha, an eighteenth century mathematician of Jaipur.

So, we have an intriguing problem as related below.

The Atharvaveda comes into being in the first millennium B.C. or earlier, with such material as can give rise to a science of architecture (Vāstuśāstra) based on it. From about the 9th Cent. A.D. we hear of the existence of such a literature. Now, a text of the same nature comes to our hand and it claims itself to be based on the AV. But in its present form it appears to be later than the 9th Century A.D.

There are many other problems with the VSU. My views on the major problems are given below.

3. The Sūtras and the explanatory text

The VSU has got two parallel divisions in the form of Sūtras and an explanatory text. They do not seem to have a common origin. The explanation of VI.26, for example, is wrong. The Sūtra runs as: *prajñārtham etad vāstūpākhyānam.* If the reading is correct, the Sanskrit here is extremely unorthodox. Literally, this would mean, "This Vāstu-story is for the sake of knowledge". The intended sense here seems to be "This explanation of the Vāstu-science is for the sake of knowledge." But this requires the reading "*vāstuvyākhyānam*" instead of *vāstūpākhyānam.* Now, the explanatory text says on this: *etadarthaṃ prajñāṃ vyākhyāpayāma iti.* Literally this means, "We explain knowledge for the sake of this (Vāstu-science)". This paraphrasing makes the confusion of the Sūtra worse and betrays very poor understanding of the Sūtra. This would not have taken place if the Sūtras and the explanatory text came from the pen of the same author.

Again I.7 says that "the mind becomes especially vitiated by diffused imagination" when attempt is made to concentrate upon the divinity without concrete form. The explanatory text does not elaborate this theme, but speaks of the same defect of diffused imagination on I.9 in a different case.

Again III.10 says that one should assume *parṇa*-amulets for protection. AVŚ III.5.1, 2, 5 mention *parṇa*-amulets. The VSU explanatory text does not cite this, but mentions AVŚ II.25.1 which has no connection with *parṇa*-amulets. The explanation seems to have been based on the assumption of some connection of *parṇa*-amulet with the term *pṛśni-parṇī* (a plant with spotted leaf) which occurs in AVŚ II.25.1.

4. Connection of the Sūtras to the Atharvaveda

The Sūtras are never explicit about their Atharvavedic origin. However, this can be inferred from a few Atharvavedic words used by them. Such a word is *parṇamaṇi* (III.10), as mentioned above; we have *diśāpālana* in V.22, which seems close to Āśāpāla of AVŚ I.31. *Ākarṣaṇīvidyā* of VSU II.17 is the name of one of the ten magical works of the AV.

Such words occur in the Sūtras very rarely and may, at best, indicate the growth of the Sūtras among people with some acquaintence with Atharvavedic priests or some knowledge of Atharvavedic rites. But there is no indication of any deep link between the Sūtras and the AV.

A loose connection between the Sūtras and the AV can be testified also by some of the ritual enjoinments in them. For example, the above-mentioned prescription in VSU III.1 that one should assume *parṇa*-amulets for protection is not usual. *Parṇa*-amulets are mostly used for general prosperity.

5. The explanatory text and the Atharvaveda

The explanatory text is more explicit about its Atharvavedic affiliation. Its frequent citation of Atharvavedic mantras, the occurrence of words like *jaṅgiḍa* (II.3), *mahīlukā* (II.3), *tarda* (V.17), Yātudhāna (II.17), many words in the explanatory text on VI.24 and the explicit statement of its tradition in the introduction to I.1 etc. indicate the involvement of the author of the explanatory text with the AV. But here too, certain anomalies should be noted.

The explanatory text asserts that the work belongs to the "Pippalādakalpa" (I.10). This word is not orthodox. But the Paippalāda recension of the AV was very well-known in ancient times. The VSU's claimed affiliation to that branch of the AV is not corroborated by internal evidences from the VSU. For, the citations made in it from the AV prove beyond any shade of doubt that the author knows only the Śaunakīya recension of the AV but not the Paippalāda recension.

The following list of citations with my observations may make my standpoint clear.
Explanatory text on

(1) III.5: *Cakṣur asi cakṣur* etc. = AVŚ II.17.6–7
This charm is not found in the AVP.

(2) III.10: *Śaṃ no devī* etc. = AVŚ II.25.1
The variants in the parallel AVP verse, viz., AVP IV.13.1 are ignored in the VSU.

(3) VI.16: *Puroḍāsavatsā sudughā* etc. = AVŚ XII.4.35

(4) VI.26: AVŚ XIX.17.7 is cited and variants are found in the parallel AVP VII.16.7

The claimed allegiance of the VSU to the AV Paippalāda is thus contradicted by its own citations. This encourages enquiry into the strength of the claimed affiliation of the VSU to the Atharvaveda. We cite a few other instances below which might indicate that the explanatory text, too, like the Sūtras, has only loose and shallow grounding in Atharvavedic tradition.

The VSU (I.1, IV.17) equates Vāstoṣpati and Viśvakarman or Prajāpati. This is not a Vedic tradition. In the Yajurveda Vāstoṣpati is Rudra; in the Amarakośa (C. 1st Cent. A.D.) he is Indra. But his identity as Viśvakarman is not known to me. In any case this is not a Vedic or even early classical tradition.

In II.15 the symbol of fire is a triangle. The idea seems to be a post-Vedic development under the influence of the triangular fireplace of the Tantras. The Sūtra, too, refers to the post-Vedic connections (*smaryate loke*) of the idea.

Again, IV.17 equates ten sacrifices (*daśayajña*) with a ten-part Puruṣa. The Gopatha Brāhmaṇa (I.1.39/II.6.2) enumerates ten *prāṇas* and equates *prāṇa, puruṣa* and *yajña.* This might give some justification for a *daśāṅga puruṣa* and *yajña.* But it is difficult to see how that becomes the ten-part Yūpa (post at the sacrifice). Moreover, the concept of the ten sacrifices does not figure in the Vedas.

6. The Atharvaveda and the Origin of the VSU

The inconsistencies mentioned above do not allow us to speak highly of the VSU's connection with the AV. If it at all originated among Atharvavedic circles, the circles consisted of priests with little traditional training and the author of the VSU knew the AV very loosely.

This negative statement, however, does not explain the origin of the VSU. The explanation is a difficult task. What seems one of the possibilities is given below.

From a certain period in Indian history the Atharvaveda seems to have become an instrument for the diffusion of Vedic culture by way of absorbing local cults into the central official cult partronised by the state, that is to say into Brāhmaṇism. The earliest texts of this Veda, namely the AV Paippalāda and AV Śaunakīya themselves indicate that such a future awaited this Veda. These texts highly praise the Vrātyas – people who had culturally diverged from the Vedic people. They were re-enlisted among the sacrifice-performing official Vedic group with certain rites. Their praise in the AV, it appears, is indicative of the shape of things to come in future.

From about the middle of the first millennium A.D. we come to hear of sectarian Upaniṣads not recognised in earlier traditions. These become fully recognised in the early second millennium A.D. Most of these are Atharvavedic. They praise different forms of Viṣṇu, Śiva, Śakti etc. in sectarian spirit, describe esoteric practices, or emphasise upon aspects of later Vedānta. It is only rational to infer that here one finds traces of huge absorption, in the first millennium A.D., of locally developed cults into the Brāhmaṇical society. The Atharvaveda was instrumental in this, as all these new Upaniṣads are Atharvavedic.

The instrumentality of the Atharvaveda in such acculturation process seems to have prevented the maintenance of rigid control over its ancillary literature so that the entrance of extra-Atharvavedic elements into its range went on till late. Later even an Upaniṣad of Allah came to be known as Atharvavedic.

The said long drawn process of absorption of extra-Vedic elements into the fold of Vedicism through the Atharvaveda seems to have brought the nucleus of a Śilpa-Vāstuśāstra into the range of Atharvavedic literature and given rise to the AV-Vāstuśāstra tradition of the Bhāgavata.

Unfortunately for us we do not know whether the supposed nucleus of a Śilpa-Vāstuśāstra existed in Sanskrit or some local dialect. Also we cannot prove that the VSU grew around such a nucleus. However, it is obvious that the AV was used to give the theories of the VSU an official stamp.

Thus, while the inclusion of the VSU with the stream of AV tradition is plausible, all of our problems are not solved. For, it is strange and striking that the medieval movement would continue for centuries. Another problem is the loose connection of the VSU with the AV.

The last-mentioned fact requires explanation. Should we suppose that the existing Sanskrit version of the VSU grew on the foundation of popular codes in some local dialect? One may consider whether the facts lead one to the same conclusion.

(i) The ten sacrifices in VSU IV.17

As told above, the concept of ten sacrifices is not Vedic. But in later Vedic literature one finds the ten domestic rites (*daśakarmāṇi*). These remained very popular during the medieval period. It is highly probable that the idea of ten sacrifices in the VSU grew out of that of the ten domestic rites and that the terminological aberration reflects its growth among people with loose traditional training regarding the Vedas.

(ii) The idea of fourteen *bhuvanakoṣas* (VSU V.20) is a similar instance. *Bhuvanakoṣa* meant the circular flat of the earth. It is one and not fourteen in number. The fourteen worlds – *lokas* or *bhuvanas*, on the other hand are well-known (Bhartṛhari's Vairāgyaśataka, 23, the Purāṇas etc). But the VSU V.20 speaks of fourteen *bhuvanakoṣas* within the body. Two aspects of the idea are to be noted –

(a) The *bhuvanas* are presented as *bhuvanakoṣas*;

(b) the body is a microcosm of the Universe. Such presentation easily encourages the inference of acquaintance with popular theories (macro-micro symmetry) without the same with books.

The hypothesis of the VSU's origin in popular circles among semi-orthodox, semi-literate elements, among architects knowing about the AV from traditions floating among Atharvavedic priests with poor training, explains VSU discrepancies with the AV and other inconsistencies.

The hypothesis of a popular origin of the VSU is somewhat supported also by the recent observations of Biswadev Mukherjee in "A study of the legend of Nālagiri as depicted in an Ajanta fresco".[3] A series of events has been depicted in the fresco. Taken sundrily, some of them might be found in one literary version of the legend or another. But when they are taken together, the fresco version does not tally with any known text version. Mukherjee explains this discrepancy with the hypothesis of a popular version of the legend widely known to the people, which had been used by the painters at Ajanta.

---

[3] Dr Siddheshwar Bhattacharya Felicitation Volume, Varanasi, not yet published.

Just like the apparent concoction of different literary versions of a story in the Ajanta fresco, in the VSU one finds the concoction of different religio-philosophical ideas. And their uncouth and quite unorthodox handling as in the VSU, shown above, encourages the inference of the utilisation of an oral, popular version, before presenting them in Sanskrit, by the authors of the VSU.

VĀSTUSŪTRA UPANIṢAD

ENGLISH TRANSLATION

Now begins the Atharvavedic

VĀSTUSŪTROPANIṢAD

FIRST CHAPTER

THE SIX BRANCHES OF ART

Ātharvaṇāṅgirasa[1] and Śilpakāśyapa[2] spoke to Pippalāda of great wisdom: Among the sixteen Tāpinī (Upaniṣads)[3] this is the Vāstusthāpakavidyā (the science of the architect and sculptor).[4] The one who knows it...The priests (*hotṛ*), the chanters (*udgātṛ*) and the students of Śilpa in the Ātharvaṇa tradition –

Sūtra 1: (They) should know Vāstoṣpati (the divinity of Vāstu).[5]

He is the divinity Viśvakarman. His doctrine (*vidyā*) contains the enquiry into the six branches of Art (*śilpa*).[6] To those, Āṅgirasa and others who were keenly looking up to him, Pippalāda explained – what the artists (*śilpakārāḥ*) propound in whom all kinds of works of art originate and how many types (of art) there are. (Then) that very Kuvitsa, the one who uproots (*kuśa* grass) with strong hands[7] (and) Śilpakāśyapa, having resolved (in his mind): "I shall ask according to my desire" (asked): "Who is Vāstoṣpati Viśvakarman?"[8] (Further)

[1]In the Atharvaveda, (AVŚ) XI.4.16 he is mentioned as a Ṛṣi. In the 19th Kāṇḍa Aṅgiras is the Ṛṣi, author of the 5th Anuvāka (AVŚ XIX.34–35).

[2]The author of the Kāśyapa Śilpasūtra is the Ṛṣi Śilpakāśyapa.

[3]The sixteen Tāpinī texts of the Atharvaveda are: Avadhūta-tāpinī, Tripuratāpinī, Nṛsiṃhatāpinī, Puruṣatāpinī, Vṛṣatāpinī, these and others are all Atharvavedic.

[4]Sūtras dealing with the subject of Vāstu (Art=architecture and sculpture).

[5]The divinity of Vāstu is Vāstoṣpati, that is the meaning.

[6]In the Kāśyapa Śilpasūtra there are the following subjects (topics): making of divine images, temple building, town planning, fort construction, metal-work, calligraphy and other arts. [N.B. This is a wrong interpretation, for the six disciplines are enumerated in Sūtra 8.]

[7]This is an Atharvavedic *brāhmaṇa* for setting up the stone for the image at an auspicious moment on *darbha* grass.

[8]The divinity of Śilpa, as mentioned in the Atharvaveda (AVŚ) XIX.18.7: "Praise Viśvakarman with the seven Ṛṣis".

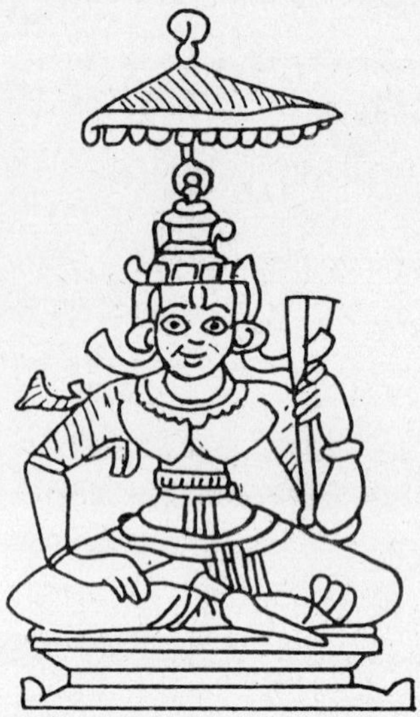

Fig. 1: Viśvakarman
(from the illustrated MS of the Ṭippaṇī)

he said to him: "I think you will teach us, who are members of the Vedic community."

Pippalāda answered: "Those who are about to depart from this world (desiring liberation), they all aspire for knowledge."

Sūtra 2: Art-forms[9] are produced by means of six disciplines.

Forms (sculptures) are made in stone[10] or in *khādira* wood (*akacia katechu*), this much is the knowledge of form in this world. In the Veda (it is said): Every form is an image (of an original form) (cf. ṚV VI.47.18), this is the difference (between the conception of form in the world and in the Veda). This knowledge is divine knowledge.

[9]In the Paippalāda Saṃhitā I.26.5 it is said: "The Dark One (Śyāmā) who gives a beautiful form (*rūpa*) was borne on the earth. Accomplish it in these bodies (*mūrtiṣu*) and create again complete forms (or colours)." (Charm against leprosy). (See also AVŚ I.24.4.)

[10]"There are four types of images: those made of clay, of stone, of metal or of wood, these are specially for worship." (Note of MS घ).

Sūtra 3: The Yūpa[11] (sacrificial post) is this light.

That very Yūpa is made of *khādira* wood or of stone, as said in the Vaitāna (Sūtra).[12] Circular is the head of the Yūpa since it is the whole universe (*viśvam*), it is at the top of the Yūpa. (And) the actions (*karmāṇi*) are of proportionate shapings in a straight line – that is the Yūpa-pillar, the trunk of the Yūpa. By their connection (i.e. of the head and the trunk) the Yūpa is made (complete). He who knows this, declares this knowledge, and he is verily Viśvakarman, the presiding divinity of Art (*Śilpa*).[13] He who knows this is the best of architects.

Sūtra 4: Who has the knowledge of circle and line is a sthāpaka.

Holding in hand a measuring rod of *khādira* wood and a cord of *darbha* grass fitted with a ring, that is his outer aspect. This knowledge is the knowledge of Art (*śilpajñāna*). From this knowledge arises divine knowledge, and such knowledge leads to liberation. This (liberation) is verily the essence of the knowledge of Art. He who knows this [attains the essence].[14]

Sūtra 5: By Śilpa images are produced.[15]

---

[11] "Āditya (the Sun) is the Yūpa", thus it is said in the Aitareya (Brāhmaṇa V.28) and Taittirīya (Brāhmaṇa II.1.5.2).

[12] The Vaitāna-Sūtra of the Atharvaveda. In the Atharvaveda XIII.1.47 it is said: "He established heat and cold, he made the mountains sacrificial posts." Again it is said by Indra in the mantra "The mighty Yūpa is a Māruta pillar." Again in the Atharvaveda (X.7–8) the Yūpa is glorified as the Skambha, the pillar upholding the universe in the form of a divinity.

[13] That is mentioned in the Gṛhyasūtra and the Atharvaveda [wrong reference: cf. ṚV X.81 and 82]. In the Śatapatha Brāhmaṇa (I.7.3.7) it is said "Vāstu is that part of the sacrifice what (is left) after the oblations have been made." [read *huteṣu* instead of *ghṛteṣu*. The context of the quotation is the oblation to Agni Sviṣṭakṛt and the shares in the offerings. Rudra is called Vāstavya "for he was left behind on the (sacrificial) site (*vāstu*)" (ŚB I.7.3.1)]. This divinity is the Vāstupuruṣa, Śikhinī and others [i.e. the deities of the Vāstupuruṣa maṇḍala].

[14] The bliss of Brahman is honey, as said in the Atharvaveda (AVŚ I.34.1): "From honey sprang the plant to life, with honey now we tied thee up. Make us as sweet as honey, for from honey hast thou been produced." (Griffith).

[15] *Pratimā* is mentioned in the Atharvaveda, (AVŚ IX.4.2): "He who in the beginning became an image of the Waters, the Originator of all, like Goddess Earth, the Father of the calves, the husband of the cows, may he bestow on us a thousand-fold prosperity." In the Vājasaneyi Saṃhitā it is said: "What is this image in yonder world, is the same image in the mid-space (*antarikṣa*)."

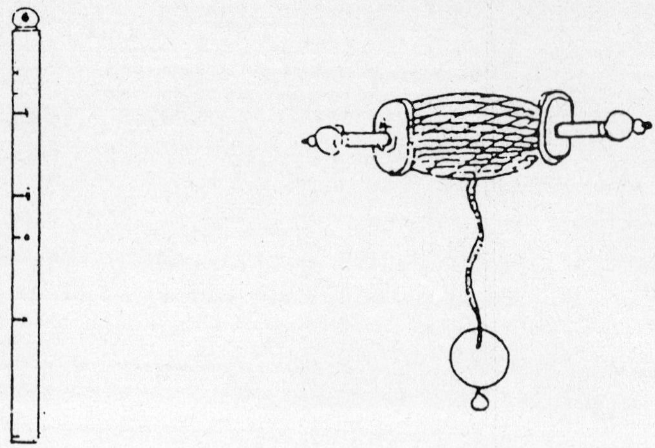

Fig. 2: Measuring rod and cord

By images arises faith, from faith firm devotion, from this comes knowledge which results in liberation. These are the five steps of Vāstu. He who knows this has an all-embracing knowledge according to the Ātharvaṇa tradition – this is the teaching. Then Śilpakāśyapa, Ātharvaṇāṅgirasa, Kuvitsa and others[16] became proficient in the chanting of the Udgītha,[17] and they asked Pippalāda: Explain us the six branches of Vāstu according to your conception. He said: Yes, being desirous to teach them.

Sūtra 6: He, the carrier of the tradition, proclaimed (to them) the teaching of the Śilpasūtra (called) the sthāpakavidyā.

This is the best science which originated from Prajāpati in the beginning (of creation). From Prajāpati (it was passed on) to Nārada, from Nārada to Maya, from Maya to Vaiśravaṇa,[18] from Vaiśravaṇa to Pippalāda. (A disciple said:) I will listen (to this science), the revelation of all these is truth.

Then Āṅgirasa said: "I will ask you." – Pippalāda replied: "Ask!" – "How does an image come into being? How in this world forms

[16]They are certain Ṛtviks, priests of the Atharvaveda.

[17]Arisen are the (two) blessed stars called the Unfasteners (*vicṛt*), AV II.8.1 (Whitney).

[18]The descendant (grandson) of Paulastya was Rāvaṇa, the son of Viśravā.

and images arise? My Lord, I cannot see this."

Pippalāda spoke in the way of Prajāpati; "Āṅgirasa, put your heart at rest. In this mortal world this (universe) was Being in the best act of sacrificing.

> "He who in the beginning became the archetypal model
> of the waters,
> the originator of all, like Goddess Earth,
> the Father of the calves, the husband of the cows,
> may he bestow on us a thousandfold prosperity."[19]
> With this mantra one should worship for fulfilment. This
> is the sense.

And this sacrificing and worship,

Sūtra 7: When worship is done without bodily images, the mind becomes particularly vitiated by indiscriminate imagination.

From the archetype gradually arises the knowledge of the principle of images, from the knowledge of the principle (*tattvabodha*) comes clear conception (*dhāraṇā*), from clear conception sacred songs (*gāthā*) and myths (*kathā*) arise among the people. From the sacred songs (*gāthā*) the *sthāpakas* derive the images." Thus he said to him: "For the purpose of creating form and acquiring the practice of an artist (now) the specific (means is):

Sūtra 8: Six disciplines of Art are essential.

(They are the following:) Knowledge of stones (*śailam*), compositional diagrams (*khilapañjara*)[20] made with a peg, a net-work of lines for housing the image like a cage, in which the limbs of the image depend on the vital points (*marmāṇi*), the carving of stones (*śailabhedana*), the arrangement of the limbs or parts (*aṅgaprayoga*), the emotional disposition evoked by the composition (*nyāsabhāvanā*) and the understanding of the integration of the composition (*sambandha-prabodhana*)."

Āṅgirasa spoke: "How do the six branches of the Art of image-making (*rūpavāstuṣaḍaṅgaṃ śilpaṃ*) become established and made

[19] AVŚ IX.4.2 (AVP XVI.24.2), see above note 15.
[20] *Khila* is a Sūtra containing the application (*prayoga*).

manifest? May the Lord satisfy my desire of knowing this." Having heard this, he (Pippalāda) replied: "The order in which this *sthāpakavidyā* has come down to me and is being passed on," that very order of the six branches was told by him:

[STONE]

Sūtra 9: Six kinds of stone are to be known.

Six kinds of stone are known in this region to people, namely: *hiraṇyarekhikā, samavarṇā, tāmrā, dhātupuṭitā, vajralabdhā* and *saikatālikā.*

(*Hiraṇyarekhikā*): When curved lines of golden colour show up in the stone, it is of bad quality, not fit for image-making, it will cause deformations, from whose sight diffused imaginations arise. On account of their aspect they are called unfit. So it is said, and such it is. Because of this the image becomes deformed.

(*Samavarṇā*): When the entire stone is of one colour, either black, dark-brown or turmeric yellow, it is considered best (fit) for the main image, that is *samavarṇā.*

(*Tāmrā*): Very hard stone of copper-red (*gāḍhapiṅgala*) colour should not be considered. When the stone is not severed from the rock, then it can be used in sculpture-halls.[21] When detached from the rock it becomes useless. Where only *līlāvigrahas* (mythological scenes) are made on the walls (it can be used).

(*Dhātupuṭitā*): When the stone has metal-like sores of smoky colour it is worst for image-making.

(*Vajralabdhā*): When between the layers of the stone soft mineral lines of shining yellow colour are running, they are always considered to be inferior by the best sculptors (*śilpakāras*).

Saikatālikā (sandstone) is especially good for Yūpas, Yonis, Mithunastambhas[22] and Kuṇḍas, it is (also) to be taken for making images.

The sculptors who possess this knowledge are found among the people and are greatly honoured as accomplished.

[21] Just like *līlā-mūrtis* of divinities are carved out in a big rock-wall as a sculpture-hall for the pleasure of ascetics (*tapasvin*), this is a saying of Kāśyapa.

[22] Stambha is a Yūpa, Yūpa verily is Stambha (Skambha), this is said in AVŚ X.7. In practical use there are three distinct types: for sacrifices to Brahma the Skambha is the Yūpa, for sacrifices to ancestors the bull-pillar (*vṛṣa-stambha*), for sacrifices to fulfil desires a Mithuna-stambha, that is the difference.

Sūtra 10: By the type of stone the colour (rāga) of the image is known.

In all the worlds there is freedom (for the sculptor).

This is the first Prapāṭhaka called the knowledge of the six types of stones, which is the tradition of the Vāstusūtra in the Pippalāda Kalpa of the Atharvaveda, in the discourse passed on by the Muni to the hearers by way of word, body and mind.

SECOND CHAPTER

COMPOSITIONAL DIAGRAM

Now follows the knowledge of the *khilapañjara*[1] (compositional diagram) of which I explain the procedure. Āṅgirasa[2] should make efforts (to study it) like a sculptor (*grābhakāra*).

Sūtra 1: An image should be envisaged to express a specified meaning.[3]

After selecting a suitable stone it should be laid on *darbha* grass in the workshop at an auspicious moment (*abhijit*).[4] Then the stone should be fixed with pegs of *udumbara* wood.

Sūtra 2: Setting the stone is the first action.

After setting and fixing it the *hotṛ* and the *adhvaryu* together with the sculptors should polish the stone for the image to make it smooth.

Sūtra 3: Polishing it is the second action.

Beginning with the mantra[5]:

> "OM! So have I glorified with praise strong Dadhikrāvan
> conquering steed.
> Sweet may he make our mouths, may he prolong the days
> we have to live." (Griffith)

---

[1] That secret method by which images obtain their measure and proportion, (*prāmāṇyam*) is the *khilapañjaravidyā*. It means that it is uncommon, a secret knowledge of lines.

[2] (Āṅgirasa) worshipped the Udgītha. He is known as Āṅgirasa, who is the essence (*rasa*) of the limbs (*aṅgānām*). He is a Ṛṣi who is a knower of the Self (*ātmajña*).

[3] An image proper (fit) for worship.

[4] The Taittirīya Brāhmaṇa (I.5.2.3) says: "That special auspicious constellation is called Abhijit, above (the constellation Aṣāḍha)", this is the quotation.

[5] AVŚ XX.137.3.

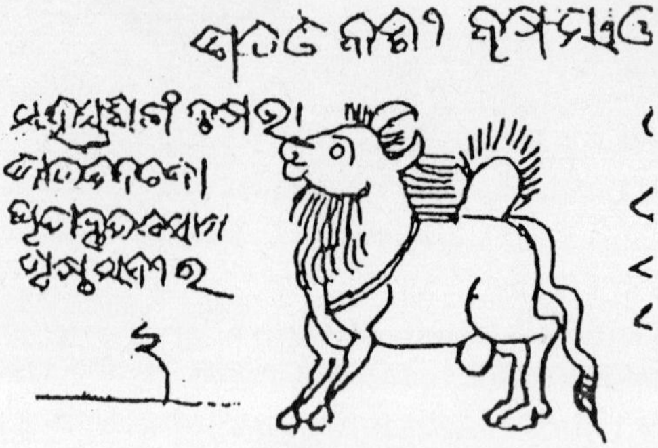

Fig. 3: Śatakeśī Vṛṣa
(illustrations from Nigama Ḍiṇḍima Ṭippaṇī)

Then the stone is washed with the milk of the Mahīlukā cow,[6] in order to release it from the Kumbhīkās[7]. Then Śatakeśī Vṛṣa[8] should be meditated upon from foot to head and invoked with prayers: "OM, (adoration) to the hundred-haired Bull! Protect me, protect me, *svāhā* !" thus he should say.

With this (mantra) Jaṅgiḍa[9] and others protect. It conduces to well-being and mental joy; one becomes immortal. Then the circle is traced: drawing a circle with a stick of *yujuva* wood[10] (ber-tree) attached to a ring and a peg by means of a rope (while uttering the mantra)[11]:

[6](Mahīlukā) is a cow of uniform yellow or variegated colours. In the Daivatantra (?) the cow is indicated as Śakti. AVŚ X.10.6 it is said: "*Svadhā* is her breath, Mahīlukā".

[7]For releasing from Kumbhīkā it is said: *OM kumbhīkā dūṣīkāḥ pīyakān.* (AVŚ XVI.6.8).

[8]The great Bull of a hundred hairs (or horns) in the form of Rudra. See AVŚ V.22.8. [N.B.: This hymn has nothing to do with Śatakeśī Vṛṣa, but refers to the tribe of Mahāvṛṣas.]

[9]A kind of being giving affliction (demon) [N.B. wrong definition.] AVŚ XIX.35.2: "So may this *jaṅgiḍa* (a protective charm or amulet) guard us, even as a treasurer guards wealth."

[10]In the Kāśyapa Saṃhitā Śilpaśāstra, 1st Adhyāya, it is said: "With a stick of *yujuva* wood encircled by a ring, having a rope of two *muṣṭi* with an iron point or peg at the end, that is the *ghūrṇikā* (in function of a pair of compasses)."

[11]This mantra is found in AVŚ VI.19.1: When determining the *marma* the *upādhyāyas* should recite the Pavamāna Sūkta, this is the practice.

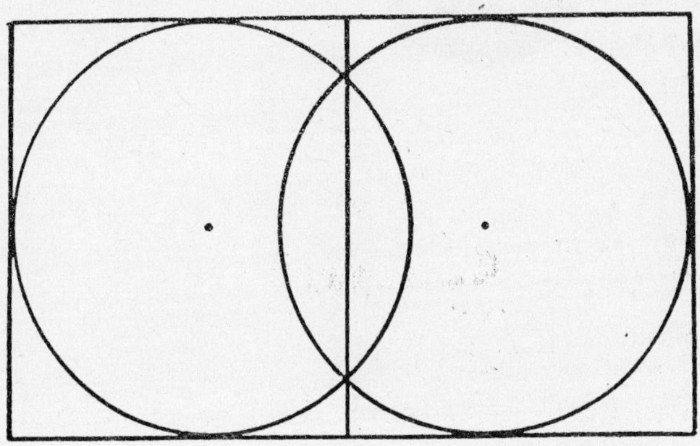

Fig. 4: Double circle

> "Let the gods purify me, let men purify me with a prayer. Cleanse me all creatures that exist! May Pavamāna make me pure."
>
> (AVŚ VI.19.1, Griffith)

With this mantra the central hole should be established.

Sūtra 4: This hole is considered as the central point (marman = core).

This is the third action.[12] On this place on the stone panel, on both sides of the central hole, the *sthāpakas* draw a double circle from different *bindus* on a line by joining them in the model of Prakṛti and Puruṣa. That is the twin circle, by 'one' is meant that the two (circles) are on one line, this should be noted. Listen, O students of Śilpa, in what way the lines are to be drawn with *vajra* (white powder)[13] whence the glorious abode (of the image) is born.[14]

Sūtra 5: For kṛtya-images (clay figures)[15] a line-diagram need not be made.

---

[12] "Setting, polishing, tracing the lines, these are the three processes. Carving is the last work, the *sthāpaka* should always remember." Kāśyapa Saṃhitā I.14.

[13] *Vajra* is white stone powder, this is the material for drawing the *vajra* lines (of the diagram).

[14] The image whose base is a line-diagram (*rekhā-pañjara*) is the form of glory.

[15] For clay-images no line-diagram is required.

Sūtra 6: In the beginning is a circle. The circle[16] is the All (universe).

The breath of life (*prāṇa*) is (contained) in its form, even as the mind is in Man. The circle is Time, according to the Vāstuveda. The movement of the circle is restricted (by its circumference), like the fluctuation of the mind. The support of the circle is the immortal, the *bindu* is its firm position (station) like the Ātman (in man). Starting from the *bindu*, by connecting it with another point arises the circumference (enclosure) surrounding it. He who knows this is the supreme Lord, the Overseer, Union (*yoga*), he is intelligence (*kratu*), he is truth.

Sūtra 7: By the connection of one with one a unity is formed. This is the meaning: The circle verily is the Plenum (fullness, pūrṇam).

The *bindu* is its support. As the sacrificial offering (*āhuti*) it is the life-breath of the world, it is its position, just as the Gāyatrī is the Vedic mantra (par excellence). The circle is made on the stone, while tracing the circle the Vāstugāyatrī[17] or the mantra of eight syllables[18] should be recited. Thus it should be done.

I consider the circle within the field to be the support. Just as all living beings revolve, thus many forms originate. That is the breath of life. The field has to be divided in order to obtain the limbs (or parts) of the image. Therefore –

Sūtra 8: All limbs have to be set along the lines.

This is the dividing action. The lines are to be drawn with white powder (*vajra*) on the stone, not on earth and not on brick.[19] Then Āṅgirasa said: "I am asking the *brāhmaṇa*, the venerable Pippalāda, two questions, whether he may tell me: What is the line? What is its

---

[16]The subject of circle and *bindu* is clearly explained in the Paippalāda Praṇavatāraka (Upaniṣad) (note MS घ).

[17]*Om viśvakarmāya* [!] *vidmahe kārukārāya dhīmahi tanno śilpī pracodayāt.* (OM We reflect on Viśvakarman, we meditate on the great Artist, may he, the Śilpī, impel us!).

[18]*OM viśvakarmāya namaḥ* (Salutation to Viśvakarman), this is the mantra of eight syllables.

[19]That means: not in the practice of the sacrificial Śulva-Sūtras which are used for fabricating *viśvajyotis* and other bricks.

character (*bhāva*)? How many varieties are there? Please tell, O Pippalāda." To them the Ṛṣi said: "O Āṅgirasa and Śilpakāśyapa, hear the explanation of the lines and their character (*bhāva*). The line is the support (determinant) of the composition, it is like a boundary (or: like a stream, *dhārā*). It is that which corresponds to the fundamental elements (*adhibhūta*) and to the gods (*adhidaivata*) in the realization of action.

Sūtra 9: Straight lines are as rays of light.

By the line they (the *sthāpakas*) divide the circle, as the creators by their action divide the world. From these (lines) in this way all the parts of the image become visibly manifest[20], for the sake of the whole image in accordance with the myths of the country[21], and the harmony of the limbs arises.

Sūtra 10: The creation of the image starts from the navel.

All limbs should be determined to achieve harmony, according to Brahmā's design. As is the realization of Brahman (*brahmavidyā*), such is the knowledge of form (*rūpaprajñā*). With this knowledge the artists manifest Brahman indirectly in the creation of form, enjoying it as a very ancient wisdom. Setting the limbs along the proper lines is praised like the knowledge of Brahman (*brahmavidyā*). The *sthāpakas* who know this are honoured as wise, he who knows this. By this knowledge the *sthāpakas* become knowers of form.[22] Those who are wise, these experts attain the realisation of Brahman in the work of Art. As in the creation of the world arise the five great elements, similarly with the circle as support Śilpakāśyapa and other priests of art conceived and dispose the features of beings and elements.

Sūtra 11: Following the order of Prajāpati[23] the circle represents light (tejas) while the square indicates water.

[20]Visible forms arise in the stone, that is the meaning.

[21]The plays of the gods are produced in their respective forms according to the various regions.

[22]In the Śilparahasya Āgama IV.2 it is said: "A *śilpī* who knows the proportions of all the parts is called a *sthāpaka*. He who knows the setting of lines becomes a knower of forms (*rūpajña*)."

[23]"He is Prajāpati and all the gods and also the five fundamental elements: (earth), wind, ether, water, light and the subtle mixed elements." This is said in the Aitareya (Upaniṣad III.5). [N.B. *pṛthivī* has been omitted.] Even so in the Vāstuveda the same distinction is known and seen.

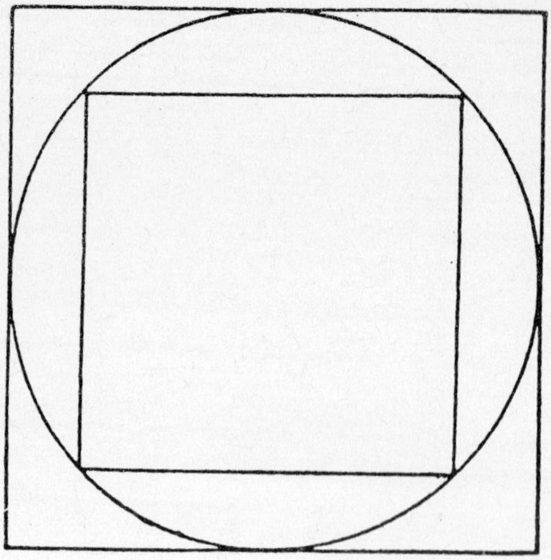

Fig. 5: Square and circle

The area is enclosed by four lines. Like a water-tank, so also the relief panel is a square. The Vedas show that the entire world including all its quarters,[24] follows the way of Prajāpati (cosmic laws).[25] Thus in the panel too that (cosmic) form is contained. Because of repetition (of cosmic laws) the students of Vāstu place this (the square or rhombus) again inside the circle (even in the symbolic representation in the panel).

Sūtra 12: Two diagonals are drawn in the nature of wind.

As from the contact of water and wind foam arises, again in the foam bubbles arise, thus when the square is joined with the diagonals that relief-field becomes active. This is the understanding of the action of the diagonal (wind) lines.

Sūtra 13: The sthāpakas trace the karṇikakṣetra (rhombus) as the earth.

Then the *sthāpakas* draw the rhombus, starting from the centre,[26] and they trace two centre-lines within the circle, they are the vertical

[24] For all figures in stone the square is the support.

[25] "From the rock water springs forth" says the Śatapatha Brāhmaṇa (IX.1.2.4).

[26] Hanging on the centre-points of the vertical and the horizontal middle lines (touching the border lines).

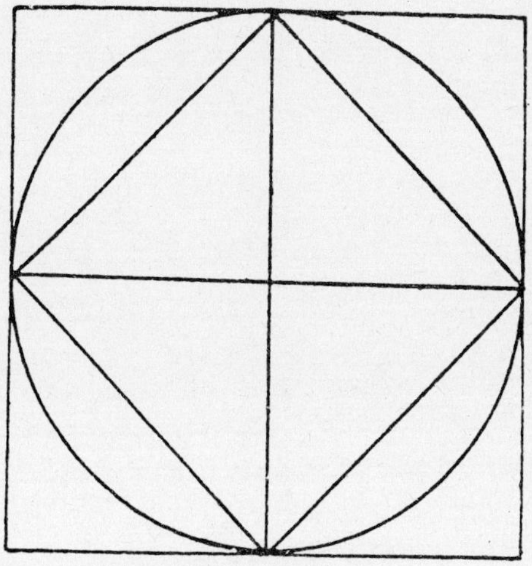

Fig. 6: Karṇikakṣetra

middle line (*madhyarekhā*) and the horizontal middle line (*madhyaprastharekhā*). There they obtain four parts of the same measure, like the four continents of the earth. This is the conception (*bhāvanā*) of the earth-field. There,

Sūtra 14: The bindu obtained in the centre is the life-breath of the earth.

The *śilpakāras* call it *marma* (core). Listen to its meaning (*bhāva*), O you all sons of immortality and disciples: As from the union of Water with Earth arises the Light of heaven (*dyauḥ*),[27] as said in the Śruti,[28] thus in that ether the Sun circulates in the form of Light. As the movement of the Sun travelling in the firmament is unbroken, thus the course of the wind (the diagonals) is oblique.

Taking the broken lines (crossing each other) the knowing *sthāpakas*, conceiving them for the sake of the composition of Śilpa obtain two or more *bindus*, they multiply the *bindus*.

[27] Firmament is its meaning.

[28] "You direct heaven and earth and it rains", says the Śatapatha Brāhmaṇa. See also AVŚ XII.1 [wrongly quoted], cf. "She (Earth) who at first was water in the ocean, whom with their wondrous powers the sages followed.
May she whose heart is in the highest heaven,
Compassed about with truth and ever-lasting,
May she, this Earth, bestow upon us lustre, and grant us power in loftiest dominion." AVŚ XII; 1.8: (Griffith)

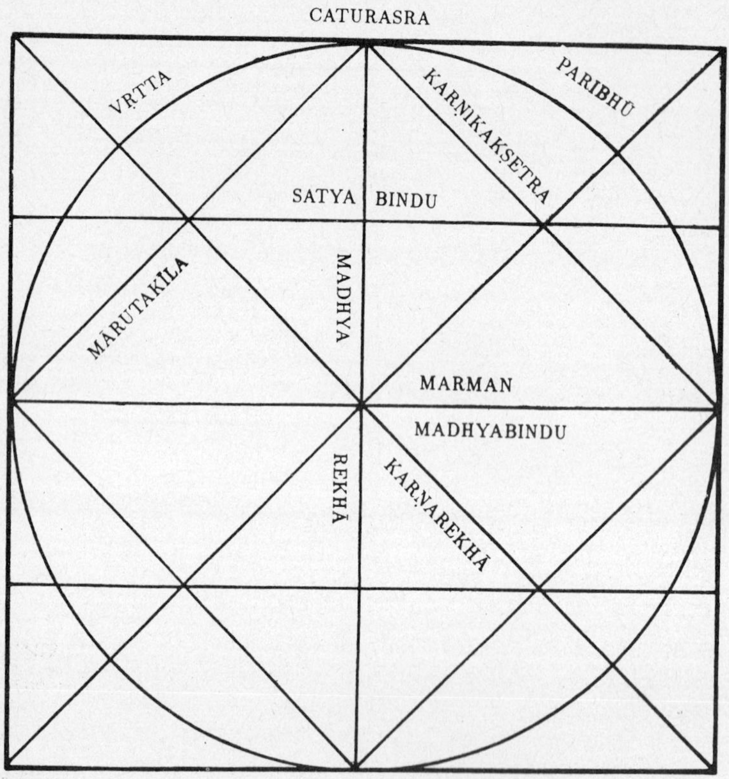

Fig. 7: Khilapañjara

Knowing this the artists draw a field[29] in the abode of the circle making it into three from below upwards according to rule, in the form of fire, sometimes it is established within the circle as a triangle (*trihuta*).[30]

Sūtra 15: Fire in the form of a triangle is known even in the (non-Vedic) world.

Sūtra 16: The inverted triangle is water.

When both are conjoined arises the state of union (*mithuna-bhāva*). Those who realize this become perfected. This is the state of awakening. By the joining of Fire and Water (man) becomes

[29]The form of Agni is a triangular field.

[30]*Huta* (oblation) means a line, that area which is formed by three lines is a *trihuta* (triangle).

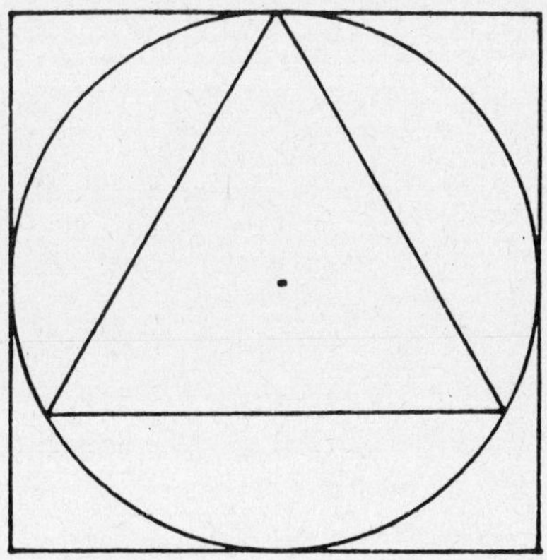

Fig. 8: Fire-triangle

divine,[31] which the *hotāras* know as the 'great union' (*mahacchandas*) and they use it in sacrifice. They draw it on the altar and on the platform. By this they satisfy with offerings the worlds of the gods and of the ancestors,[32] and it bestows on men union with the divine (*sāyujya*) – this is learnt in many ways. All artists who are knowers of Brahman set the lines in the centre of the panel within the circle with six *bindus* starting from six points at equal distance (and connected by lines).

Sūtra 17: The hexagram is the special science of attraction.[33]

By means of the *mithunacchandas* Yātudhānas[34] are warded off. Māṇḍavya[35] and other (Ṛṣis) worship many gods. They attract the

[31]'Divine' means 'divine nature', as said in AVŚ II.12.4: "May the felicity of the Fathers guard us. I seize that man with divine fire."

[32]According to a secret practice, when establishing the fire for giving Brahma-instruction, a hexagram is drawn on the *sthaṇḍila*, then two seats (of sacred grass) are spread. On this the sacrificial fire is established. This is the method of establishing the fire (*agnisandhānavidhi*).

[33]In the Tantra and the Kālikā Upaniṣad it is said: "The *bījamantra hūṃ* is the sixth sound of heaven, its form is joined with a *bindu*, two (*bījas*) are two forms of *māyā*, in the *dakṣiṇā kālikā* (mantra found in the Kālikā Upaniṣad)."

[34]In the AV Yātudhānas are said to be born from Nirṛti and similar creatures of mixed birth causing trouble (AVŚ VII.70.2).

[35]Māṇḍavya is born from the lineage (*vaṃśa*) of the Maṇḍus, a disciple of

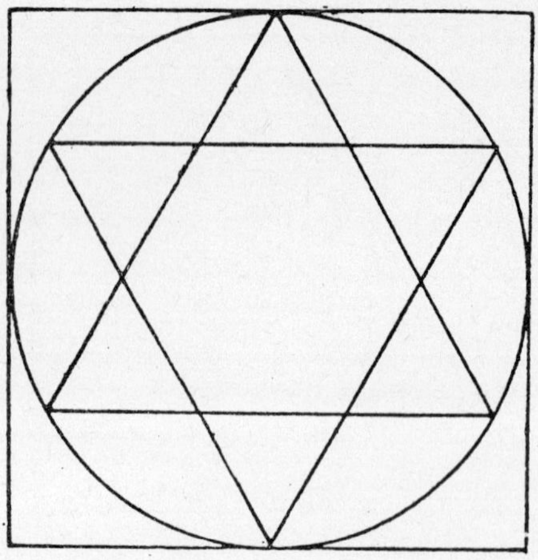

·Fig. 9: Hexagram

Rudras, the Ādityas and the Vasus. In the tracing of the lines (in the compositional diagram) according to the Vāstuveda the (science) of attraction (in the form of the hexagram) is the best means of revealing the character (of the image or *deva*).

Sūtra 18: As for images thus for Yūpas cutting along the line divisions should be done.

The sacrificer in the Yūpa and the sculptor in the image proceed in the same way.[36]

Sūtra 19: Observe the method of (using) the chisels.

By means of the chisel the sculptors divide that field of the *brahmamaṇḍala* according to the principle of sixteen divisions into sixteen parts.[37] A plain Yūpa[38] whose post is divided into eight sec-

Kautsa, a Ṛṣi mentioned in the Bṛhadāraṇyaka (Upaniṣad VI.5.4).

[36] "For achieving this purpose six line-diagrams are transmitted. The *maṇḍala* (circle) as a reflection of the sky (firmament), the square considered as water, the diagonals as wind, the rhombus as the earth, the upright triangle as the form of fire, the hexagram as the abode of gods," as is said by Kāśyapa.

[37] They cut with the chisel into the relief-field, they carve the base on the lines drawn with white powder with an iron (instrument).

[38] For starting a construction a plain stone Yūpa is used. For a sacrifice to Viṣṇu a particular sixteen-angled stone Yūpa is the practice, for offering sacrifices to the ancestors a wooden Vṛṣa post is used.

tors serves for fulfilling the desire of the sacrificer. Sometimes when it is divided in this way, it serves according to inferior knowledge (*aparāvidyā*) for Vṛṣastambhas or Agnistambhas, which can be made according to desire of stone or of *udumbara* wood. Stone Yūpas are permanently fixed as Śilpakāśyapa should know. The plain Yūpa is for (ordinary) sacrifices, the Yūpa of eight divisions is for sacrifices to Viṣṇu, for fulfilling desires the Yūpa of sixteen divisions should be considered.[39]

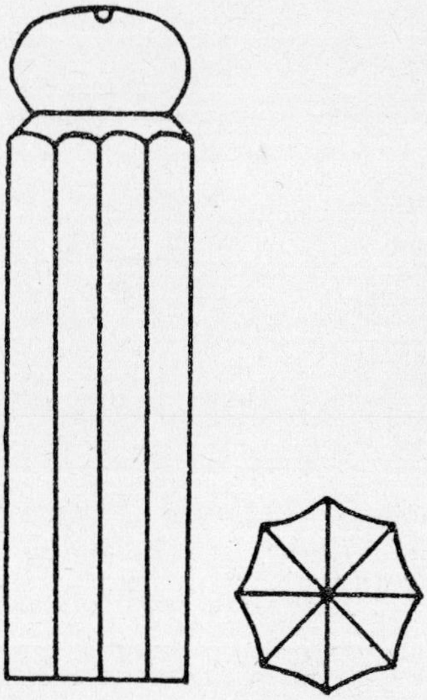

Fig. 10: Aṣṭāṃśa Yūpa

Sūtra 20: Lines following the Sūtra[40] become harmonious.

It conveys the character (*bhāva*, of the image). This knowledge is a secret knowledge, it is the *khilavidyā* (supplementary science). That drawing of the lines –

Sūtra 21: The knowledge of the compositional diagram (khilapañjara) is the best.

Those who know it, who are knowers of form, create the essential forms (*tattvarūpāṇi*) according to the principle of form (*rūpatattva*). It should be remembered that without tracing the lines (of the diagram) the form becomes deficient.

Sūtra 22: Vertical lines[41] have the nature of fire, horizontal lines[42] have the nature of water, diagonal lines have the nature of wind (māruta).

[39] In the AVŚ X.7.30 it is said in many ways: "On Indra Fervour rests, on him the worlds and Holy Law recline. Indra I clearly know that all of thee on Skambha (or: on the Yūpa) findeth rest." (Griffith).

[40] The lines which are regularly drawn with a thread become harmonious.

[41] The vertical lines (*dairghyarekhā*).

[42] The horizontal lines (*prastharekhā*).

With the different lines the differences of characters (of images) arise. That form shines forth as determined by the lines and the form becomes perfect (*surūpa*).[43] By depending on the essential lines (*tattvarekhā*), the soul of form becomes manifest, and also that of the represented image. As by sacrificial offerings rain is produced, thus by a harmonious form the mood of meditation is induced. As from rain food is produced, thus from meditation arises absorption (in the divinity). By absorption men become divinised. As from food the life (-breath) arises, thus from the state of absorption they experience union with That (the object of meditation). The mind becomes steady. For them there is no return to further births. For this purpose Ṛṣis create images in this world. The lines in the image are like sacrificial offerings.

Sūtra 23: By a harmonious form a meditative mood is induced.

This is rain, the flow of cosmic order. As from rain many types of grain are produced,[44] so too various forms arise from the lines.

Sūtra 24: On the fire (vertical) lines upright forms are produced.

All the upright forms are harmonious and convey a feeling of elevation.

Sūtra 25: On the water (horizontal) lines forms expressing longing are produced.

These are producers of a feeling of fluidity.

Sūtra 26: On the diagonal (wind) lines fiery (energetic) forms are produced.

They are givers of a violent mood and produce fighting figures. For giving them all a terrifying form or expression diagonal lines have to be used. This is for the purpose of the creation of form. (See end of chapter IV.)

---

[43] In the Paippalāda Saṃhitā I.28.3 it is said on the subject of the essence of form: "Each several form, each several force– with these we compass thee about." (Griffith). Thus is the conception of forms (cf. AVŚ I.22.3, actually a prayer for cure from jaundice).

[44] "From food come the creatures, from rain comes food," thus it is said in the Gītā III.14, and also in the Taittirīya Up. II.2 (cf. Praśna Up. VI.1).

Sūtra 27: The knowledge of the line is to be known as all-comprehensive.

Those who possess all this knowledge become famous as priests of Art (*sthāpakodgītha*).[45]

This is the second Prapāṭhaka of the Pippalāda Vāstusūtra, called the science of tracing compositional diagrams (*khila-pañjara*), transmitted from the Muni to the hearers by means of discussion by word, body and mind.

[45]The image-maker is a *sthāpaka*, and they are called "priests of art" (*sthāpakodgītha*).

THIRD CHAPTER

CARVING

"Listen to the exposition of Śilpa which within the six branches of Vāstu deals with the processes of stone-carving."

Saying yes, Ātharvaṇāṅgirasa and Śilpakāśyapa approached the venerable Pippalāda and asked: "Do tell us what in the practice of art is the best method of stone-carving? How many (methods) are there? As this knowledge is difficult for us to obtain, we are asking you." – "Ask," he said.

"What is the process of stone-carving? By whom is it practiced? Tell us what is the purpose of making a preliminary compositional diagram (*khilapañjara*) by making lines on the stone?" Pippalāda replied: "The limbs of the images follow along the lines."

Sūtra 1: The character (bhāva) of the form is essential.

From the character arises inspiration,[1] from that inspiration divine vision, the action for this is the science of carving (*bhedanavidyā*). As from highest knowledge arises divine nature, thus men can obtain divine nature through perfect form. In order to manifest the character of the image to the minds of the people, the *sthāpakas* proceed with great care in the creation of forms. Amongst images some are peaceful (*saumya*) and some are fierce (*ugra*).

Sūtra 2: The lay-out of the lines has to be established according to the character (of the image).

He who knows this has the fundamental knowledge of the centre (*marman*).[2] He is honoured in the world and in the village he is famous as a priest of art (*vāstūdgītha*). Before the king he has the title of *cākra*.[3]

---

[1] What feeling is aroused in the mind by the mere sight of an image that is the inspiration (impress) of the form.

[2] Who realizes what is the point in the centre of the image and how the limbs are depending on it, who understands the significance (*bhāva*) of this, is considered as a *marmajña* (expert). This is said in the Śilparatnakośa, v. 455.

[3] The best *sthapati* is called *cākra*. *Pāṭavacākra* is mentioned in the Śatapatha Brāhmaṇa (XII.8.1.77, XII.9.3.1).

Sūtra 3: For these (artists) many work-processes are important.

They cut stones, carve various forms and place limbs according to the lines. They carve narrow incisions between the limbs. The stones severed by these incisions between the elevated parts of the stone are cast away with a mantra of dismissal.

The limbs consist of elevations and depressions. This is the knowledge of composition (*nyāsabodha*).

Sūtra 4: One should observe the proper time for setting the stone (nyāsa).

The best sculptors would not do it at night, not at new moon, not at the junction of sun and moon (eclipse), nor at evening or morning twilight. For fixing or securing the stone for the image they hold it between two pegs of *udumbara* wood[4] for sprinkling it with ghee. This is the rite for fixing the stone. While fixing (the stone) he should recite the Vedas in the *jaṭā*-order[5] in Parjanya-worship; and thus, by reciting and worshipping, and by the rules of the science of *rasa* (chemistry), the sages, masters of the (art concerning) stones, cut the stone.

Sūtra 5: For carving the chisels must be consecrated with a mantra.

OṂ Goddess arise! Why are you sleeping?
I am overcome by fear,
Whether I am capable or incapable,
Huṃ (Durgā), Goddess, appease it. *Svāhā* !

This is the mantra to be employed for the chisels. Death is averted and fear is overcome by this mantra. With this knowledge the *agnihotra* sacrifice is offered to Vaiśvānara. Just as one should offer all evils into the burning coals for reducing them to ashes so too should the sculptors perform the *agnihotra* and offer into Vaiśvānara for the sake of their works of art. Impediments to the chisels are

---

[4]The stone should be firmly fixed with wooden pegs of one *muṣṭi* length on all four sides, this is the fixing of the stone. Thus the Śilparatnakośa explains the action of fixing.

[5]The chanters chant the *gāthās*, like the Kuntāpasūktas in the Atharvaveda: (XX.127) *idaṃ janā upaśruta narāśaṃsastaviṣyate*, etc. This the chanters recite according to the rule of the *jaṭā*-recitation (repetitions and inversions).

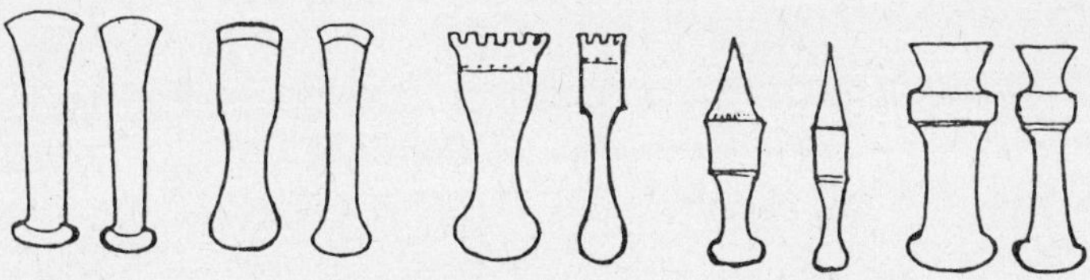

Fig. 11: Chisels

removed and fears are eliminated by this sacrifice of Vāstu. They should meditate on the following mantra in their mind in order to overcome weakness while working with the chisels:

> OṂ You are eye, give me eye-sight !
> You are protection, give me protection ! *Svāhā* !
>
> AVŚ II.17.6–7

This action should be remembered by him who knows it thus. Now Āṅgirasa and the other *udgātāras* asked: "How many types of chisels are there ?"

Sūtra 6: Five types of chisels are the best.

Listen in what way the *śilpodgātāras* practice carving, chiselling etc. Chisel-work is not just for sculpture of figures, the *hotṛs* use it in the hall of Soma sacrifices for making altars, platforms, as it was said earlier in the Veda in the description of secular architecture (*lokavāstu*) in the section on houses and (sacrificial) halls of Bṛhaspati.[6]

By the inexpert use of the chisels the image becomes deformed. Such primitive images are worshipped by tribals (*kukkuṭikās*),[7] not by *brāhmaṇas*, (Therefore) I will explain to you the best types of chisels and their use for carving.

These are the different varieties: *lāñjī, lāṅgalī, gṛdhradantī, sūcīmukhā, vajrā*, all are made of iron and each one is of two types, narrow and broad. The chisel-work for cutting the stone is effected by

[6] AVŚ III.12 (says about dwelling houses:) Of the house the firm foundation is the *stambha* (pillar), "rich in horses" means the wall, the post (*sthūṇa*) means the bamboo post, the *kumbha* (water-pot) means the supporting beams, and even in the construction (of the house) chisels are used.

[7] Forest-dwellers.

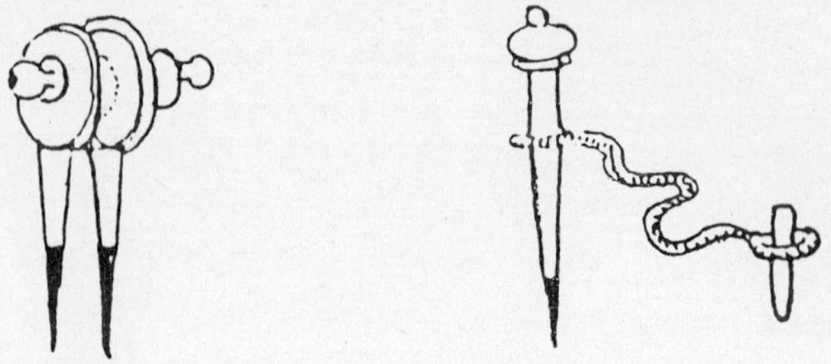

Fig. 12: Dvimukhī and ghūrṇikā

striking it with short and long mallets (*muṣaladharubha* and *muṣala-daṇḍa*). All instruments are sharpened by dipping them in cow's urine, then smearing them with *iṅgiḍa* oil (*terminalia catappa*) and whetting them on leather.

Sūtra 7: The limbs of the images should be smooth to bring out a clear form.

Those who carve with the instruments proceed gently. They have a two-pointed instrument and a compass which have iron points and rods (or pegs) of *palāśa* wood.[8] That is their form.

Then Āṅgirasa asked: "Venerable Pippalāda, what instruments do sculptors use to cut stones as hard as diamond ?" The teacher answered.

Sūtra 8: The śilpakāras apply a softening mixture.

They use the chisel after applying a mixture of four substances consisting of shell-solvent (*śaṅkhadrāva*), *kuṣṭharasa* (*costus speciosus* or *arabicus*), sea-salt, powder of the bark of the *ukatsa* tree,[9] in order to soften the stone, with a mantra. After rubbing the stone for ten days, the *sthāpakas* can use the chisels and carve with ease.[10]

Sūtra 9: This is the best method of (using) the instruments.

Sūtra 10: For protection parṇamaṇi should be worn (in an amulet).

[8] For making circles, the special instrument is like a needle connected with a rope, applied on a red (?) stone surface.

[9] In the forests of the Mahendra mountain a tree is found, whose bark is called stone-breaking (*prastara-bhedi*).

[10] This is the proper means to lay out the prescribed features.

For protecting themselves during chisel-work they wear an amulet of *pāṭhāmūlikā*. They wear an amulet (*parṇamaṇi*) with a mantra. By reciting the mantra:

> The Goddess Pṛśniparṇī hath blest us, and troubled Nirṛti. Fierce crusher of the Kaṇvas she: her have I gained, the mighty one.
>
> AVŚ II.25.1 (Griffith)

Sūtra 11: Perfection of limbs is achieved by carving.[11]

As in the human body thus in the body of divinities there are ankles, folds, bellies and other features, turbans, belts and other ornaments. They are carved out in perfect form. The stones are removed from the depressions and cast away (with the proper ritual).

Sūtra 12: Placing the limbs along the compositional lines is the best method (action).

In this science of Vāstuveda the rule is to place the limbs along the lines.

Sūtra 13: In the sacred songs the features (of the gods) are revealed.

As from the sacred chants the legends are derived, in the same way the knowing sculptors represent the features of the images, and so their form becomes visible (*vyaktarūpa*). When attractive gestures (*hāva-bhāva*) and other states become visible in the image, that is the manifest form (*vyaktarūpa*). The worshippers realize a perfect feeling through the (divine) form, by means of which they do their meditation. This is the application.[12]

Sūtra 14: The excellence of form becomes clear in the act of meditation (by applying the dhyāna of the divinity).

Therefore the *vāstukāras* declare it to be a meditation image (*dhyānarūpa*).

---

[11] According to nature one should make the body beautiful with folds and joints made by curved lines, as is proper, this is considered the harmony of the limbs (or body). Thus it is said in the Śilpāgama, II.14.

[12] "That image which is done according to meditation that is called meditation-image (*dhyāna-rūpa*)." Śilparatnakośa v.455.

Sūtra 15: The features of images conform to nature.

The forms of images are according to their own nature. They manifest their qualities corresponding to each form as they arise in the heart of those who are moved by creative impulse (*kāmacārin*). Desire is the most permanent impulse of human beings.[13]

Sūtra 16: Figures in half relief[14] are beautiful (suitable) for meditation.[15]

Full figures in the round are best for worship, but are not indicated for the wall.

Sūtra 17: Figures in half relief should not extend beyond the borderline on both sides and above.

Turbans, belts and other ornaments are shown by an extremely curved raised line.

During the period of carving the sculptured stone should be sprinkled with shell-solvent (*śaṅkhadrāva*) and it should be protected from destructive forces. This is the procedure.

Sūtra 18: Obstacles are removed by the protective covering.

Obstacles are destroyed by this particular method of protection. While beginning the carving the sculptor should utter (the mantra):

> OṂ *hojā, hojā*, O Śatakeśī Vṛṣa (hundred haired bull),
> do protect me !

Being free from obstructions the lines of the hands and other features of the limbs are to be made on the stone according to the divine character (*daivabhāva*).

(The sculptors) obtain perfection (*siddhi*) by (creating images) with (divine) attributes. Union (with the divine) is obtained whether (worship is done) for worldly (*kāmya*) or for purely spiritual ends (*akāmya*). For this purpose the art of carving is the highest.

The most important thing while carving is to set the limbs along the lines (of the *pañjara*).

---

[13] "In the beginning was desire, the first seed of mind", Nāsadīya Sūkta (ṚV X.129.4).

[14] When all limbs are not detached but connected with the stone surface, that beautiful (form) is half-relief.

[15] The image is called beautiful when the body is young and does not show muscles and articulations and is endowed with divine features. Thus it is said in the Āgama.

Sūtra 19: There are four known ways of carving (the limbs) along the lines.

According to rules of composition they are *ekāśrayi*, *yugalāśrayi*, *khaṇḍāśrayi* and *sparśitā*. When a limb is entirely set on one line, it is *ekāśrayi*; when the prominent limb of the image and the limb facing it rest on different lines, that is *yugalāśrayi*. When a separate limb of the image touches only with a part of a limb a subdivisional line (*bhinnarekhā*) or a fundamental line (*mūlarekhā*) above or below, that is *khaṇḍāśrayi*. When a part of a limb only somehow slightly touches a line, that is *sparśitā*, but this is inferior. A limb following the outer circle is sometimes the best.

Sūtra 20: No limb of the image should exceed the circle.

This is the rule for setting the limbs.

At the time of carving one should keep silence, always meditating on the sacred myths. Before starting carving the chisels should be consecrated with a consecration mantra, by whose power faults and misfortune are overcome.

Sūtra 21: The method of handling the chisels should be studied particularly.

Holding the chisel firmly in the left hand it should be controlled by the little finger, it must be done in this way. One should hold the mallet for carving in the right hand. Divine features are made known by form-work (sculpture). This is the explanation of the science of carving (*bhedanavidhi*).

This the third Prapāṭhaka called the process of carving the stone, transmitted from the Muni to the hearers by discussion through word, body and mind.

FOURTH CHAPTER

DISPOSITION OF THE PARTS OF THE IMAGE

Then Pippalāda said cheerfully: O you three who art anxious to learn about Śilpa ! (The Ṛṣis) told about the forms of speech and the knowledge of the body: Formerly there was Brahman (only), the One and the Truth. Through its knowledge, the light within the space of the heart is Brahman itself. His knowledge is supreme knowledge. Those who thus attain supreme knowledge, whatever they attain through word (language) the same (they can attain also) through form, accomplished through the word of (the said) supreme knowledge, (as also) he who knows this. Where the conception (contemplation, *bhāvanā*) is void, that is *nirguṇa* (Brahman without qualities). By a conception (contemplation) endowed with qualities it becomes *saguṇa* (Brahman with qualities). From *saguṇa* the mind materializes (becomes concrete).

Sūtra 1: From the realization comes the symbol.

Pratīta (realization or intuition), *pratīka* (symbol), *pratimā* (image), in this order these three are essential. When in the reflection of an aureole of light Brahman is realized, that is realization (*pratīta*), like the Puruṣa consisting of consciousness, who is not seen by the eye, by whom the eye sees. That which manifests the experiences in the manner of the relationship between the resemblance and the thing to be known [taken as *upamopameya*], that is the symbol (*pratīka*), as for example "the Puruṣa of the size of a thumb" and others. That which in worship bestows bliss, that is the image (*pratimā*).

Unmanifest, manifest, visible, in this order; unqualified (*nirguṇa*), subtle and gross, in this way people are induced to a sense of the divine (*daivabhāva*). This is the theory of worship (or sacrifice) of the Gods, as said in the Śatapatha Brāhmaṇa and in the Chāndogya (Upaniṣad). This is the order, this is the theory of worship, which by means of worship giving bliss to the soul (*ātmā*) (worships) the thirtythree gods, thus is said in Tārkṣya Brāhmaṇa.

As the nature (*bhāva*) of the Puruṣa is conceived of the size of a thumb, and in imagination the thumb means only light,[1] so it is like the post of the Yūpa.

Sūtra 2: From the form (of the symbol) arise the limbs (of images).

The images corresponding to every (original) form arise on the basis of that nature (*bhāva*), as in the case of the Puruṣa. This knowledge is most excellent. Where there is duality with others, it becomes a firm knowledge of another, this is verily truth. There one smells another, one sees another, one hears another, one talks to another, one thinks about another, one knows another. Where there is no other, he who sees this, what should one know and through what? Thus it was said by Yājñavalkya (Bṛhad. Up. II.4.14), he who knows this.

Sūtra 3: Thus, on account of having two aspects Brahman acquires form.

The *sthāpakas* fashion images in stone for worship.[2]

Sūtra 4: For making images a grid is most important.

As in Śulva (construction of altars), thus it is also in Śilpa: Without a grid the character of the image will not be correct and the worship becomes impaired. The science of making the grid for sculptures is to use vertical and horizontal lines made with white powder to divide (the panel).

Sūtra 5: Making squares is the principal work.

This is to be known as Śulva for sacrifices and as Śilpa for making sculptures and it makes the work easy. Thus it is said in the Veda. The meaning is to measure out the square by means of the thread. The *śilpakāras* trace lines perfectly on the measured out stone-panel using the measuring rod. Thus the big square is divided into many

---

[1]In the symbolic conception the thumb means light.

[2]By the knowledge of the principles thought is transformed, without it the mind is not transformed. By the understanding of the principles (*tattvabodha*) thought becomes firm. When it is inspired by feeling (*bhāva*) the mind merges in the realization of reality (*tattvabodha*) as the *visarga* whose two points become one (8). Duality is transformed into unity.

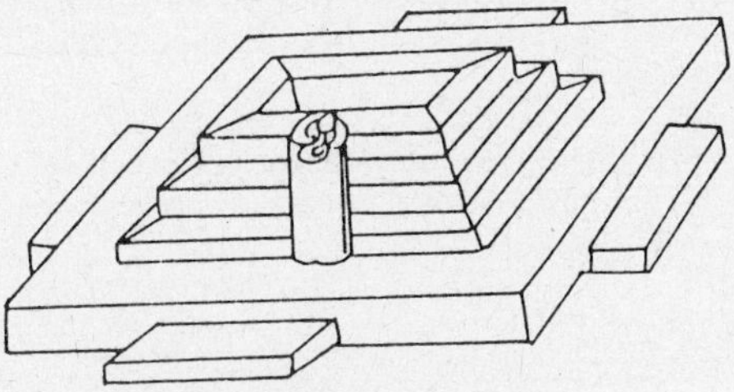

Fig. 13: Kuṇḍa

smaller compartments: One into two, two into four, four divided in two become eight. In this way the compartments are multiplied in number. As in the partition of altars (Śulva) the layers etc. are increased in even and uneven numbers by half a measure for the enclosure according to the design, in the same way (it is done by) the *sthāpakas*.

Sūtra 6: One should imagine the various parts of the image within the grid.

The *sthāpakas* measure out and place the measured limbs and parts, in the desired order, this is the law of proportion (*tāla-niryāsa*).

Sūtra 7: The features of the character (bhāva) arise from the measured gestures of the body (or limbs).

Limbs transgressing the measure assume a defective character, that is the fault. When an altar (*kuṇḍa*) transgresses the measurement of the grid, the *hotṛs* become dumb. The same happens with images:

Sūtra 8: By transgressing the grid the image becomes imperfect.

The *sthāpakas* obtain the nature of a *piśāca* (evil spirit). Then Śilpakāśyapa asked: What is the difference between the science of Śulva and the science of Śilpa ? What connection is between them ? What are their particularities ? Tell us, Pippalāda, embodiment of *dharma* !

Sūtra 9: Śulva is the discipline for sacrifice, Śilpa is the discipline for form-creation (image-making).

This is the difference. The *śulvakāras* construct altars (*kuṇḍa*), platforms (*sthaṇḍila*), sacrificial halls, *yonis*, layers (of the firealtar, *mekhalā*), Yūpas and other things with a measuring rod and thread.

Sūtra 10: The śilpakāras make image-halls in cave-temples and such things.

This is their speciality. There is no essential difference.

Sūtra 11: From the Yūpa comes the (human) form, from the (human) form comes the Yūpa, that is their (common) fundamental nature.

The students asked: In what way do the *śulvakāras* build the Yūpa according to the method of art, following the practice of the ancient Veda?

Sūtra 12: Study the measurement of the Yūpa.

The *vāstukāras* should hear: (First) draw a line measuring three *muṣṭis* of the sacrificer, (then) to the left make a triangle of the same length, with two shorter lines, this is the making of a triangle. Then making a triangle in the left upper corner, draw a quadrangle lengthwise, this is making a division (or squaring). Dividing the quadrangle into two parts, the smaller part should be known as the elevation of the Yūpa.

Sūtra 13: The function of six parts should be understood.

The side-field should be divided in order to obtain six subdivisions.[3] The lowest part of these six divisions is the earth-part for establishing it (the Yūpa), its divinity is Bhūmidevatā. The two parts above that (earth-part) constitute the lower limb for tying the belt for consecration. That is the part of procreation, its divinity is Rudra. The two parts above that are the upper limb for calling the life-breath, its divinity is Prajāpati. One part above that is the top-part for fixing the flag, its divinity is Savitṛ. In this order –

Sūtra 14: The four parts (of the pillar) become eight parts in the form (image) of the Puruṣa, in their respective order.

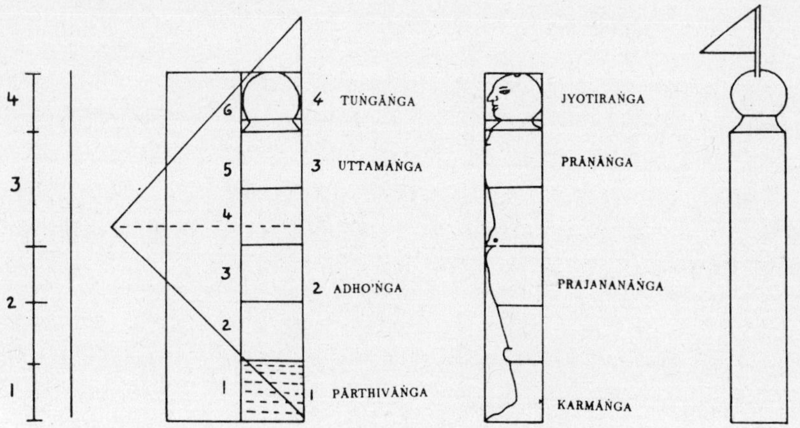

Fig. 14: Yūpa

(These are:) The earth-part (= the feet), the action-part (lower part of the leg), the lower part (thigh), the procreative part, the belly-part, the breath-part, the neck-part (from neck up to the eye-brows), the light-part (from the eye-brows to the top of the head). Thus there are eight limbs in succession in the form of the complete Puruṣa.

The wise Śilpakāśyapa (and others) asked: Pray tell us what are the measurements of the image, what is its character (*bhāva*), what are its features and what is the connection (of all the parts)? Being told this, Pippalāda spoke in the order invented by him.

Sūtra 15: Draw the lines with a measuring rod of palāśa wood and a rope.

The skilful (artists) should draw the lines on the stone for the grid in ascending order, they should make the grid with a mixture of water and red stone powder. Inside the grid the forms are obtained proceeding from foot to head.

Sūtra 16: Lines and other (forms) are always to be traced from below upwards.

---

[3]Making a triangle is meant for determining the measure of the flag of the *Yūpa*, the lower and upper parts are for determining the middle line and this is the measure for obtaining the measurement of the subdivisions; this is the meaning.

This is the action of rising, that is Rudra, the Lord, the Puruṣa according to the Veda.

Sūtra 17: The Puruṣa is like the pillar (of the universe), the pillar is the very symbol of sacrifice.

It is the support of the ten sacrifices.[4] The bull-pillar (*vṛṣastambha*)[5] is used for ancestor-worship for pleasing Rudra. Prajāpati is verily Vāstoṣpati, he is the awakening of the life-breath.

Sūtra 18: As there are ten parts in the pillar, thus the Puruṣa is understood as consisting of ten sacrifices.

Below are the feet, the belt of *darbha* grass twisted in a rope, above that there is a post-like belt in form of a ring of *pippala* or *udumbara* wood, above that the post of the pillar whose divinity is Viṣṇu. Above that the hip of the pillar in form of a sacrificial vessel (*śarāva*), in front of that is the navel in the shape of the cavity of a sacrificial ladle, like the hoof of a deer in mud. Above that a plain pillar whose divinity is Ambālikā, above that a square niche like an abode, this is the heart of the pillar. Rudra is the divinity of that chamber, as the hundred haired, hundred headed bull.[6] He is light, the saviour in the form of the *praṇava* (OM). Above that is the neck of the pillar in the form of a sacrificial vessel, its divinity is Svāhā. Above that is the head of the pillar in the form of a sphere whose divinity is Savitṛ. In this order the priests (*hotṛ*) show the pillar of ten parts according to the model of the ten sacrifices.

---

[4] "Man (*puruṣa*) doubtless is twenty-four fold: ten fingers of the hands, ten toes, and four limbs; and Prajāpati is the Puruṣa..." as said in the Śatapatha Brāhmaṇa (VI.2.1.23, Eggeling; quotation partial and incorrect). The Puruṣa is the support of the ten organs, that is the meaning. As there are ten parts in the Puruṣa, so in the ancestor-worship of the Pippalādīyas the Ṛṣis conceive the Yūpa in form of a pillar (*stambha*) as of ten parts.

[5] The divinity of a Yūpa of eight divisions (lit. spokes) is established at the begining of a work of construction (of a temple). A Yūpa of 16 divisions is used for the great Viṣṇu sacrifice, a bull-pillar is used in ancestor worship on the eleventh day of the decease, the *mithuna-stambha* is not in use. (Addition in Oriya:) The first and the second should be made in stone, the bull-pillar should be made of the wood of Banyan, *bilva* or *udumbara*. (note of MS ঘ).

[6] In the Śukla Yajurveda Rudra is said to be in the form of a bull as the *dharma*-bull. "The Bull verily is *dharma*" (AVP? cf. Manusmṛti VIII.16). "The bull with golden horns who arises from the ocean." [cf. AVŚ XIX.36.5] "The bull with a hundred hair is the friend Indra" (AVŚ?). That Bull is worshipped in the niche of the *pitṛyūpa* in the form of the Fathers. Its meaning is that Rudra is for the Fathers.

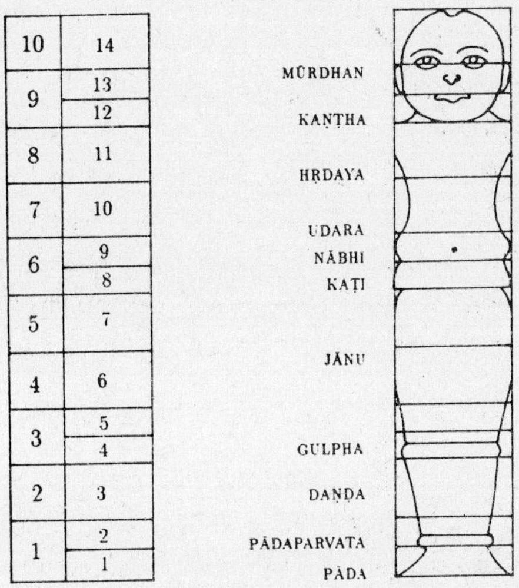

Fig. 15: Puruṣa derived from the Yūpa

Sūtra 19: The masters of art understand the (human) image as derived from the pillar.

They build up the complete form of the Puruṣa in the height of ten parts with the same ten divisions according to the same law of the Puruṣa, as said in this Veda.

Sūtra 20: Those who have desires set up pillars of three types.

Sacrificers set up pillars in the north-east corner for ancestor-worship.

Sūtra 21: A Yūpa is set up for sacrifices to the gods.

The *śulvakāras* (altar-builders) make the head and the post in the body (of the Yūpa). The post may be plain, or octagonal, or with sixteen angles, according to desire. Rulers defeat their enemies by performing animal sacrifices and make offerings for gaining complete power (*kṛtsnasiddhi*).

Sūtra 22: Those who want to fulfill desires set up bull-pillars (vṛṣa-stambha) for ancestor-worship and mithuna-stambhas in homa-ceremonies.

On the upper part of broad stone pillars the figure of pairing boars (is represented). By its ritual application enemies become paralysed like pillars. Rulers obtain success by performing animal-sacrifices, as indicated in the Veda and in the ritual. Pippalāda said: O Ātharvaṇāṅgirasa, (I shall tell you) whatever is to be known about the Yūpa, how from its form the image of the Puruṣa becomes manifest (and) how the Puruṣa becomes visible in the sections of the grid.

Sūtra 23: By knowing this, men become knowers of Form.

The venerable Pippalāda said: I will tell him.

Being pleased, the gentle Pippalāda spoke: The masters of Art say that this is the truth: As the sun rises in the eastern quarters and makes the life emerge, in the same way–

Sūtra 24: In the complete figure of the Puruṣa (human body) the form expressing its character (bhāvarūpa) arises from the lower compartments of the grid.

This is the action of elevating the pillar in ten sections, just as action becomes manifest in the ten actions of the ten sacrifices.[7]

As the Puruṣa, who is the actor, understander, taster, thinker, creator, hearer, seer and knower, being the knowing Self becomes Brahman, in the same way men perform the ten actions in ten organs (limbs). In this way the Puruṣa becomes visible to the eye in the ten compartments: Foot, ankle, shin, knee (*daṇḍagulpha*?), these are the lower limbs. From the knee up to the hip elevation, these two are the middle part, belly and heart (chest), these two are the upper part, neck and head, these two are the topmost part. The sculptors (*rūpakārāḥ*) conceive it in this way. These are the ten limbs of the Puruṣa, the Puruṣa being of the size of ten fingers, this is the meaning, as said in the ancient Veda (cf. ṚV X.90.1). In imagination he is the visible form of Brahman.[8]

[7]The five invocations in the worship of the Gods, *ājyabhāga, pradhānayāga, sviṣṭakṛt, prāśitrāvadānam, iḍāvadānam, bhāga-prāśanam, anvāhāryā-dakṣiṇā*, the three *anuyājas*, the arrangement of the hymns and of the *śaṃyuvāka, patnīsaṃyāja*, these are the ten different actions in the order of Viṣṇu, joined with the parts of the ten sacrifices. This is the meaning of the ten parts.

[8]It becomes a direct vision.

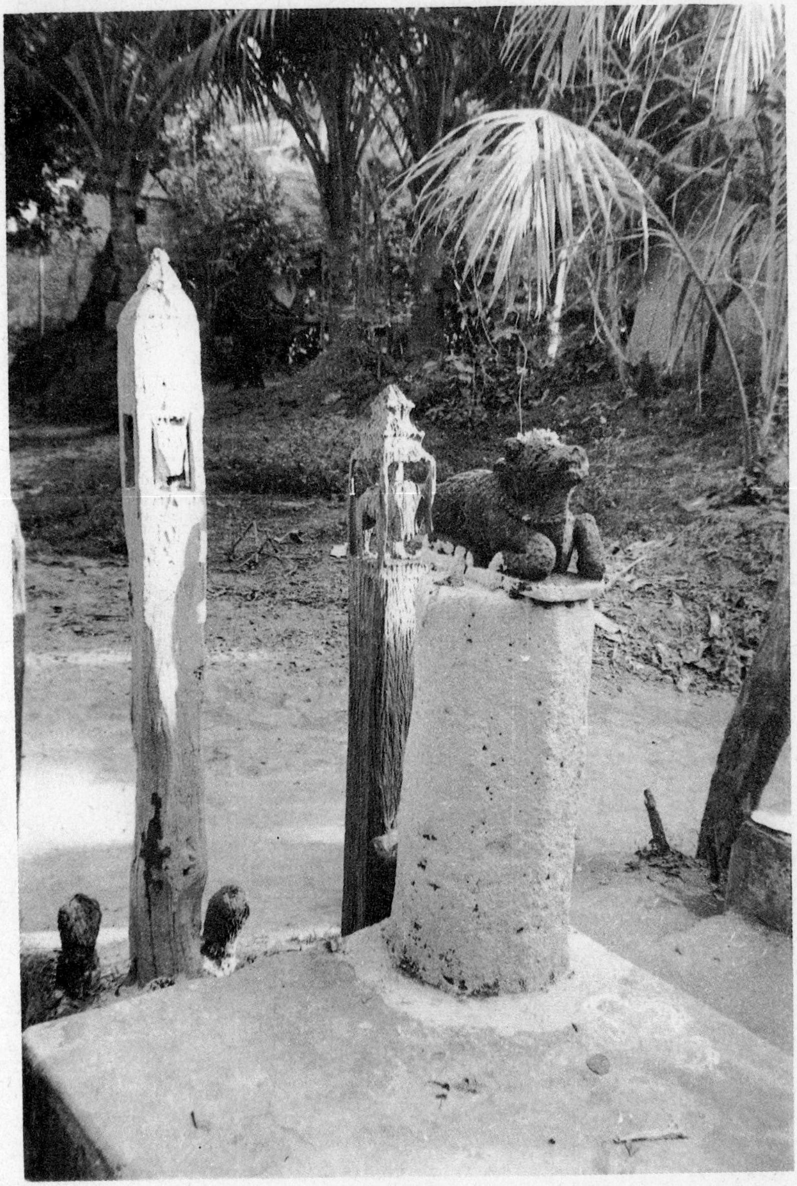

Fig. 16:
Wooden Vṛṣastambhas of Jadupur village
(near Koṇārka)

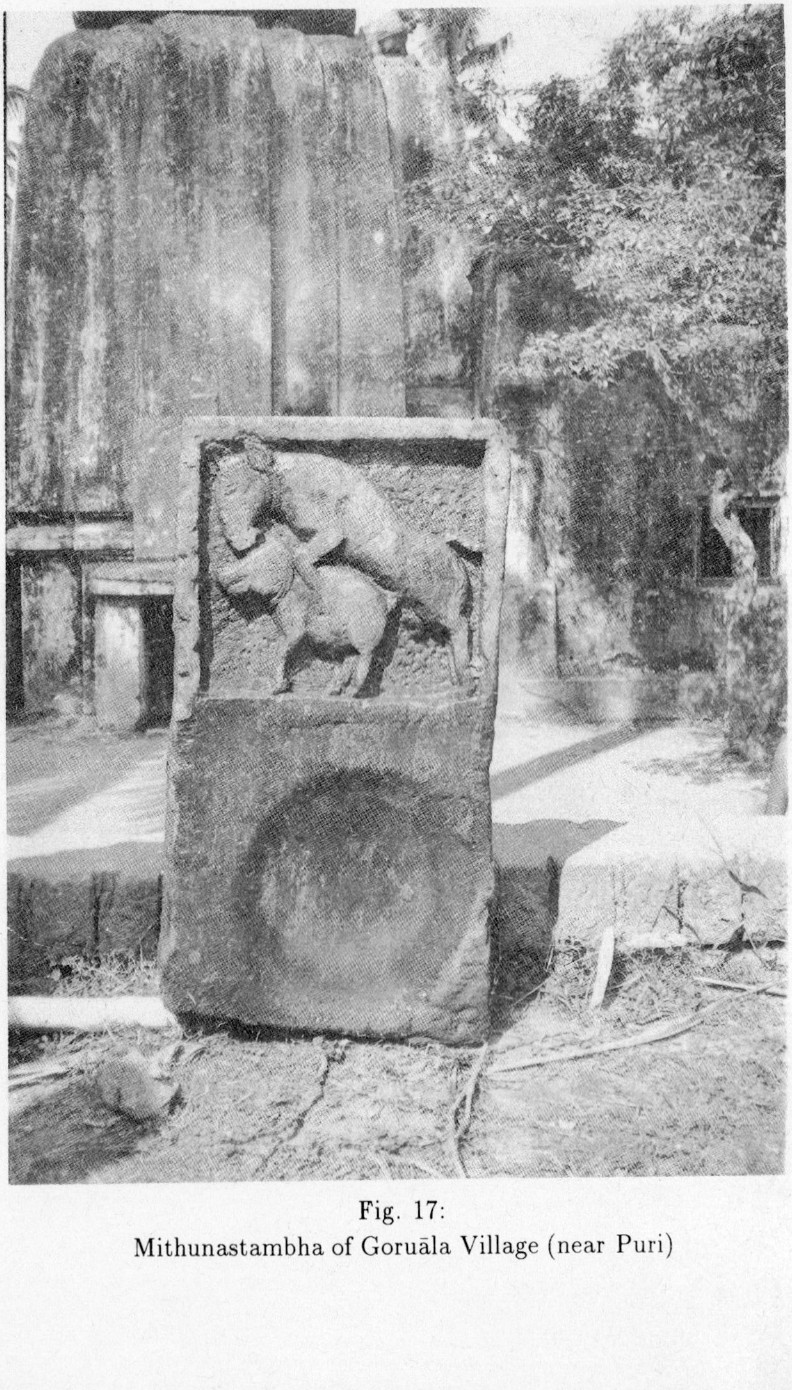

Fig. 17:
Mithunastambha of Goruāla Village (near Puri)

Sūtra 25: The significance of the ten sections is the same in both the Yūpa and the human form (image).

Therefore the sculptors conceive these divisions.

Sūtra 26: The middle-line (brahmakīla) is the support, and the field (panel) should be divided by this middle line.[9]

They divide the field (panel) in two parts by the *brahmakīla* which is the vertical middle line, like the post of mount Meru (*merukīla*) on the earth, like the backbone in the animal, like the marrow of the tree, like the soul in the living being. Thus the line is verily a fundamental reality (*satyam*), it is the origin of form. Therefore, division in ten sections should be made by lines from below upwards, by which equal subdivisions may be obtained, thus some sections are divided. The experts (*kārujñāḥ*) divide the first, third, sixth and ninth compartments in two for obtaining narrow and broad divisions, (thus) four of the ten compartments are divided in two, and six remain intact (undivided). Thus the ten compartments become fourteen (*bhuvana-saṅkhyakā*), as the Ṛṣis conceive the (fourteenfold) cosmos (*brahmāṇḍa*) within the body (*piṇḍa*). As the Atharvavedins make a *maṇḍala* with white powder for offering rice-cakes (*piṇḍa*) at the *śrāddha* ceremony,[10] the ancestor sacrifice, thus (also) in the *vaiśvadeva* ceremony they draw (a diagram) of ten compartments,[11] in this order: (first) the foot, above that the ankle of half a part, above that the shin of one part, above that the knee of half a part, above that the thigh in two and a half parts, above that the hip in half a division, above that in two and a half parts the belly with a navel in the form of a hole like a lotus-root, the round part of the belly being one and a half part, and above that the heart (chest) reaching to the eighth division. Above that is the neck in half a part, above that the head in one and a half divisions which is the uppermost part. In this way the figure becomes manifest in the ten divisions.

---

[9]The *brahmakīla* is the middle-line.

[10]In the *aṣṭakaśrāddha* (*śrāddha* of the eighth day) the Pippalādīya *brāhmaṇas* (worship) Indra, the Viśvedevas and Prajāpati for the seven Puruṣas (cf. ŚB VI.1.1.1 ff.).

[11]"As in the human embryo these ten elements are mixed: worms, marrow, bones, flesh, fat, sinews, blood, hair, blood-vessels, skin etc., in the same way the Atharvavedins conceive (the image) in ten compartments." Śiśuveda Up. (note of MSS घ, ङ).

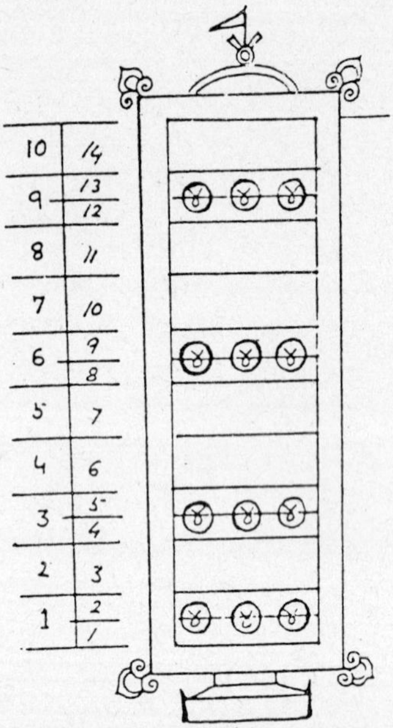

Fig. 18: Śrāddha maṇḍala

Sūtra 27: From one limb arises the other limb.

It is verily this form-creation which is composition. The measured limbs go from below upwards towards the divine, hands and feet arising in order.

Sūtra 28: When the limbs in that panel[12] adhere to the lines they become well-proportioned (harmonious).

On vertical lines erect limbs, on horizontal lines restful and quiet limbs, on diagonal lines limbs showing speed (movement). Setting them in this way the forms (images) attract the mind. After that –

Sūtra 29: One should establish the circle of the panel.

The *sthāpakas* make the grid inside the four border lines. Śilpakāśyapa and others should consider the compositional diagram (*khilapañjara*) for images according to this order. This is the explanation which the venerable Pippalāda gave to illumine the three *vāstūdgīthas*.

[12]As it is said in the Śatapatha Brāhmaṇa (VII.4.1, 15), the priests make the figure of Prajāpati in the form of a golden Puruṣa.

This is the fourth Prapāṭhaka of the Pippalāda Vāstusūtra, called the instructions for setting the limbs (of figures) with proper measure and proportion, transmitted in the discussion from the Muni to the hearers by way of word, body and mind.

FIFTH CHAPTER

THE INNER SENSE OF FORM

Then Ātharvaṇāṅgirasa and Śilpakāśyapa asked him (Pippalāda): "If Śulva (sūtra)[1] is for the purpose of sacrifice, Śilpasūtra is for the purpose of Art (*śilpa*) related to image-making. Please tell us about this". – Pippalāda answered: Students of Śilpa and priests of Śilpa, listen:

Sūtra 1: In image-making the infusion of feeling (bhāva) (into the image) is enjoined.

The science of Śulva is best for making sacrificial halls and altars (or platforms, *sthaṇḍila*), there one should know the technique of making the sides of the altar (*śroṇisādhana*),[2] of dividing the parts etc. and setting the bricks. In the same way in image-making (the geometry which consists of) drawing triangles, diagonals and angles on the panel is most important. For this purpose the understanding of the emotional attitude (*bhāva*) (of the image) is necessary. Hear what is meant by its emotional attitude and what is its relationship to form (i.e. the relation between the different *bhāvas* and the image). The body is the support of action, so say the adepts of sacrifice. It bestows feeling.

Sūtra 2: Action bestows the mood (bhāva).

Sūtra 3: The support of the emotional attitude (bhāva) (of the image) is rasa.

The *rasa* being the impelling force of action, it is expressed in the body manifesting respectively through speech, mind, eyes, ears, hands, feet and other organs. Thus (the *rasa*) becomes the defining characteristic of the body. The *rasas* of the body come forth establishing the emotional attitude. From the *rasa* –

---

[1] The Śulva (sūtra) is by Maharṣi Kātyāyana, the Śilpasūtra by Bhagavān Pippalāda.

[2] Laying the bricks (for the altar) according to the (out-)lines, that is *śroṇi* (cf. Śulvasūtra I.5–7): "In the Jyotiṣṭoma *śroṇi* is the great arranger, etc.".

Sūtra 4: Many fluctuations arise in the mind; by their different rasas, forms become manifold.

Sūtra 5: There are nine rasas.

For the (expression of the) nine *rasas* different kinds of lines are used.

Sūtra 6: The first rasa is love (śṛṅgāra).

Just as in a man (on seeing a woman) due to infatuation there arises a desire to unite with her. This is the common truth of all living beings.

When a feeling of delight (*muda-bhāva*) arises, it takes the form of a love-image. Thus two bodies are carved as the playful image of god and goddess. Where there are two figures (a couple) playful activity is the means (of depicting this feeling of delight). Therefore playing at dice or other (playful activities) are for the sake of producing a joyful image.

Sūtra 7: For love-images horizontal lines should be used.

A cheerful countenance is their characteristic feature. When desire is fulfilled the mind rejoices and bursts out in laughter.

Sūtra 8: Laughter (hāsa) is the second rasa.

Images bestowing the mood of laughter give joy to the heart of men. In the work of art they are made with parted lips and tender eyes as their features.

Sūtra 9: By seeing the features of the face all people can know the rasa.

Men worship for attaining happiness of the mind. Where there is sorrow there is also happiness, that is the truth, (they are) like night and day. Happiness changes into depression, and due to depression all the senses become slack.

Sūtra 10: Compassion (karuṇa) is the third rasa or sentiment.

Half-closed eyes are its characteristic features. From affliction the mind becomes inactive. This is exhaustion. From exhaustion again results depression and from that arises anger (*krodha*).

Sūtra 11: The furious sentiment (raudra) is the fourth rasa.

The artists call the furious mood *ugra* (fierce) in the image. The mouth (face) is expanded, the eyes are dilated, the hands hold fighting weapons, these are their features.

Sūtra 12: This sentiment becomes evident in the oblique lines in the image.

This is the specific feature. By the furious sentiment (*raudrabhāva*) the body becomes distorted.

Sūtra 13: The heroic sentiment (vīrabhāva) is the fifth (rasa).

In these (figures) the body, face and eyes are asymmetrical, this is its characteristic. The lines (movement) of their feet are swift, as in the features of a Kauṇapa (demon), stretched out on straight lines, like the fighting between gods and demons. Their face has the expression of heroism, they are as if overwhelmingly terrifying.

Sūtra 14: When the heroic sentiment becomes excessive it becomes terrifying (bhayaṅkara),[3] this is the sixth rasa which is different (from vīra).

One should be attentive to the asymmetry of the limbs on both sides of the figures. Those (images) where these features are still heightened turn into disgust (*bībhatsa*), they are exhausted figures.

Sūtra 15: The deformed figures with their limbs in disarray are placed on diagonal lines, this is the seventh sentiment (bībhatsa, disgust).

When desires are given up a divine sentiment arises, this is the last means (of expression). Due to realization one becomes detached.

Sūtra 16: The sentiment of peace is the eighth rasa.

In this way by the eight transformations of a living being (*jīvasya aṣṭavikāra*) the eight emotional states (*bhāvāḥ*) are produced.[4]

---

[3] Here the sentiment of wonder (*adbhuta*) merges in that of fear. In Śilpa the sentiment of wonder is to be inferred.

[4] What is shown in the body that is *bhāva*, what through the eye is entering the heart that is *rasa*.

Sūtra 17: In conformity with the sentiment images are of four main types.

All those having a peaceful character depend on vertical (*agni*) lines. All those in a sorrowful mood depend on the horizontal (water) lines. Inactive images are all lying on horizontal lines. Those whose limbs depend on the diagonal lines are expressing anger (*raudrāḥ*). The angry, mixed and heroic figures are supported on oblique lines. Here the canon is to be observed.

Then Śilpakāśyapa spoke: For what purpose do forms (images) make known the sentiments? What is the cause (of the evocation of the *bhāva*)? From their differentiation arises the conception of the gods and other results too. May the Lord, the seer of truth, tell us how to understand the sentiments.

Pippalāda spoke:

Sūtra 18: In this world mind is the cause of experiencing sentiments.

From its (the mind's) differentiation arise the different (classes of beings) like the gods, the fathers, Soma, the eight guardians of the quarters (*āśāpālāḥ*), the Viśvedevas, demons (*rākṣasāḥ*) and evil spirits like Hiṅga (?) and others. All have their different attitude (*vṛtti*), all have a different character, some are friendly, some are fiendish. The inimical mood constitutes their connection. The priests (*hotṛ*) worship the gods in order to deliver from *piśācas* and offer sacrifices in order to free (themselves) from (the danger of) the Tarda birds and others[5]. That is the connection between living beings. By sacrifice *piśācas* are destroyed. *Brāhmaṇas* wear *parṇamaṇi* in an amulet as protection against enemies. The different castes shine by their (proper) activities: *brāhmaṇas* by the power of sacrifice, *kṣatriyas* by the power of weapons, *vaiśyas* by knowing the quality of the soil and *śūdras* by service. Just as *brāhmaṇas* perform sacrifice for the sake of liberation, the (other) three castes attain liberation by worshipping images (*rūpasaparyā*), through *bhāva* they are released. Thus form (image) is to be meditated upon as a means of (spiritual) ascent. Therefore there is no objection to the meditation of images.

Sūtra 19: Of humans it is the mental modification (vṛtti) which is important.

---

[5] *Tarda* (*kharvata*): AVŚ VI.50.1 it is said to be a special bird (or insect) which destroys food.

From the mental modification arise inactive and active sentiments, this is the way (which is) the result of actions. With this aim the *sthāpakas* meditate on form with the knowledge of Śilpa and become *brāhmaṇas.*

Sūtra 20: The intention to worship (saṅkalpa) is the cause for the imagination (vikalpa), (of the particular form of God in which he is worshipped).

Vikalpa (in the Sūtra) means the particular. As the particular (imagination) arises from intention, at the end of the desire for enjoyment the desire to overpower enemies arises, the end of overpowering enemies is enjoyment. This is the cycle of the senses. From the state of imagination (of a particular form of God) comes faith, from faith the establishment in reality (*sattābhāva*), from establishment in reality comes worship with emotions. By this state (of imagination) arise the images corresponding to the archetypes.

Sūtra 21: This arrangement of the (fourteen) worlds (stages) constitutes the order of bodily realization.

Students of art (*śilpa*), listen to the order. Then the students asked: O venerable one, what are the fourteen worlds (stages)? What is their true nature? What is their particular order? Śilpakāśyapa and others asked: Tell us O Pippalāda, embodiment of *dharma*, of great wisdom, the characteristic of the fourteen stages of the body (which is) the bodily realization. Then the venerable Pippalāda gave them this instruction: The *śilpakāras* initiate all work by an invocation of Śatakeśī Vṛṣa (the hundred-haired Bull):

> "OṂ (Praise be) to Rudra of a hundred hairs, O Rudra, remove my fear, hundred-headed Rudra, appease my fear!
>
> Praise to you in the form of a hundred-haired Bull, who are the embodiment of Dharma!"

After uttering (this mantra) Pippalāda spoke: Hear the relationship of the expanse of the fourteen stages.[6] The word with which the priests (*hotṛ*) offer sacrifice to Prajāpati and other gods in the

[6] *Bhuvana* means the number fourteen.

Vaiśvānara (fire), that is the mantra,[7] that is *dhvani* (mantra-sound). By that *dhvani* they visualize the divine attributes. That attribute (appears in the vision) of the Ṛṣis only.[8] That characteristic (attribute) is verily cosmic order (*ṛtam*). According to this characteristic (attribute) they choose the form in the world of men.

From sacrifice emanates *dhvani*, from *dhvani* the (divine) attributes, from the (divine) attributes comes the archetype (*rūpa*), from the archetype comes the nature (*bhāva*), from the nature the quality, from the quality comes action, from action comes religious practice (*ācāra*), from religious practice comes the method (*upāya*), from the method comes the ritual performance, due to the ritual performance the way is found. From the way come the forms (of divinities), from forms come the derived forms (images).[9] From the understanding of the science of form image-making is born. This order of worship are the fourteen universal stages in the way of the Vedas.

Sūtra 22: From the formless arises form, that is the result (of the fourteen stages).

Āditya verily is Brahman, for his sake there are sacrifices. Its origin lies in the relationship of the space-directions to the earth. "Āditya verily is Brahman", that is his *dhvani* (mantra). From the *dhvani* comes the characteristic attribute: "The various divinities pertaining to the rays of the sun, (of them) there was one Lord"– this is the characteristic. The twice-born sacrifice through the rays (of the sun and) with the chariot of immortality, that is the archetype. The Sun is the Lord of light, this is his nature. From the nature comes the quality. That Sun (Sūrya) is heating the world, that is his quality. According to that quality the *brāhmaṇas* recite the Gāyatrī. Those who on earth worship thus proceed towards the light (day), that is action. When the *brāhmaṇas* arise when the stars are still visible, that is religious practice, the *brāhmaṇas* performing the

---

[7] "The word verily is mantra", as said in Śatapatha Brāhmaṇa (VI.4.1.7; cf. I.4.4.6 and 11). By the sentence they express it.

[8] The characteristic is given in AVŚ VI.141.3: "O Aśvins, make the mark for a thousandfold prosperity." [wrong application!]

[9] AVŚ XIX.1.3: "Each several form, each several force I seize and compass round this man" (Griffith). Therefore it is also said about the form of Viṣṇu in the Paippalāda Saṃhitā: "Women are worshippers of images (*pratirūpa*), for them the (secondary) images are created."

sandhyā rites thrice a day with mantras. In protecting the living beings the *brāhmaṇas* accept wealth, that is the method. The rites they perform with a certain number of mantras etc., that is their ritual performance; as this is said to be diverse, that is the way. Thus due to diversity of conceptions arises the form of the image (*pratirūpa*, or: secondary form). This knowledge is the science of form (*rūpavidyā*) which is the Śilpasūtra. These are the fourteen stages of form (corresponding to the fourteen stages) of the universe, in the way of the Veda. Thus the space-directions are responsible for creating forms. From the formless arises form, that is the result (of these stages), as said in ancient times by the Veda.[10]

Sūtra 23: According to space-directions the guardians of the quarters are worshipped.[11]

Āditya in the East, Yama in the South, Varuṇa in the West, Soma in the North, Agni in the centre, thus say the praisers (*ahallikāḥ*),[12] as it was said before in the Veda. Then there are the ten wise gods (*daśapracetasaḥ*),[13] the Ādityas and the guardians of the quarters;[14] he who knows thus...

[10]It is said in the Ṣaḍviṃśa Brāhmaṇa V.10 [wrong reference corrected]: This is the abode of divinities, they are not shaking (moving). The images of Gods laugh, weep, dance, grieve, appear suddenly, open the eyes, close the eyes." [quotation not literal]. In the Aitareya Brāhmaṇa the knowledge of form is said to be in the form of metrical (rhythmical) divine art. [N.B. the reference given is wrong, it refers probably to AB VI.5.1, (VI.37) without being a literal quotation: "There are such wonder works of the gods, and the arts in this world are to be understood as an imitation thereof." Transl. Haug] In the Śatapatha Brāhmaṇa III.2.1.5 it is said about form (that) a reflected image is art [quotation not literal]. *Rūpa* means an image for worship, *pratirūpas* are the secondary divinities, others are for decoration.

[11]As it is said in the Jaiminīya (Upaniṣad) Brāhmaṇa: "The space-directions are the Viśvedevas", (II.11.5), "the space-directions verily are the life-breath (*prāṇa*)" (IV.22.11).

[12]*Ahallikā* (talker) means one who praises *bhāṭa* in Oriya, the Kuntapīyas are a kind of women (who chant the Kuntāpasūktas of the Atharvaveda).

[13]They are the divinities of the stars etc. AVŚ VI.53.1 it is said: "May Heaven and Earth, wise pair (the two Pracetas), may lofty Śukra (Venus) grant me this thing by reason of the guerdon. May Agni, Soma mark through this libation: May Vāyu, Savitar and Bhaga guard us (Griffith)." Sūrya (Sun) is the meaning [he is one of the ten Pracetas].

[14]It is said in AVŚ I.31.1: "Here will we serve with sacrifice the great controllers of the world. The four immortal Warders who protect the regions of the sky." (Griffith).

Sūtra 24: Thus from different divinities arise different ways (traditions).

And from these ways originate the forms. These are not natural (*aprākṛtam*) and yet not untrue. From the God Viṣṇu come the Vaiṣṇavas,[15] from Rudra the Raudras, from Iḍā the Aiḍas, from Ambā the Ambinas, from Savitā the Sauras. With this differentiation the *brāhmaṇas* worship images. He who knows this is a knower of form, and those who carve images[16] in stone are sculptors (*rūpakārāḥ*). They create images according to their knowledge of form. They worship[17] those images (of the divinities) freely according to their desire; he who knows thus.

The transmission in the Pippalāda Kalpa by way of speech, body and mind, this fifth Prapāṭhaka, called the chapter on the knowledge of the conception of form has been presented before the hearers of the Muni in the form of a discussion.

---

[15]Worshippers of Viṣṇu. It is said in the Śatapatha Brāhmaṇa: "Puruṣa Nārāyaṇa desired." (ŚB XIII.6.1.1) "For the dwarf (Vāmana) belongs to Viṣṇu." (ŚB V.2.5.4). (cf. VS XXIV.7).

[16]As it is said in the Śatapatha: "In the light form is produced." [may be a mistake for *yoṣityeva rūpam dadhāti*, "on the woman he bestows beautiful form", ŚB XIII.1.9.6].

[17]As in the domestic sacrifice and in the worship (*upāsanā*) Prajāpati (is the divinity), the sacrificial fire *sviṣṭakṛt* is the auxiliary divinity and in the morning the sun (Sūrya) becomes prominent, so the sacrifice to the gods is for all gods (*viśvadevāḥ*).

SIXTH CHAPTER

INTEGRATION OF THE COMPOSITION

Then Ātharvaṇāṅgirasa, Śilpakāśyapa and others approached the hermitage of Pippalāda and asked: "Venerable Lord, how do differences in form arise? We want to hear this most excellent (teaching)." To them Pippalāda spoke the following:

Sūtra 1: The conception of the composition (nyāsadhāraṇā) is most essential.

That conception is creation. Thus spoke the kind Pippalāda, being very pleased: As Prajāpati, when he was desirous of offspring, performed austerities, and having performed austerities he brought forth a couple, Matter and Energy, (thinking) 'these two will bring forth many creatures for me', as I have told earlier in the Praśna (Upaniṣad, I.4 ff.), in the same way those who follow the way of desires desire happiness, unlimited happiness. In this wheel of happiness –

Sūtra 2: According to the (differences of) mental modification (vṛtti) a difference arises in the conception of divinities.

It is twofold. Owing to this differentiation, they conceived the images (*pratirūpāṇi*), this is the teaching.

Then the three disciples, Ātharvaṇāṅgirasa and the others asked him: "Venerable Lord, in what way do *brāhmaṇas* establish a connection between the divinities and the entire form? how do they compose them?" Whereupon the perfect Puruṣa Pippalāda said: "Hear, you sons of immortality!

Sūtra 3: The science of Śilpa is to make manifest the (divine) features.

The *śilpodgīthas* (and) the priests make many types of composition (*nyāsa*) in due order and so do the *sthāpakas*.

Sūtra 4: One should remember the nine elements constituting images in their order: composition, ornamentation, gestures, weapons, postures, vehicles, secondary divinities, enemies and devotees.

They conceive it in this way: composition of line-diagrams, ornamentation, gestures, (weapons), postures, vehicles, secondary divinities, enemies and devotees. Listen, my three beloved disciples, to the instruction about the nine elements of composition", said Pippalāda. For obtaining the correct disposition of the limbs, the wise *sthāpakas* make lines on the stone. These nine elements are not for human images, but are important (only) for divine images. The turban-clad sculptors trace the lines on the stone-panel with white stone-powder according to the attitude of the god.

Sūtra 5: Three (types of) lines are essential.

Vertical lines are fire-lines like a flame soaring upwards, horizontal lines are water-lines, like the flow of rivers, diagonal lines going to the corners are wind-lines, like the transversal motion of the wind. With the above-mentioned lines one should make a grid (*koṣṭhaka*) on the stone panel, which is called *pañjara*. This grid is the combination of the vertical, horizontal and oblique lines.

Sūtra 6: The sequence of lines of the grid on the image panel is most important.

By tracing small compartments on the walls of the rock-cut caves, the positioning of the figures is easily obtained. As the Puruṣa is of sixteen parts[1] (the grid) becomes complete with sixteen parts. Thus –

Sūtra 7: The forms appear within the grid of sixteen compartments, this is best for making images.

(First) trace a circle on that panel with white powder with the help of the *ghūrṇikā* (compass) for fixing the centre. That is the circumference which is the manifestation of Brahman. The central hole in that form is the hole of the life-breath.

---

[1] "Brahma verily is sixteenfold", (Jaiminīya Up. Br IV.25.1–2) says the Śatapatha Brāhmaṇa. (cf. ŚB VII.2.2.17, "Prajāpati is sixteenfold", ŚB XI.1.6.36, "Puruṣa consists of sixteen parts"; cf. Chānd. Up. VI.7.1). See also AVŚ XIX.23.13,: "Hail to the sixteen-versed!" (Griffith), thus it is said about the sixteenfold.

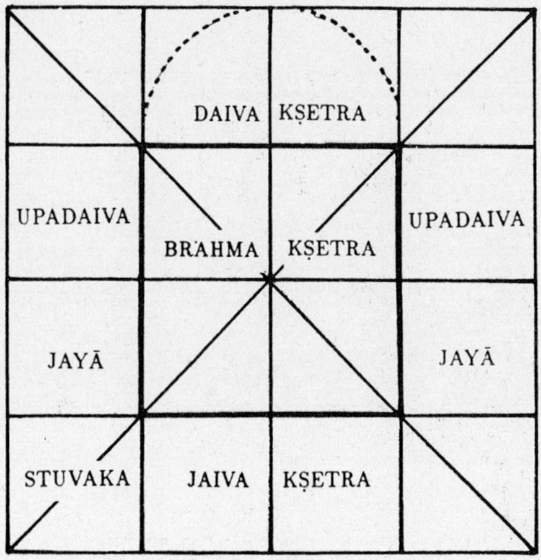

Fig. 19: Koṣṭhaka

Sūtra 8: The hole is the centre (marman), (it is to be) contemplated as Brahman.

Through this centre the unity of the composition of the figures (*aṅgabhāva*) is derived.

Sūtra 9: The compartments in the measure of the sixteen-fold grid are known to be of five types: the field of Brahman, of the gods (daiva), of living beings (jaiva), of secondary divinities (upadaiva) and of worshippers.

One should make a corner-division depending on the four corners with the help of a circle. In the two uppermost compartments of this grid Yakṣas, Gandharvas and Apsarases should be carved. The corresponding two lowest compartments are the places for adorers. In both corners human worshippers should be drawn. The two lowest central compartments are the place of living beings, for the vehicles of divinities. The four central compartments of the grid form the field of Brahman where the body of the image for worship is established, making it from below upwards, up to the head-part, from the feet to the head. The four compartments left and right of the *brahmakṣetra* are the places for the consorts.

Sūtra 10: There are four parts in the figure, this is the particularity.

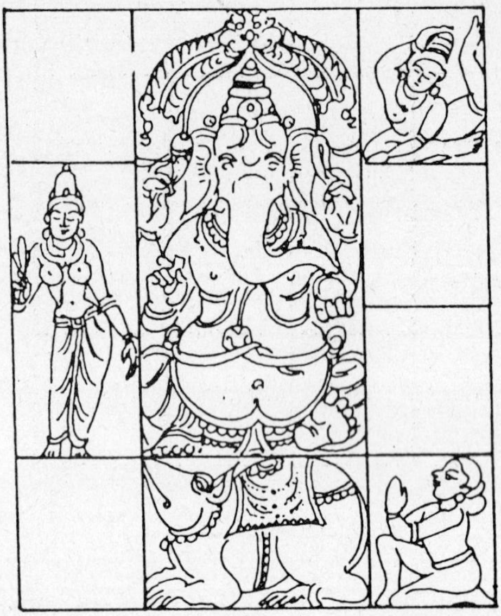

Fig. 20: Koṣṭhaka with figure of Gaṇeśa

The earth-part, the vital part, the part of the life-breath and the divine part. From foot to knees is the earth-part,[2] from knee to navel is the vital part,[3] from navel to neck is the part of the life-breath,[4] from neck to the *brahmarandhra* is the part of (divine) light.[5] That is similar to (the division of the body into the domains of) the Saviour with form (*mūrtitāraka*) and the Saviour without form (*amūrtitāraka*), as already told by the Veda.[6]

In the two uppermost (central) compartments there should be the face and the head-ornaments and an aureole of divine light which can be in egg-(oval) form or circular form. There dwells the white light which is the essence of immortality.[7] Thus there are four divisions

---

[2] The limb which moves on the earth.

[3] In the navel reigns the essence of life and thence it comes forth.

[4] In the heart the life-breath is established.

[5] In the *brahmarandhra* the light shines forth and becomes manifest.

[6] "The saviour is twofold, the embodied saviour and the bodiless saviour. Within the limits of the sense-organs is the embodied saviour, the other which goes beyond the eyebrows is the bodiless one." Thus it is said in the Advayatāraka (Upaniṣad) 10.

[7] "I am myself the light within everything, the Lord of all." It is said about

of the limbs (parts) of the image for the stone figure. In the two fields left and right in the divine field the secondary divinities are placed with the Śaktis of the gods. On both sides (they occupy) four compartments. This is the connection of the sixteen compartments of the grid. This is the most important rule (*mahāsūtra*) which should be applied to all image panels. Thus spoke the gentle Pippalāda.

Then Śilpakāśyapa, Āṅgirasa, Kośala and others asked: "Venerable Pippalāda, incarnation of architectural science (*vāstukarmāṅgāvatāra*), perfect Puruṣa (of sixteen parts) ! How do the secondary divinities contribute to the character of the image? what is their best connection (to the main divinity)?"

With hands in gift-bestowing and expounding gestures and having pronounced the blessing (*svasti*), the serene Pippalāda spoke: "Sages of Art (*śilparṣayaḥ*), hear first about the connection of the points (*bindu*).

Sūtra 11: The bindu is like Brahman, Brahman is immovable.

Inside the grid of the image there are two *bindus*. The *brahmabindu* is the central point, like Brahman. In the middle of the upper part is the *bindu* called *satya*. Both are distinct.

Sūtra 12: Brahman and satya (truth) are in the beginning.

As Prajāpati was created from the navel of the original Puruṣa and he creates (all) beings: "Brahman was first born at the beginning", (AVŚ IV.1.1), as in natural generation the embryo is formed in the mother's womb while attached by a string to the navel, in the same way it is in the image.

Sūtra 13: When the limbs of the image are depending on the brahmabindu (central point) they becomes harmonious.

The upper *bindu* is the *satyabindu*. In the centre between the eyebrows the Brahma-elixir is found in a golden vessel[8], from that elixir knowledge arises in living beings. Thus in making images the *sthāpakas* figure out the glory of the limbs and forms as depending

---

Svarāṭ (Brahmavidyā Up. 106, not in the Yogatattva Upaniṣad).

[8]In the highest golden vessel (*hiraṇmaya koṣa*) (shines) the pure formless Brahman, in this way.

on the *bindu*. In female figures one should consider the *bindu* in one third of the middle-line (*brahmakīla*) as the *marman* (vital point). By this means all forms become well-proportioned, (the image) bestows perfection (*siddhi*, power) and people become pleased.

Now, students, hear about the setting of ornaments.

Sūtra 14: Ornamentation means the decoration of divine images.

By ornamentation an attractive sight is obtained by which worshippers are gladdened. Many kinds of ornaments are to be used: one should make turbans, three-tired crowns, hair-knots, matted hair for Ṛṣis, ear-ornaments in form of serpents, pendants, upper ear-rings, rings, ear-ornaments in form of a ball and in the form of a jar. For the neck *kuśacchanda* (necklace with a double knot), necklace of gold-coins, double chains, around the hip the girdle with a knot, draperies falling from shoulder to knee, for Ṛṣis a sacred thread made of the skin of a black antelope, for the ankles of women five rings, for their wrist serpent bracelets. On the palms of divine images the signs of lotus, conch and others are made by lines as auspicious signs. For Indra a headdress, for Paśupati an elephant-hide and an upper cover in form of a serpent and other things should be made as divine ornaments. By seeing these ornaments all people rejoice.

Sūtra 15: From the ornamentation (of the image) arises delight.

From delight grows contemplation (vision, *darśana*), from understanding the image[9], the realization of Brahman[10], which is bliss, thus it is said in the Veda.

Sūtra 16: Hand gestures manifest the emotional attitude of the image.

Hear the connection between the gestures in sacrificial actions and in the divine figures according to the understanding of form. The way

---

[9]As said in the Nāradaparivrājaka Upaniṣad (VI.3): "By the eye forms are apprehended, by the ear sounds are apprehended..." In the Atharvaveda it is said: "Every form and every power..." (AVŚ XIX, I.3).

[10]It is said in the Śatapatha Brāhmaṇa (=Bṛhad. Up II.3.1): "Two are the forms of Brahman, the formed and the unformed, the mortal and the immortal." [Correct: *dve vāva brahmaṇo rūpe mūrtaṃ caivāmūrtaṃ ca, martyaṃ cāmṛtam ca.*]

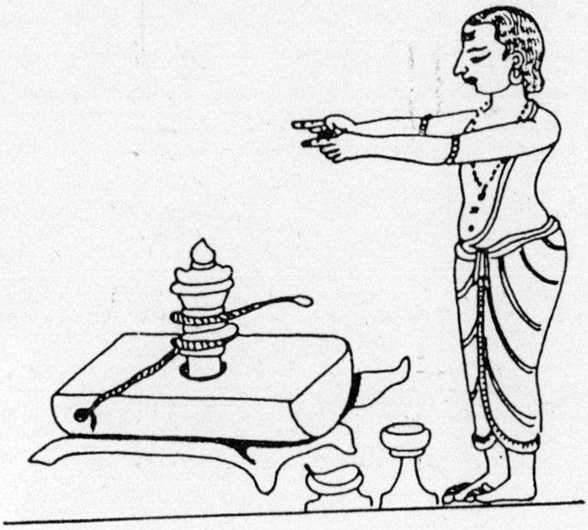

Fig. 21:
Tarjanī-Mudrā (Uttādanī)

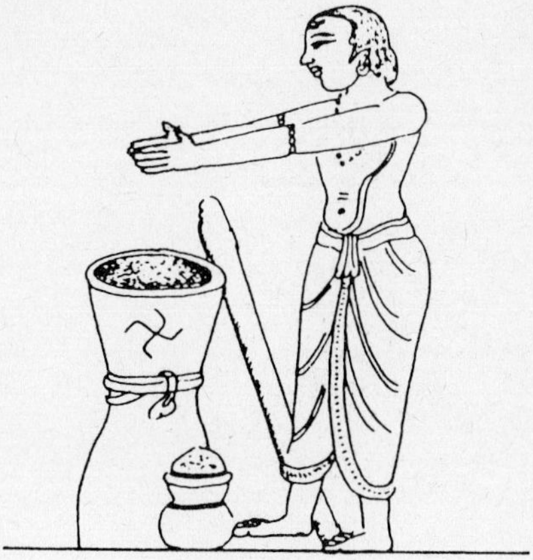

Fig. 22:
Dhvaja-Mudrā (Prasāriṇī)

in which in the sacrificial ritual the chanting priests (*udgīthāḥ*) while chanting the *gāthā* extend and show their hands, that is the *mudrā*. It is instrumental in the sacrifice. These the sculptors use for images, there is no difference between the two. That action is reflected in the body of the image. Five are the principal *mudrās*: *tarjanī, vara, abhaya, yoga, vyākhyāna*. Just as the priests (*udgīthāḥ*), the members of the Vedic assembly, extend their hands when churning the two fire-sticks (lighting the fire), when consecrating the mortar, cleansing the altar, placing the fire on the altar and consecrating the sacrificial cakes, in the same way these five *mudrās* are used. Listen, my dear disciples!

At the time of churning the fire-sticks the *adhvaryu*, pronouncing the mantra: "OṂ Utter a vow to Agni which is being kindled" (TS VI..5.3; ŚB III.4.1.22) points with his finger, that is *tarjanī-mudrā* which is graceful in the image. The way they extend their hands over the mortar for spreading the offering on the mortar, that is the *dhvaja-mudrā* which is graceful in the image. The way the *brāhmaṇas* at the time of inspecting the altar and singing the sacrificial chants (*gāthā*), uttering this sentence: "OṂ! To sacrifice, to worshipper, hymns, songs and healing charms we speak" (AVŚ XI.6.14, Griffith), pray to Vaiśvānara with hollowed hands (as in receiving), this is *āvāhanī* (welcoming gesture), that is *varamudrā* (boon-bestowing gesture) which is graceful in the image. The way the *ācāryas* in the main action, at the time of placing the fire on the altar, holding a bundle of *darbha* grass in their hand make the fire to rise by show-

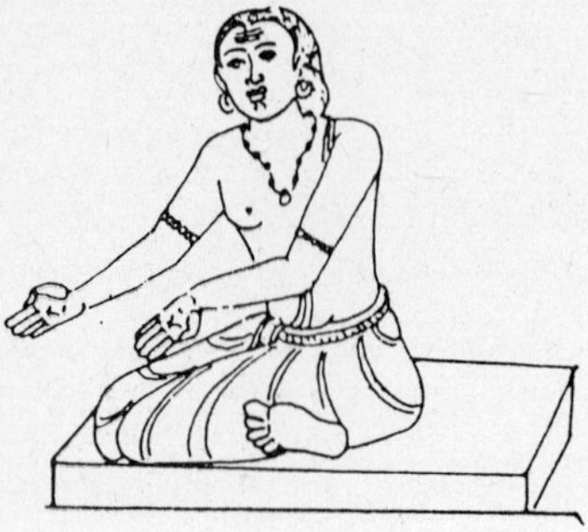

Fig. 23:
Āvāhanī-Mudrā (Vara)

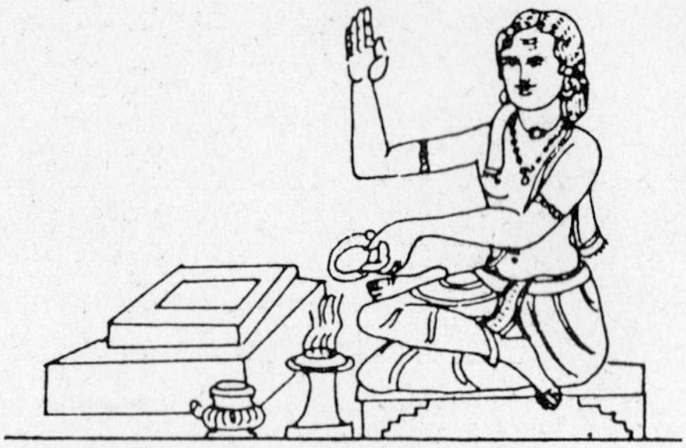

Fig. 24:
Abhaya-Mudrā

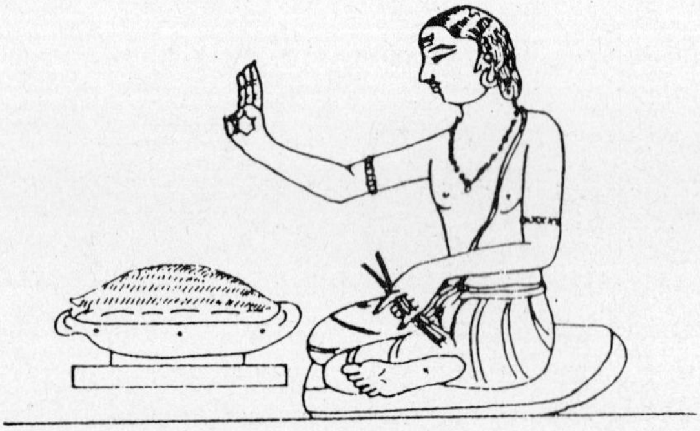

Fig. 25: Yogamudrā

ing the palms, that is (called) *abhayamudrā* in the image where it is graceful. Those two *mudrās*, *vara* and *abhaya*, are to be given only to figures in the *brahmakṣetra*, they do not appear in the (lower) field of living beings (*jaivakṣetra*) on the grid.

The way in which the participants show their hands at the time of covering the sacrificial cakes, while turning towards the sacrificer, saying:

> "Good milker, with rice-cake as calf, she in the world comes nigh to him, [to him who gave her as a gift the Cow grants every hope and wish."] (AVŚ XII.4.35, Griffith).

etc. and offer the cake with the mantra '*haviṣa* etc.' in the *sviṣṭakṛt* fire, that is the *yogamudrā* in the image, and also the *vyākhyānamudrā* which is graceful in the image. These are the five *mudrās* to be observed in the image.

Now, hear, students of art (*śilpādhyetāraḥ*) the relation of the *bādhra* (weapons, with the figures) in sculpture.[11]

Sūtra 17: The bādhra (weapons) communicate the power of the figure.

The *bādhra* means weapon (attribute).[12] Each has its (peculiar) form. The gods hurl (them) at the Kauṇapas. The *bījamantras*[13] (seed-words) of the weapons should be remembered. Without the mantras the weapons are (impotent like) clods of earth. Thus even at the time of carving the *sthāpakas* utter the mantras.[14] Twelve are the *bījas* of weapons known by the knowers of mantras. The subtle sound of the mantra is the *bīja* (seed-word). Being united with it the action of the mantra is manifested.

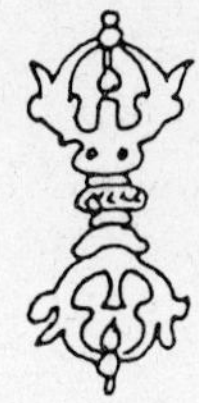

Fig. 26: Vajra

Indra's attribute is the thunderbolt (*vajra*). (Its mantra is:) OṂ VAṂ VAJRĀYA, they consecrate it with the *bīja* VAṂ. That is the power of destruction (*saṃhāra*).[15]

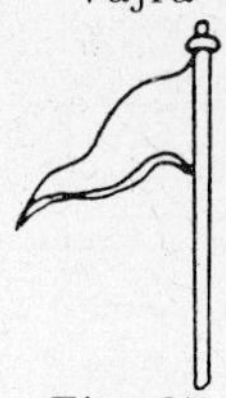

Fig. 27: Dhvaja

Marut's attribute is the flag (*dhvaja*). (Its mantra is:) OṂ DHAṂ DHVAJĀYA, they consecrate it with the *bīja* DHAṂ. That is the power of shaking.[16]

Yama's attribute is the rod (*daṇḍa*). (Its mantra is:) OṂ DUṂ DAṆḌĀYA, they consecrate it with the *bīja* DUṂ. That is the power of killing.

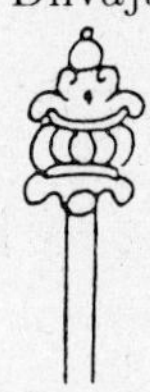

Fig. 28: Daṇḍa

---

[11] In the Kauṣītaki Brāhmaṇa *kalāvidyā* is mentioned [does it refer to Kauṣ. Br. 29.5: *trivṛd vai śilpam...*?], (also) in the Paippalāda Saṃhitā, Ist Kāṇḍa.

[12] "Thou, weapon of the Ṛṣis, art adored and served with sacrifice," it is said in the AVŚ (VI.133.2, Griffith) in connection with the subject of the investiture with the sacred girdle. "May all the deities whose might controls the fortune of the fray ! Frighten away our enemies with Drum and skin of antelope." (AVŚ V.21.7, Griffith).

[13] In the Āsurīkalpa of the Atharvaveda the use of *bīja-mantras* is explained.

[14] In the Śatapatha Brāhmaṇa (VI.4.1.7) it is said: "The word verily is the mantra." In the Kauṣītaki Brāhmaṇa (X.6) it is said: "The word verily is the mantra [*mānotā*, a part. hymn] of the Gods."

[15] *Vaṃ* means destruction, and it is the *śakti* of the previous word (Indra).

[16] Trembling is the meaning.

Varuṇa's attribute is the noose (*pāśa*). (Its mantra is:) OṂ PAṂ PĀŚĀYA, they consecrate it with the *bīja* PAṂ. That is the power of attraction (*ākarṣaṇa*).

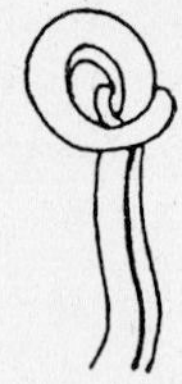

Fig. 29: Pāśa

Īśāna's attribute is the spear (*śūla*). (Its mantra is:) OṂ ŚUṂ ŚŪLĀYA, they consecrate it with the *bīja* ŚUṂ. That is the power of piercing (splitting, *bhedana*).

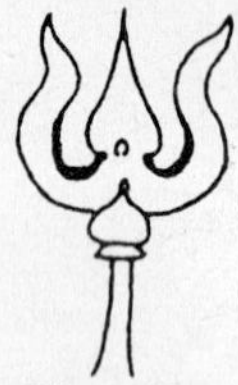

Fig. 30: Śūla

Soma's attribute is the bowl (*pātra*). (Its mantra is:) OṂ PAṂ PĀTRĀYA, they consecrate it with the *bīja* PAṂ. That is the power of life-breath (*prāṇaśakti*).

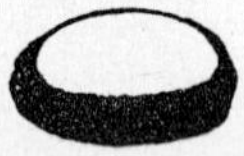

Fig. 31: Pātra

Vaiśvānara's attribute is the sacrificial ladle (*sruk*). (Its mantra is:) OṂ SRUṂ SRUVĀYA, they consecrate it with the *bīja* SRUṂ. That is the power of renunciation (*tyāgaśakti*).

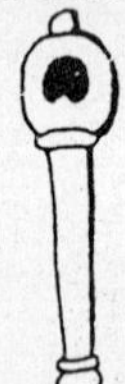

Fig. 32: Sruk

Sūrya's attribute is the lotus (*padma*). (Its mantra is:) OṂ PAṂ PADMĀYA, they consecrate it with the *bīja* PAṂ. That is the power of giving delight (*prahlādinī śakti*).

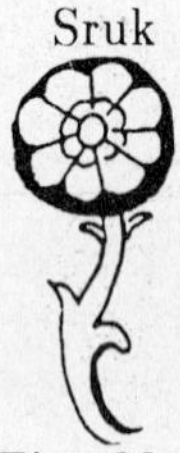

Fig. 33: Padma

Ambā's attribute is the rosary (*mālā*). (Its mantra is:) OṂ MAṂ MĀLĀYAI, they consecrate it with the *bīja* MAṂ. That is the power of meditation (*dhyānaśakti*).

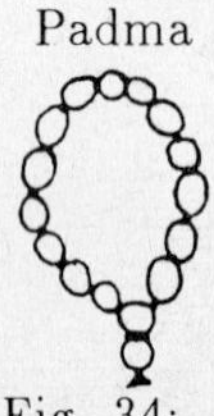

Fig. 34: Mālā

Viṣṇu's attribute is the discus (*cakra*). (Its mantra is:) OṂ HUṂ CAKRĀYA, they consecrate it with the *bīja* HUṂ. That is the power of delusion (*māyāśakti*).[17]

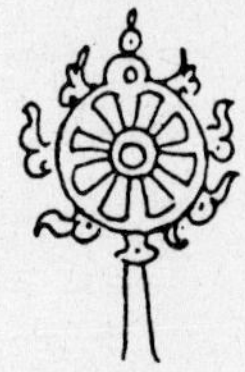

Fig. 35: Cakra

Kubera's attribute is the pot (*kumbha*). (Its mantra is:) OṂ KAṂ KUMBHĀYA, they consecrate it with the *bīja* KAṂ. That is the power of wealth (*nidhiśakti*).

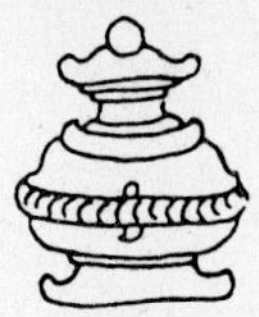

Fig. 36: Kumbha

Gaṇadaivata's attribute is the elephant-goad (*aṅkuśa*). (Its mantra is:) OṂ AṂ AṄKUŚĀYA, they consecrate it with the *bīja* AṂ. That is the power of control (*saṃyama*).

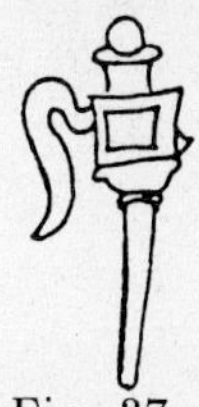

Fig. 37: Aṅkuśa

Thus uttering the sound (of the *bīja*) following the rule, the sculptors make the attributes. This sound is the essence of the mantra. That is the *bīja* which should be applied and known.

Within the sixteen compartments (of the panel) in connection with the positioning of the hands of the figure the contact with the circumference should be considered.

Now Pippalāda spoke with a serene countenance to the *vāstūdgīthas* about the connection of the stances (*kakṣā*) (with the *devas*).

Sūtra 18: Six are the principal types of postures (āsana).

The postures reveal the action of the figure. The form of the body (its appearance) is of two main types which are distinguished by standing and seated postures. Standing[18] figures are (called) *utsarga* in the image, seated figures are *āsika* in different images, this should

[17] *Māyā* means wisdom (*prajñā*).

[18] Figures standing erect, that is the meaning.

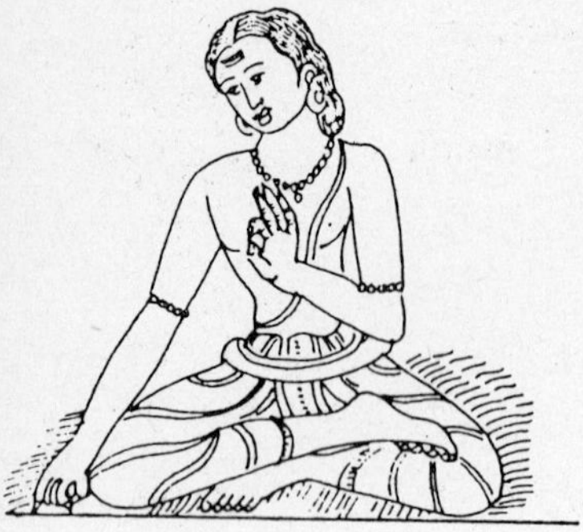

Fig. 38:
Sukhāsana

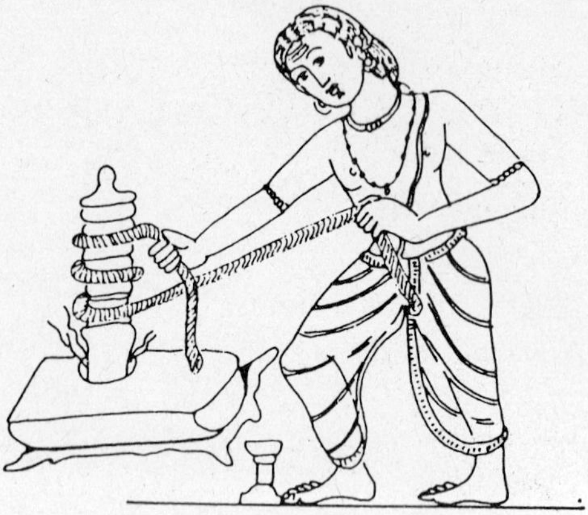

Fig. 39:
Viṣamāsana

be known. As are the actions in sacrifice, thus (the postures) are represented in stone sculpture. There are six types of *āsanas*.

The way the sacrificers are seated on *darbha* grass in their own hall, that is *sukhāsana* in the image.

The way the priests (*agnidhra*) pull the ropes while kindling the fire, that is *viṣamāsana* (asymmetrical pose) in the image.

The way the *ācāryas* seat themselves on the *vedi*, that is *svastikāsana* in the image.

The way the *brāhmaṇas* are seated with bent hips at the time of putting on the sacred thread in the rite of protection, arranging and tying the thread, that is *yogāsana* in the image.

The way the twice-born are seated while worshipping the Sun, that is *kukkuṭāsana* in the image.

The way the *udgīthas*, according to the Vājasaneyi Saṃhitā, extend their hands towards the east at the time of twilight-worship, that is *saumyāsana* in the image.

This is the application of the six types of postures in the image and in sacrifice.

Āṅgirasa, Śilpakāśyapa and the other students asked: "Venerable Sir, why do differences in posture arise? how is it to be observed for the purpose of seating (the images)? what is their connection? Tell us with faith, O gentle one, to make us understand the image which is difficult to comprehend."

(Reply:) By the posture the emotional state embodied in the action of the image is revealed. The *sukhāsana* gives a peaceful atti-

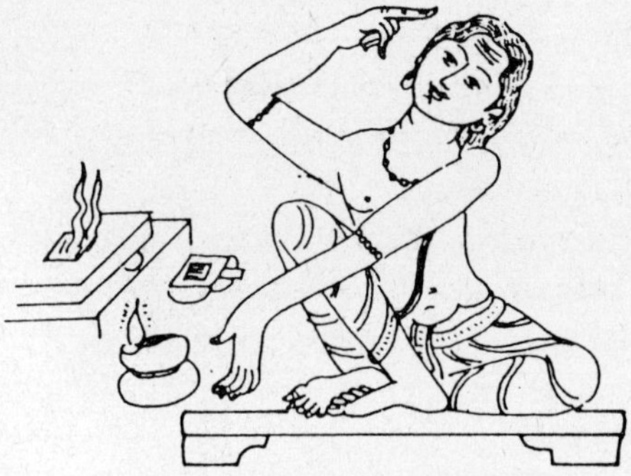

Fig. 40:
Svastikāsana

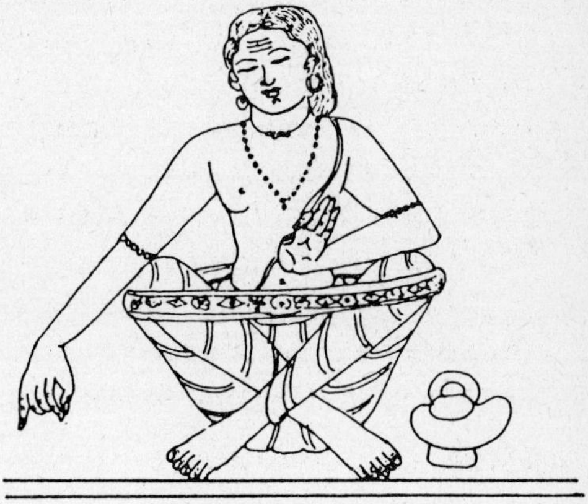

Fig. 41:
Yogāsana

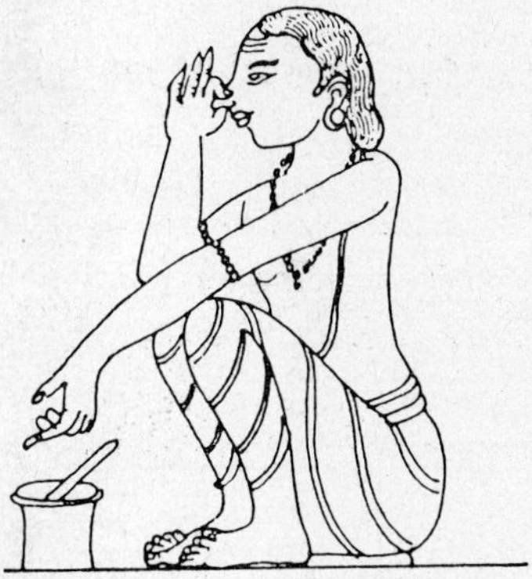

Fig. 42:
Kukkuṭāsana

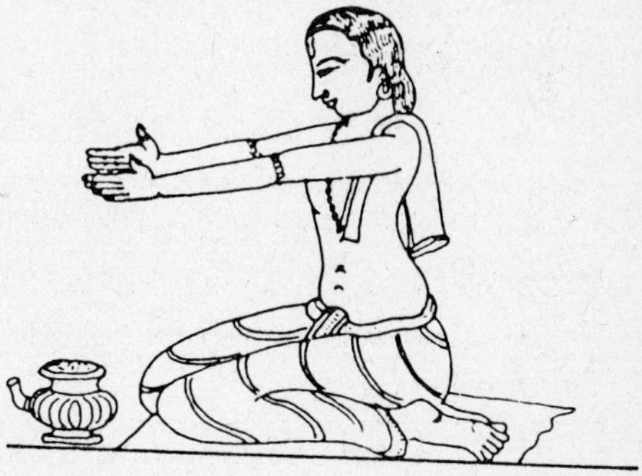

Fig. 43:
Saumyāsana

tude to the image. The *viṣamāsana* shows a heroic attitude or hurling and other such (aggressive) actions. The *svastikāsana* reveals the attitude of wisdom. The *yogāsana* shows the attitude of realization of Brahman or self-realization. The *kukkuṭāsana* reveals the attitude of longing. The *saumyāsana* conveys a feeling of firmness. This should be observed with respect to the image as a whole. All masters of Śilpa apply them in connection with the image in the *brahmakṣetra* inside the circle within the sixteen compartments.

Hear now, beloved disciples, the relationship of the vehicles of the gods[19] in the images. The vehicles show and make known the intrinsic quality (*guṇa*) of the image.

Sūtra 19: According to the quality (guṇa) there are three types of images.

From *sattva* (*guṇa*) sāttvic images, from *rajas* rājasic images, from *tamas* tāmasic images are derived, that is their distinction. Images leading to union (with the divinity) are sāttvic images. Those who procure bodily satisfaction are rājasic. Those images meant to give death to an enemy are tāmasic.[20] The science of image-making of this Vāstuveda follows the order of the qualities. He who knows this (science)... This is the exposition.

Now hear about the intrinsic character of the vehicles.

Sūtra 20: The vehicle is a special means for revealing the nature of the figure.

As Indra[21] is attracting the elephants of the quarters and causes rain, thus he is mounted on Airāvata whose nature is attraction.

As Yama is extracting the life-breath of living beings, thus he is mounted on a terrifying buffalo.[22]

As Vaiśvānara becomes enkindled by the sacrificers, thus he is mounted on a ram.[23]

---

[19]In the Aitareya (Brāhmaṇa) the special forms of vehicles are mentioned.

[20]This is the theory of worship (or sacrifice) of the Gods, as said in the Śatapatha Brāhmaṇa and in the Chāndogya (Upaniṣad). This is the order, this is the theory of worship which by means of worship giving bliss to the soul (*ātmā*) (worships) the thirtythree gods (Tārkṣya Brāhmaṇa).

[21]"Verily mighty is the net of mighty Śakra (Indra) rich in wealth. (AVŚ VIII.8.6, Griffith).

[22]"The life-breath verily is the buffalo", as said in the Śatapatha Brāhmaṇa (VI.7.4.5).

[23]"Like a ram you contract and expand", AVŚ VI.49.2.

As Savitṛ (the Sun) moves on one course with seven rays, thus he is mounted on a one-wheeled chariot.[24]

As Rudra is propagating *dharma*, he is mounted on the *dharma*-bull.[25]

As Prajāpati attracts the creatures by knowledge, he is mounted on a swan (*haṃsa*).[26]

As Viṣṇu bestows liberation, he is mounted on the divine bird (*suparṇa*).[27]

As Ambā destroys the host of enemies, she is mounted on a tiger (leopard).[28]

It should be remembered to make the *vāhanas* in the field for living beings within the sixteen compartments. When the figure of the *brahmakṣetra* is in depression, it is good to have other (figures) below (in the *jaivakṣetra*).

Now hear the relation with the secondary divinities,[29] said the gentle Pippalāda.

Sūtra 21: Attendant divinities are secondary figures.

All these gods and the five great elements earth, wind, ether, water and fire have been created by Prajāpati with their respective qualities. According to the knowledge of these elements the respective qualities of the forms embodying the sentiment (*bhāvarūpa*) are shown. The nature of the secondary divinities is corresponding to the knowledge of these elements. As Vaiśvānara[30] is Brahman, he is sacrifice, the burning power (*dāhikā śaktiḥ*)[31] of the sacrifice is

[24] "One of the Sun's rays is giver of rain", as said in the Śatapatha Brāhmaṇa (XIV.2.1.21), that is Savitā who mounts on a chariot.

[25] "Thou art a Bull that mounts to heaven: to Ṛṣis and their offspring go." AVŚ XI, I.35 (Griffith).

[26] The meaning of the word *haṃsa* is "the one who moves, having penetrated within all bodies." Thus it is said in the Haṃsopaniṣad (5).

[27] "Two birds, fast bound companions, clasp close the self-same tree." (ṚV I.164.20; AV IX.9, 20; Muṇḍ. Up. III.1.1, Śvet. Up. IV.6, transl. Hume).

[28] "These [priests], compassing the tiger [the king], rouse the lion to great joy and bliss." AVŚ IV.8.7, (Griffith).

[29] In the Vāstuveda attendant divinity (*upadaivatam*) means secondary form (*pratirūpam*). About secondary forms speaks the Śatapatha Brāhmaṇa (III.2.1.5 *yad vai pratirūpaṃ tacchilpam*). Their usage is mentioned in the Jaiminīya Brāhmaṇa (I.27.5, corrected): "The (Puruṣa) in the Sun is an image (*pratirūpa*), he is facing all forms. (One should meditate on him as an image, for all the forms are facing him)."

[30] Vaiśvānara verily is all fires, as said in the Śatapatha Brāhmaṇa (VI.6.1.5).

[31] "That which heats is that Vaiśvānara", (Kauṣ. Br. IV.3).

Svāhā, the cooking power is Svadhā.[32] Thus the character of the secondary divinity as it is manifested prevails in worship.

Indra's procreative Śakti is Indrāṇī.[33]

Māruta's Śakti of speed is Vāyunāyī. She is speedy.

Yama has two qualities, a protecting one and a destructive one. His protecting Śakti is Ākūti,[34] his destroying Śakti is Mṛtyu.[35]

Varuṇa's Śakti of flowing is Vāruṇī.[36]

Soma's power of supporting is Iḷā.[37]

Sūrya's or Savitṛ's depending Śakti is Chāyā,[38] his penetrating Śakti is Uṣas.[39]

Viṣṇu's Śakti conferring liberation is Śrī[40], the golden-coloured Hariṇī, his Śakti of enduring is Pṛthivī.[41]

Śeṣa's bearing Śakti is Dhṛti, his expanding Śakti Vidhṛti. As the earth is a carrier (Dhṛti) of food, Vidhṛti is happiness.

Hiraṇyagarbha's Śakti has the nature of Time; Gāyatrī[42] is the embodiment of knowledge, Sāvitrī[43] is the embodiment of intelligence, Sarasvatī[44] is the embodiment of wisdom. The goddess is specific (with regard to time) and she embodies the three times (morning, midday and evening, the three times of worship).

---

[32]It is that by which food is digested in man, as said in the Śatapatha Brāhmaṇa (Bṛhad. Up. V.9).

[33]She is Indra's consort, as said in the Gobhila Gṛhya Sūtra.

[34]She (Ākūti, intention personified as goddess) is an essential part of a living being.

[35]"Agni verily is death", according to the Kauṣītaki Brāhmaṇa (XIII.3; cf. Jaim. Up. Br. I.26.6). "Death verily belongs to it", says also Śatapatha Brāhmaṇa (X.5.1.4).

[36]In the Aitareya (Brāhmaṇa) Vāruṇī is said to be night (cf. AB IV.10, *rātrir varuṇaḥ*).

[37]"Iḷā verily is food", as said in the Atharvaveda (cf. AB II.4; VIII.26; Kauṣ. Br. 7, III).

[38]*Chāyā* (shadow) is darkness.

[39]"Goddess Uṣā is united with Vāk (word), Goddess Vāk is united with Uṣā", as said in the Atharvaveda (AVŚ XVI.6.5).

[40]Heaven is the meaning. The strength of past, present and future is the power of Lakṣmī, as said in the Atharvaveda (?).

[41]The Earth is the consort of the gods, as said in the Śatapatha Brāhmaṇa. (I.3.1.15).

[42]"Gāyatrī is first by way of light (*tejas*)", according to the Tāṇḍya Brāhmaṇa (X.5.3).

[43]"Sāvitrī as the Word (Vāk)", is said in the Gopatha Brāhmaṇa (I.1.33).

[44]The form of learning (*Sārasvata*), as said in the Aitareya (Brāhmaṇa III.1–2).

Rudra is by his sovereign power.[45] His generating Śaktis are Ambā[46] and Ambālikā,[47] these two.

Durgā's protecting Śakti is Sundarī and Mohinī, these two are forms of attraction.

In this way, following the order of the qualities of the main divinities the secondary divinities are created as their consorts (*jāyābhāvena*). These (Śaktis) are their attributes.

Then Ātharvaṇāṅgirasa, Śilpakāśyapa, Kuvitsa, Kośala and others, having saluted in diverse ways, asked: "Venerable Pippalāda, divine Puruṣa, how is this? what are the Śaktis (*hetayaḥ*?)? We do not understand this. Kindly explain more explicitly, O gentle one!" The divine Puruṣa Pippalāda spoke: "*Śilpodgīthas*, hear as I shall explain in detail how the canon for the work of sculpture of secondary divinities has been expounded in the ancient Veda:

Prajāpati (first) created Time, the two (halves of the year), the southern and the northern (course of the sun). From the North come the gods, from the South the ancestors, from the North Savitṛ (the sun), from the South Candramā (the moon). The Ṛṣis lead to the South according to desire. That is the way of the fathers, which is night. Brahmacārīs (ascetics) who desire liberation take the way of the North, that is verily the way of the gods (*devayāna*), which is day. From the South come the regions of Aryaman and the five generations of Fathers.[48] From the North come the twelve divine forms, thus they say. In this way according to the different qualities the one Brahman becomes twelvefold. Just as Sūrya is the Lord of all lights, according to their qualities are the (different) gods, and according to their features their forms arise, and from those the secondary divinities are derived. This is truth.

As surrender is the principal attitude arising from sacrifice,[49] with

---

[45]Savitā is the kingdom and the ruler, as said in the Śatapatha Brāhmaṇa XI.4.3.14. (Connection with Rudra?)

[46]Ambā mentioned in the Atharvaveda.

[47]Ambālikā has the form of remedy (*bheṣaja*), as said in the Vājasaneyi (Saṃhitā).

[48]"Gods are the Fathers and the Fathers Gods. I am the very man I am" (AVŚ VI.123.3, Griffith), these are the Viśvedevas as: The Fathers are the attendant divinities. The Vasus are the Fathers, Rudra is the grandfather, Āditya is the great-grandfather. AVŚ V.24 the mantras for setting up the Yūpa for the Fathers are given.

[49]They say: "Deliver us from trouble, from anxiety" (AVŚ I.31.2). "O Jātavedas, southward sacrificers as foes assail us from the southern quarter"

respect to the divinity it is *Svāhā*.[50] *Svāhā* is the embodiment of the attitude of surrender. *Svadhā* is that which is enjoyed, it is means for the fathers (*pitṛbhāva*). As Viṣṇu bestows liberation, (the Śakti of) liberation is Śrī, Pṛthivī is to be enjoyed in the form of the object of enjoyment.[51]

As from Rudra's aspect of liberation arises Ambā, from his attitude of enjoyment Ambikā, these two.

As from Indra's action of surrender comes the sacrifice, in his aspect of enjoyment (his Śakti) is Indrāṇī.

Where there are many qualities, on account of the secondary states the attendant divinities are many, as observed by the wise. As they speak about seven states of Agni Vaiśvānara from its rising to its extinction, in this order: pleasantly shining (*snigdhā*), smoky (*dhūmā*), heating (*taptā*), blazing (*uttaptā*), burning (*dāhikā*), consuming to ashes (*bhasmā*) and extinct (*nirvāṇā*). The fire burns in these stages, according to its qualities arise the seven tongues (of flames). From these flames they derive the secondary divinities which are, in the order given before: Kālī (black), Karālī (terrifying), Manojavā (swift as thought), Sulohitā (glowing red), Sudhūmavarṇā (smoke-coloured), Sphuliṅginī (sparkling), Viśvaruci (all glittering), they are all of female form and should be understood in the attitude of the image.

As the Śruti (Veda) is supreme, in the form of intelligence it becomes Bhāratī. As from intelligence speech is brought forth, thus from the Śruti originates Sarasvatī,[52] greater than the great, the embodiment of supreme knowledge.

According to the nature of these forms arose Lakṣmī with the nature of prosperity, Devahūtī and others. They are all in the *daivakṣetras* on the two sides of the sixteen compartments as secondary divinities in the form of consorts of the main divinities. O sculptors,

---

(AVŚ IV.40.2, Griffith), that is surrender (*tyāga*). "Indra and Soma, burn the demon...", thus they say (AVŚ VIII.4.1). "With deadly poison strike thou back the treacherous brood of Rākṣasas" (AVŚ VIII.3.23, Griffith) that is enjoyment (*bhoga*).

[50] "*Svāhā* is born from truth, she is the daughter of Brahman", as said in the Śatapatha Brāhmaṇa (Ṣaḍviṃśa Br. IV.7).

[51] In this way Śrīdevī and Bhūdevī are indicated as the two modes of being of Viṣṇu.

[52] "The pious call Sarasvatī: they worship Sarasvatī while sacrifice proceedeth. The righteous doers of good deeds invoke her: Sarasvatī send bliss to him who giveth." (AVŚ XVIII.4.45, Griffith).

vāstūdgīthas regard this as truth.

Sūtra 22: The (aspects of the) main image are known by the attendant divinities.

By (their) worship the magic powers are subdued.[53]

Sūtra 23: The connection (of the main figure) with adversaries should be remembered.

Sūtra 24: From the sequence of forms comes the condition (of the mind), this (procedure) is the best.

Now hear about the different attitudes derived from the flow of form, how the transformation of the attitudes takes place. Prajāpati's first state of creation was Mind,[54] from Mind developed Life-breath,[55] the evolution of Life-breath is action, action verily is knowledge.[56] This the Ṛṣis declare to be of two types, the knowledge of being and non-being (*sadasadvidyā*). What is the flow of cosmic order (truth), that is divine action, it is supreme knowledge. What is against cosmic order (untruth) is wrong action which is ungodly and lower (knowledge). The Asuras come from the lower knowledge. The gods are related to the day and the Asuras to the night.[57] Those who are full of fear and sorrow, such as Nikandins, Kaṇvajambhas, Yātudhānas, Pṛśniparṇi and others of evil birth, they all destroy the purpose of others according to their different nature. They are all enemies who destroy the sacrifice in the realm of the gods and (also) in the world.[58] They are all powerful *kimpuruṣas*, wrathful destroyers of the gods. These enemies are represented in a form as being crushed in the animal field of the panel of sixteen compartments in the worship of the secondary images. These flesh-eaters are inflicting fear to the gods and give them great trouble. They are saved by sacrifice. For this purpose some gods meditate on the Ṛṣis. By worshipping the gods Munis become spiritual. The priests (*hotāraḥ*) throw with devotion food-offerings and fuel for the gods into the fire, and Ṛṣis become singers of praises.

---

[53] The science for obtaining worldly powers is called *bhūtavidyā* (note of MS घ).

[54] "Prajāpati verily is like mind", as said in the Taittirīya Brāhmaṇa (II.2.1.2).

[55] "Life-breath verily is Hari, he seizes (*harati*)", Kauṣītaki Brāhmaṇa (XVII.1).

[56] "The wealth which husbandmen aforetime, digging, like men who find their food with knowledge, buried..." (AVŚ VI.116.1, Griffith).

[57] It is said in the Gobhila Gṛhyasūtra (?) (cf. AB IV.5; Gopatha Br. II.5.1).

[58] *śimi* means *karma* (rite) and what is born from it.

Sūtra 25: Through the (representation of the) singers of praises images become particularly beautiful.[59]

They sing sacred chants.[60] People worship the image in many ways. The knowledge of form is the support of religious action in the world of men. The sound (*nāda*) is considered as truth. The *sthāpakas*, knowers of Vāstu and the *vāstūdgīthas* create images. Praisers like Pailas, Nālandinas and Apsarases entertain the gods in diverse ways, they are givers of delight. These panegyrists praise with body, mind and speech. The Bhrājins and Yakṣas sing songs of praise. The Gandharvas[61] dance for the delight of the gods. All these beings of mixed birth should be placed in the upper two corner-fields within the sixteen compartments of the panel, in the field of secondary divinities. Those human beings who are intent on (attaining) the divine state are the worshippers (*yājakāḥ*). In their meditation their being shines as if it were divinized. They are to be placed in the fields by the side of the field of living beings (*jaivakṣetra*) in the two lowest compartments. Thus the divine image should be considered within the sixteen compartments. They are indeed fortunate and wise who offer sacrifices and worship images. It is from the knowledge of form that wisdom originates in this world.

Sūtra 26: This exposition of Art (vāstu) is for the purpose of conferring knowledge.

For this purpose we are expounding this knowledge. This is the Vāstusūtropaniṣad which is the excellent exposition given by the venerable Pippalāda. Whoever understands it becomes a Master of Form (*rūpācārya*), a *vāstūdgītha*, this should be meditated upon. Those who meditate on this become liberated.

> "Let my libations, giving boons, adoring, further the
> Twice-born's song that honours Soma.
> Go ye to Brahma's world having enriched me with life and
> breath, with children and with cattle, with fame[62] and
> wealth, and with a brahman's lustre."

---

[59] Who shall hear the praiser's words and my call. (AVŚ VI.2.1, Whitney)

[60] The Kuntāpasūktas and others are additional texts, as for example the hundred verses of Śunaḥśepa (cf. AB VI.3).

[61] "Gandharvas are lovers of women", they move by smell and by forms, thus it is said in the Śatapatha Brāhmaṇa (III.2.4.3).

[62] Fame (*kīrti*) (relates to) temple, image etc.

AVŚ XIX.71.1 (Griffith)

OṂ, praise to Viśvakarman !

> "May Viśvakarma with the seven Ṛṣis be my protector from the northern region. To him I go, in him I rest: this fort I seek for refuge.
>
> May he protect me, may he be my guardian. I give my soul – all hail! into his keeping."

AVŚ XIX.17.7 (Griffith)

Here ends the sixth Prapāthaka.
Salutation to the supreme Ṛṣis! Salutation to the supreme Ṛṣis!
This completes the Ātharvaṇīyā Vāstusūtropaniṣad of Pippalāda who is an embodiment of Art (*vāstukarma*).
Here ends the gloss Pariśuddhi Ṭippaṇī written by the Ātharvaṇa Udgātṛ Somabhaṭṭa of Orissa.

Colophon:

This Vāstusūtropaniṣad of the Atharvaveda along with the gloss Viṣayabodhinī ('Illuminating the subject') Ṭippaṇī by the teacher of Atharvaveda Somabhaṭṭa has been copied by me, Kāmadeva Udgātha, teacher of Vāstu (*vāstuśāstri*), of the village Kurumacaini of Baṅkī, in the 15th year of the reign of king Rāmacandra Deva for the Rājā Haricandana.
OṂ, praise to Mahādevī (the great goddess)!

CRITICAL AND EXEGETICAL NOTES

The numbers refer to Prapāṭhaka and Sūtra (with Commentary)

I: "The one who knows it...": *ya enāṃ veda* does not form a complete sentence, like *ya evaṃ veda* it is a stereotype phrase taken over from the Brāhmaṇas and Upaniṣads, sometimes out of context. The basic meaning is that the one who knows this (in this case the science of Śilpa or Vāstu) attains the same degree of realization of Brahman (see Comm. on Sūtra 4).

I.1. Vāstoṣpati: the Lord of the house, the tutelary god of architecture. See ṚV VII.54. Sometimes identified with Viśvakarman.

Viśvakarman: "the all-doer", creator of the first sacrifice at the beginning of creation, the Architect of the gods. See ṚV X.81.

"Six branches of Śilpa": those expounded in the six chapters (see I.8), and not those wrongly given by the note of the Ṭippaṇī. The number six is a traditional division, e.g. the six Vedāṅgas (auxiliary texts of the Veda), and similar divisions in other Śāstras (e.g. Saṅgīta-Ratnākara). In Āyurveda the whole body is formed of six *aṅgas* (limbs). Since the six subjects are dealt with in the six Prapāṭhakas the VSU follows the model of the Praśna Upaniṣad.

The following passage in form of questions and answer has been confused in all the MSS, it has not been rearranged.

Kuvitsa-valabhujottolaka: according to the Ṭippaṇī, Kuvitsa, the third disciple of Pippalāda, is a *brāhmaṇa* who collects sacred grass (*darbhotpāṭaka*).

yathākāmam: probably an allusion to Praśna Upaniṣad I.2.

"Those who are about to depart...": *prayānti* can also mean advance, but since the meaning implied is not merely secular ("those who want to advance in this world"), the other meaning has been preferred. I.4 also stresses that this knowledge leads to liberation, and the text ends with a reference to the same knowledge (VI.26). Here the worldly and spiritual progress have to be taken together.

I.2. Here the Comm. does not follow the Sūtra, which is again taken up in I.8, it only comments upon the word *rūpa* and expounds its two meanings which will reoccur throughout the whole text: *rūpa* in the technical sense of sculpture or image, and in the abstract meaning of form.

Loke, vede: the worldly (*laukika*) knowledge is often contrasted with the Vedic, here the first relates to the visible form (art) and the second to the divine archetype.

rūpaṃ rūpaṃ pratirūpo bhavati: referring to ṚV VI.47.18 (not a literal quotation), in Griffith's translation: "In every figure he hath been the model: that is his only form to look on. Indra moves multiform by his illusions..." (*māyā* would be better rendered by "powers"). See Geldner's translation: "Jeglicher Gestalt hat er sich angepasst; diese (wahre) Gestalt von ihm ist (in allen) wiederzuerkennen. Vermöge seiner Zauberkünste geht Indra in vielen Gestalten ..." There are two possible interpretations of *pratirūpa* in this verse: either as the archetype or original form (model) of every form, or as the replica, likeness, image (the word image is related to imitation), the prefix *prati* indicating that it is a reflected image (like *bimba* and *pratibimba*). In the first case it would mean that there is a divine prototype or model (cf. in another tradition the Biblical "He created man in his own image and likeness", Genesis I.26–27) after which all created forms are fashioned. In the second case it would refer more to the divine immanence (a principle of incarnation rather than creation), the Divine having penetrated every form. This theme has been developed in Kaṭha Upaniṣad V.9–12:

9. As the one fire has entered the world
And becomes corresponding in form to every form,
So the Inner Soul (*antarātman*) of all things
Is corresponding in form to every form, and yet is without.

10. As the one breath (*prāṇa*) has entered the world
And becomes corresponding in form to every form,
So the Inner Soul of all things
Is corresponding in form to every form and yet is without.

11. The Inner Soul of all things, the one Controller,
Who makes his one form manifold
The wise who perceive Him as standing in oneself,
They, and no others, have eternal happiness.
(transl. R.E. Hume, replacing 'outside' by 'without' acc. to Max Müller)

Unlike in the ṚV where the sentence refers to Indra, the VSU always uses the neuter form, applying it to its theory of form and image.

The terminology of *rūpa* and *pratirūpa* is not consistent throughout the text: sometimes the Vedic and metaphysical meaning seems to be implied (*rūpa*: original form, archetype; *pratirūpa*: corresponding form, representation, image), sometimes the meaning is more technical (*rūpa*: main image; *pratirūpa*: secondary image, in the sense of *upadaivata*, see VI.21).

I.3. Yūpa: post set up to the east of the Uttaravedi in the sacrificial compound for tying the victim of the animal sacrifice, described in the Vaitāna Sūtra X.1–10 of the AV. It is mostly made of wood. The Vaitāna Sūtra describes how it is prepared, washed, anointed, decorated, erected and set into the ground, all accompanied by the proper mantras in the name of Viṣṇu. See also ṚV III.8., AB II.1–3.

Light: the *idam* may be referring to the sun, as the note of the Ṭippaṇī suggests, since the Yūpa is a solar symbol.

The Yūpa symbolises the *skambha* or *axis mundi* which is extolled in AVŚ X.7 and 8. "In him are all the lights – the three abiding in Prajāpati" (AVŚ X.7.40 Griffith). For the close association of the Yūpa with Viṣṇu, see J. Gonda, *Aspects of Early Viṣṇuism*, Delhi, 2nd ed. 1969, pp. 81 ff.

The Yūpa is here taken up as the first and most fundamental sculptural form, since it combines circle (sphere) and straight line (post), the two main form-elements according to the following Sūtra (I.4). From the Yūpa the representation of the human figure has evolved (*puruṣa*, in IV.11.14,17 etc.). D. Bhattacharya gives the following note to this passage: "The technical terms used here are of late and popular origin. In the Śrautasūtras the top of the Yūpa is a hemispherical cap (*caṣāla*) which the VSU seems to have understood as a microcosm of the concave vault of the sky covering the world and hence *viśva*."

The circle... etc.: in the Vedic ritual of setting up the Yūpa, the sacrificer had to touch the post uttering the verse of VS VI.4 (ṚV I.22.19): "See the works of Viṣṇu...", and looking to the top he had to recite VS VI.2 (ṚV I.22.20): "The patrons ever see that highest step of Viṣṇu, laid as it were an eye in heaven." (transl. Gonda). The *skambha* is the great link between earth and heaven (cf. AVŚ X.7.32 and 35). Hence the top of the Yūpa symbolises the light of heaven: "He (the sacrificer) then touches the wheat (top-piece) with 'we have gone to the light, O ye gods'." (ŚB II.2.1,12, transl. Eggeling). In the ritual of setting up the Yūpa (*yūpasthāpana*) at the Vāstuyāga the post is worshipped with *aṣṭakarma pūjā* (the post being considered as *karman*, ritual action), and the top is worshipped as the All (with the mantra *viśvāya namaḥ*). Therefore the Yūpa is considered a representation of Viśvakarman: *karman* is the post and *viśva* the top. The Śilparatnakoṣa summarises the symbolism thus (cf. v. 457–461): *yūpaṃ sākṣisvarūpeṇa vāstukarmasya pūrṇataḥ śilpādhidaivata sākṣāt karmādhyakṣasvarūpavān. sarvakarmamayadaṇḍa mūrdhnā viśvasya dhārakaḥ, viśvakarma svarūpeṇa sthāpakas sthāpayet śubhe.* "The *sthāpaka* should set up the Yūpa at an auspicious moment, (the Yūpa) which is of the form of a witness of the work of Vāstu (building), an embodiment of the presiding deity of Śilpa, of the supervisor of the action (of construction), its post consists of all actions (*karman*), and its head upholds the All (*viśva*), (hence) it is the very symbol of Viśvakarman."

"He is Viśvakarman": may refer both to the Yūpa and to the knowing *sthāpaka* who is identified with the original, divine architect as his "representative." See also Mayamata V.13f. where the *sthapati* is called Viśvakarman (quoted by S. Kramrisch in *The Hindu Temple*, Vol. I, p. 9, note 18).

I.4. The two main instruments correspond to the two fundamental form-elements which are to be known by the *sthāpaka*: the measuring rod is for the line and the compass for the circle.

Essence: *madhu*, lit. honey, the quintessence. Cf. ṚV I.116.12, Bṛhad. Up. III.1–2 (*madhuvidyā*). It can also mean *amṛta*, the nectar of immortality (since the Ṭippaṇī explains it as the bliss of Brahman).

I.5. Compare these "five steps of Vāstu" with the *rūpacakra* mentioned in Nigama Ḍiṇḍima Ṭippaṇī VI, where the sequence is: *rūpa, śraddhā, pratyaya, nirmalabuddhi, jñāna, dhyāna, rūpa*. Both, *pratyaya* and *nirmalabuddhi* may correspond to *niṣṭhā*. Whereas in the "five steps" *jñāna* leads directly to *mokṣa*, the sequence given in the Ṭippaṇī leads again back to the world of form. It is not clear whether the Ṭippaṇī version has another source or whether it is an elaboration of VSU I.5.

I.6. *Pravahaṇa* ('vehicle') can in this context of the line of teachers only refer to Pippalāda as the bearer of the tradition of Śilpa or *sthāpatya*.

The chain of the tradition starts from Prajāpati, the creator and hence originator of all form. Nārada is a Ṛṣi who is associated with all kinds of arts, especially music. He is mentioned as an authority of Śilpa in the Matsya Purāṇa. Some treatises on Śilpa are attributed to him, such as the Nāradīya Saṃhitā which contains much material on iconography and temple-architecture; the Vāstu Vidhāna, the Nārada Śilpaśāstra, the Bhūpāla Maṇḍana, in which latter work the pleasure of the *citraśālās* (image-halls) and the *raṅgaśālās* (theatre-halls) is described. Nārada again quotes as authorities on Śilpa: Kāśyapa, Bṛhaspati, Prajāpati, Anuloma, Marīci, Bṛndaka, Nādadhvani, Bhārgava, Uśīnara and Śukrācārya who also in the Matsya Purāṇa is mentioned among teachers of Śilpa. He is most probably the author of the Śukranītisāra. All these teachers are either Ṛṣis or gods.

Maya, the master architect of the Asuras, is well known as the author of the Mayamata, a fundamental text on South-Indian architecture (first published by T. Ganapati Sastri, Trivandrum 1919, then a Tamil translation by K.S. Subramanya Sastri, Tanjore, Sarasvati Mahal Series, 2 Vols., 1966–68. English translation by Bruno Dagens: Mayamata, New Delhi 1985).

Vaiśravaṇa: half-brother of or identical with Kuvera, who originally was a chief of evil spirits and had the name of Vaiśravaṇa (son of Viśravas, cf. AVŚ VIII.10.28), later he became the lord of riches and the regent of the northern quarters, the father of Rāvaṇa, king of Laṅkā. Here he is evidently considered a legendary master architect, and a short treatise Vaiśravaṇa Śilpācāra is attributed to him.

"In the way of Prajāpati": according to the law of creation, to cosmic Order. The expression *prājāpatyamārga* or *-rīti* occurs several times in the VSU. Since Prajāpati is the first propounder of this *sthāpakavidyā*, it also means "in the tradition of Prajāpati" (see II.11).

"In this mortal world...": answering the question about the origin of form, Pippalāda first refers to the beginning of creation (Prajāpati) which is related to sacrifice. Not only is creation conceived as an original sacrifice (Puruṣa, Prajāpati, cf. ṚV X.90), but the sacrifice also represents, hence re-enacts creation. Sacrifice is a microcosm of creation.

"was Being": See ṚV X.72, 2–3, Chānd. Up. VI.2.1 ff. Through sacrifice Being (*sat*) assumed form. Every form-creation is in a way a sacrificial act, as the text suggests in various ways.

"He who in the beginning", (*apāṃ yo agre...*): AVŚ IX.4.2. This mantra shows how the creator, the fertilizing agent, in-forms the waters, the original unformed substance and source of all forms. He becomes their 'archetype', *prati-mā*. As Goddess Earth is the mother of all forms, so he is the father. This quotation, along with the Ṛgvedic phrase *rūpaṃ rūpaṃ pratirūpaṃ bhavati*, is often used by the VSU when it refers to the origin of form. The two terms *pratimā* and *rūpa* are also most frequently used to indicate both the original form (archetype) and the image, the term (*mūrta* and *amūrta* in I.5).

I.7. The VSU propounds several theories about the derivation and development of image-worship (see also VI 20–21). Here the sequence is: *rūpa* (original form), *tattvabodha* (insight into the essence or principle of form), *dhāraṇā* (concentration, holding firmly the object of meditation, conception), *gāthā* (mythological songs) and *kathā* (legends) which describe the characteristics and deeds of the gods, which in turn are represented in images by the *sthāpakas* (*rūpāṇi*) (cf. III.13). See also the development of the fourteen stages (V.20), although there the movement is from the formless to form (V.21), whereas here it starts from form.

I.8. In this list of the six topics to be treated in the six Prapāṭhakas or chapters of the work, the only topic which is given some description is the *khilapañjara*, which shows the importance the text gives to the knowledge of the *pañjara*. The names of the topics differ in some cases: thus chapter IV is called *aṅgottiṣṭhādimānabodhana* instead of *aṅgaprayoga*, chapter V is called *rūpabhāvanā (bodha)* instead of *nyāsabhāvanā*, and chapter VI starts with the Sūtra giving *nyāsadhāraṇā* as the theme.

samāvarttate: the reading *samāvartane* (on returning from studies) does not make much sense. The meaning of *samāvarttate* may be that by passing on his knowledge (*prapātinī*) to his disciples he remembers or revises it.

I.9. It is striking that among the six types of stones in fact only two are recommended for sculpture, i.e. *samavarṇā* (specially for the image for worship) and *saikatālikā*, the others being discarded. It is also strange that sandstone is not given more importance, since innumerable images are made of sandstone throughout India.

I.10. *aṅgarāgajñāna*: lit. "the knowledge of the colour of the body (of the figure) is derived". Obviously the colour of the stone determines the colour of the figure. Thus generally speaking Vaiṣṇava images are of dark colour and Śaiva images of light colour (with exceptions, especially in monumental sculpture like cave temples etc.).

Here again the Comm. does not elaborate on the Sūtra at all.

sarveṣu lokeṣu kāmacāro bhavati: cf. Chānd Up. VII.15.2 where it relates to the freedom of the liberated soul or *jīvanmukta*. In the Śāstras this phrase is sometimes used to indicate the freedom of the artist in spite of the rules and prescriptions. Cf. Saṅgītaratnākara of Śārṅgadeva, Vol. II, ed. by S. Subrahmanya Sastri, Adyar 1944; 11.2.2.: *deśitvam nāma kāmacārapravartitatvam* (in *deśī* music there is more freedom than in *mārgī*).

II: *grābhakāra*: derived from *grāvan*, stone, hence the stone-worker, sculptor.

II.1. *nirdiṣṭārthaka: nirdiṣṭa* means also ordained, enjoined, i.e. the image should conform to its meaning as laid down by the scriptures and tradition. Only an image conforming to the enjoined meaning will be fit for worship, according to the note of the Ṭippaṇī. Compare also *nirdiṣṭabhāvanā* in Nigama Ḍiṇḍima Ṭippaṇī on chapter II which is related to the unmanifest form (*avyaktarūpa*).

If this Sūtra is in its original place, it indicates that even before selecting and fixing the stone the sculptor should envisage what he is going to express. In the words of the Nigama Ḍiṇḍima Ṭippaṇī, meditative visualization of the *avyaktarūpa* has to precede the whole working process of creating the *vyaktarūpa* (manifest form): "Form is twofold: manifest and unmanifest. When there is a specified meditation, this is the unmanifest form; as by the meditation on Brahman arises the realisation that Brahman is all pervasive. The all-pervasiveness is the essential form (*tattvarūpa*) of Brahman... But when this meditation becomes manifest, it assumes form, this is the form embodying the feeling (*bhāvarūpa*) ... These manifest forms bestow ever new feelings. For this purpose the image has been created. These very forms give rise to forms and corresponding forms... That is the image, the origin of the science of Vāstu." The three stages are Brahman (unmanifest, all-pervading), Puruṣa (light-form within), manifest form (Yūpa, image), and corresponding to the visible form there is also a sound-form (*nādarūpa*). The Śilparatnakośa simply relates the *avyakta* form to meditation and the *vyakta* form to worship (*pūjanakarman*) (V.453).

The Comm. does not elaborate on the Sūtra.

II.3. Dadhikrāvan: or Dadhikrā, see ṚV IV.38–39; III.20; VII.44; X.101.1; AVŚ XX.137.3 etc. A mythical being, described as a divine horse, sometimes with wings, emerging from the ocean, identified with the morning sun. Considered sometimes as a creation of Heaven and Earth, or of Mitra-Varuṇa, invoked in the morning together with Agni, Uṣas and the Aśvins. Here Dadhikrā is invoked to bless the beginning of a new work, done in the early morning, when the stone is purified with curd and milk (the connection lies in the word *dadhi*, curd). This mantra is used even today by *sthapatis* in Orissa while rubbing the stone with curd.

Mahīlukā: the divine cow glorified in AVŚ X.10 hence an epithet of a sacred cow. She is the cosmic cow whose every part corresponds to one part of the created world: Earth, Water, Sky, Sun, Moon, the Quarters, Plants and all living beings. Even today the symbol of the cow is used at sacrifices, mainly at the sacred thread investiture, when mantras are recited on every part of her body, in analogy to the above-mentioned hymn. In the Nigama Ḍiṇḍima Ṭippaṇī the cow-symbol is represented in connection with the symbol of Śatakeśī Vṛṣa, the hundred-horned Bull (see below).

Kumbhīkā: in the AV a kind of evil spirits or demons (cf. AVŚ XVI.6.8).

Śatakeśī Vṛṣa: the hundred-haired or hundred-horned Bull, a solar symbol (the hairs or horns are the rays), representing Rudra or Dharma. Cf. Nigama Ḍiṇḍima Ṭippaṇī II: "The cow is the earth, the bull is the symbol of Dharma, the four Vedas are his four feet, his mouth is Agni... The four teats of the cow's udder are the four feet of the Gāyatrī. She is the supporter of the sacrifice and the mother, who has thousand hairs like horns... This is the cow in the form of the mantra, this is the cow's husband whose hundred hairs shine like horns, his golden hair is like the sun, the Bull with a thousand rays." See VS VIII.49, where the Bull is the Sun and also Soma. Mainly a symbol of fertility the Bull later became the *vāhana* of Rudra-Śiva (see *dharma-vṛṣabha* in VSU VI.20).

Jaṅgiḍa: a plant used as a protective amulet against demons (cf. AVŚ II.4; XIX.34 and 35), wrongly understood by the author of the Ṭippaṇī as a kind of demon similar to the Kumbhīkas etc., which shows that he is not very familiar with the AV tradition. Therefore he (or the copyist) must have changed the verb to fit this meaning: *palāyante* ('run away, flee') can be easily restored to *pālayanti* ('protect'). In the translation the latter reading has been accepted.

II.4. It is not clear why after setting the *marma* a double circle should be drawn first. Following the sequence of the Sūtras alone, it seems to be more logical that first a circle is made (Sūtra 6).

'Double circle' : the text does not make it explicit whether the two circles are only touching each other on the middle line or whether they are intersected. But since they are drawn for the composition of an image of the God and his Śakti (see Prakṛti-Puruṣa below), they have to be intersected (as in the illustration). This is confirmed by the Śilparatnakośa (on the topic of *yugmamaṇḍala*, the twin circle): *viṣamacaturasrasya pañcabhāgasamākṛtiṃ sārdhikabhāgatyaktaṃ ca ubhayapārśvataḥ kramāt, tanmadhyabindum ākramya kartavyaṃ maṇḍaladvayaṃ, yugalamaṇḍalakhyātaḥ madhye dhānyākṛti sthalam, prakṛti vāmabhāgāṃśe puruṣadakṣiṇatayā.* (MS p. 122, not in the printed text, since the MS consulted here was no longer available at the time of editing Śilparatnakośa): "Making five equal divisions in a rectangle, leaving one and a half divisions on both sides, fixing the (two) points in the centre, one should draw two circles. This is known as the double circle, in the middle there is a field of the shape of a grain: Prakṛti is on the left side and Puruṣa on the right."

'Prakṛti and Puruṣa' : the two complementary principles of creation, the Female and the Male, fundamental in all Indian cosmology and philosophy. In the Sāṅkhya doctrine they constitute the two poles of the entire reality: Matter or primordial Nature and Spirit. This scheme of composition may serve for images of the God and his Śakti, such as Lakṣmī-Nārāyaṇa (Elura), representing the fundamental polarity of existence.

"It is drawn by one...": it is again not clear whether the double circle is drawn by one continuous line, in which case they could not be intersected.

vajra: the note of the Ṭippaṇī explains *vajra* as white stone powder. But if the lines were drawn only with powder, they would be wiped away in the process of carving. The traditional practice even today is that the lines are slightly engraved with some hard instrument (which could also be called *vajra*). This is confirmed by the description of *vajra* given in the Śilparatnakośa: After cleaning the stone surface, the *pañjara* should be drawn first by a mixture of white stone powder with the juice of *kapittha* (*feronia elephantum*) and then by slightly engraving the lines with an instrument. (MS p. 23: *tadā kṛtvā pañjara sāvadhānataḥ vajrarekhānte sūkṣmeṇa rekhāṃ kṛtvā'strayuktataḥ, atisūkṣmam iti rekhā vajrarekhā itīryate.*) In the Vedic ritual *vajra* means a wooden sword (*sphya*).

II.5. Kṛtya-images: images made of clay for special festivals which are immersed in a sacred river (or in the sea) after being used for *pūjā*, as is still the practice e.g. at *Durgāpūjā*. The Śilparatnakośa gives four types of *murtis* (see also Nigama Ḍiṇḍima Ṭippaṇī): *dhyānamūrti, bhāvamūrti, kṛtyamūrti* and *grāmyamūrti. Dhyānamūrti* is the image made according to the *dhyāna*, it conforms to iconographical rules and hence is fit for worship; *bhāvamūrti* corresponds to *līlāvigraha* in the VSU (illustrative panels depicting myths and legends, not as main images for worship), *kṛtyamūrtis* are clay figures for temporary use and *grāmyamūrtis* are primitive idols worshipped in the country-side.

II.6. Here follows a series of comparisons with the two constituents of the circle, the central point and the circumference. The centre is the life-breath of the circle, as the mind is in relation to the *cittavṛttis*, which could be explained in the following way: as the central point contains in itself the potentiality of all the possible circle(s), thus the mind is only a potential organ, as such of unlimited possibilities. As the circle becomes defined and limited by the actual mental states and activities, thoughts etc. (*vṛtti*: there is also a kind of pun between *vṛtta* and *vṛtti*, both indicating a circular movement, from the root *vṛt-*, to turn, revolve, move, etc.). Hence also the centre is the timeless (immortal, the Ātman), the circumference is time.

vṛttasya gatiravadhāritā: the circumference of the circle limitation, whereas the *bindu* represents its stability.

"He who knows this": the vagueness of the sentence makes it possible to relate the series of terms to the circle as well. However, the realization of this relation (of centre and circumference) actually penetrates into the heart of reality, embracing the two opposites (*yoga*), this is the characteristic of Parameṣṭhī and *draṣṭā* and is Truth.

II.7. "One with one...": probably refering to the two points of the compass, one being set in the centre and the other at the circumference.

The relation of the circle (*pūrṇam*) with its centre-point (*bindu* as *prāṇa, ādhāra* or *sthiti*) is compared with two other relationships: as the *āhuti* (offering) is the *prāṇa* of the world, and the Gāyatrī is the quintessence of the whole Veda.

jaganmayaḥ prāṇaḥ: this phrase has to be taken as *jagataḥ prāṇaḥ*, otherwise it would not make much sense. Similarly the Vāstugāyatrī is the quintessence of the Vāstuveda, as is not expressly said but suggested by the context.

Vāstugāyatrī: the wrong form *viśvakarmāya* instead of *viśvakarmaṇe* indicates that the circles of the architects and sculptors were not well versed in Sanskrit grammar!

Summarizing II.6–7, the following correspondences can be established:

bindu	–	circle (circumference)
mind	–	*cittavṛtti*
Ātman	–	man
stability	–	time
immortal	–	mortal
āhuti	–	world
prāṇa	–	universe
Gāyatrī	–	Veda
Vāstugāyatrī	–	Vāstuveda

The recurring comparison with *āhuti* has a further implication, since the lines of the *pañjara* are compared with *āhutis* and the triangle is called *trihuta* (II.14–15).

II.8. "The line is the support": pun between *ādhāra*, and *dhārā* the latter could also be taken in the meaning of 'flow'.

adhibhūta, adhidaivata: two levels of correspondences in the universe (the third being *adhyātma*, related to the Self of man) and of sacrifice, which are a key to Vedic interpretation in the Brāhmaṇas and Upaniṣads. The lines of the *pañjara* correspond to cosmic and divine laws.

II.9. Divisions of the circle: this is the only place where divisions of the circle in diameters are mentioned, which is of great importance for the *pañjara*.

II.10. Navel: the navel is the origin of all life, see ṚV X.82.6: "The Waters, they received that germ primeval wherein the Gods were gathered all together. It rested set upon the Unborn's navel, that One whereby abide all things existing." (Griffith). Cf. also Chānd. Up. VII.15.1, etc.

Brahman's design: *vikalpa* has many meanings, it could also be translated by imagination (as creation of manifold forms in the mind of the creator).

"Manifest Brahman indirectly": *vakrataḥ*, lit. in a crooked way, the 'straight' way being *brahmavidyā*, but the result of both is identical.

II.11. "Order of Prajāpati": see note on I.6.

"the square indicates water": lit. appears like, is a reflection of water. The symbolism of the square which is here brought in relation to water is not clear, but none of the MSS has a better version. "The passage reflects confused understanding of Vedic cosmology, according to which the heaven is square-shaped, the atmosphere hemispherical and the earth circular. The VSU idea of a square-shaped symbol of waters in the panel (*apāṃ bhāse caturasram*) might be reminiscent of the idea of heavenly waters in Vedic cosmology. But such symbolic/microcosmic representation is unorthodox." (D. Bhattacharya) The short explanation of the Comm., comparing it with a water-tank would rather show that it does not follow the cosmic laws but those of human creation. The other forms and lines have a clear cosmic symbolism. The relation of square and circle is at least twofold: the outer square represents the entire universe, and perhaps the original waters which filled it before creation. The circle inscribed in it is light, i.e. the sun in heaven (for heaven as a square cf. ŚB VII.3.1.27, Uttaravedi). Within the circle either another square or a rhombus (acc. to MS ख) is inscribed (reminding of the Gārhapatya altar, ŚB VII.1.1). The space between the inner and the outer square would form a frame. Though the symbolism of this Sūtra and Comm. is extremely cryptic, the basic idea is that the panel is a microcosm reflecting all the elements of the macrocosm, it is a 'repetition' of the cosmos (*bhūyastāvat* has been understood in this sense). Cf. also ŚB VII.1.23–24 for the relation of Agni-Sūrya to the heavenly and earthly waters.

II.12. The comparison wants to demonstrate the movement of the wind which is otherwise invisible, but becomes visible in contact with water where it creates bubbles, foam etc. Similarly, the diagonal lines in the panel bestow energy, movement and speed to the forms.

II.13. The corner ears are obtained by a rhombus drawn within the circle. In these corner-ears either the four corners of the earth, seen as a square, are represented, or the four quarters of space. After this only comes the division of the circle by two lines which produce four parts similar to the four continents of the earth, as understood by Indian cosmology. From the crossing of the two central lines the *madhya-bindu* is obtained. This division by the vertical and horizontal middle lines should have come before making the corner-ears because it is from their ends that the rhombus can be traced.

II.14. The *madhya-bindu* existed from the very beginning when the first circle was traced, hence it is strange that the Sūtra speaks of *labdhabindu*. The symbolism is the same as in Sūtra 6.

"Union of Water with Earth": it is not clear to what symbolism this refers. Cf. Gopatha Brāhmaṇa II.3.2 (*dyaur antarikṣe pratiṣṭhita, antarikṣam pṛthivyām pṛthivyapsu*), where the earth is established in the waters, whose union is therefore the basis for all other creation. If in the panel it is related to the diagonals (*māruta*) in relation to the square field and the inner circle, it would be strange, since the points where the inner circle touches the square could be used for obtaining the corner-ears but not the diagonals. Is the image perhaps suggesting the vision of the sun rising from the ocean, where it touches the earth and then traverses the sky in two oblique lines, the ascending and the descending half of the day? There seems to be some confusion regarding the description of the various lines.

trihuta: rare term, of sacrificial connotations, the "threefold offered", referring to the three offerings of ghee in the fire of sacrifice. The upright triangle is the symbol of Agni. However, it may also refer to a triangular fire-place (*tryasrakuṇḍa*), in which case the translation would read: "(They) draw an area as for fire." (see D. Bhattacharya, p. 39) The note of the Ṭippaṇī (30) explains *huta* as a line (that which is offered). It had to be traced with the appropriate mantras, hence the *sthāpaka* is often called a priest (*hotṛ, udgātṛ*). See also the comparison of the circle with *āhuti* in Sūtra 7.

Divine images inscribed in an upright triangle represent the irradiation of divine light and the upward rising of the mind to the Divine.

II.15. "Even in the world": in contrast to the Vedic Agni, *loka* may refer to Tantric sources.

II.16. This and the following Sūtra refer to the hexagram which is one of the fundamental *yantras*, consisting of the two intersected triangles representing the union of fire and water and hence of all pairs of opposites, the divine and the human, the male and female principles, etc.

"By the joining of Fire and Water": in Vedic symbolism the two elements are mutually interacting (Agni is born from the waters, etc.), cf. above Sūtra 11 for a different version of the same idea.

mahacchandas: that *chandas* is not only metre in poetry but a principle of order and rhythm in all arts is already shown in the Aitareya Brāhmaṇa VI.5.1 where the term *chandomaya* is applied to all kinds of Śilpa (cf. the commentary given in: Niharranjan Ray, *An Approach to Indian Art*, Chandigarh 1974, pp. 63 ff.). The Comm. on the following Sūtra calls it *mithunacchandas*, the "metre of union".

But *chanda* could also be understood in the sense of delight, i.e.

the union of the two fundamental elements produces great delight in the worshipper or *sādhaka*.

II.17. *ākarṣaṇī vidyā*: all the thirtythree gods are attracted by this *yantra*, and human worshippers are drawn to it and their minds are concentrated by looking at it. This diagram has been profusely used in the later Tantric tradition, including the Tibetan Buddhist iconography.

Yātudhānas: a class of demons or evil spirits, like Rākṣas, but particularly related to sorcery. Even the demons use the hexagram for magical purposes.

Māṇḍavya: name of a Vedic Ṛṣi.

II.18. The subject of the Yūpa has been inserted here and in the Comm. on the following Sūtra, but it does not fit into the context of the *pañjara*. The line-divisions of the Yūpa are quite different, they will be given in IV.4–5.

II.19. This is another confusion between the line-divisions of the *pañjara* (given above), the *koṣṭhaka* (sixteen divisions, given in VI.7.9, etc.) and the diametrical divisions of the Yūpa.

"Permanently fixed": *dhruvā* is fem. !

II.20. "Following the Sūtra": i.e. the rules given by the Sūtras. *sūtrāyane* could also be translated 'traced with a thread", as it has been understood by the Ṭippaṇī, but this would not mean anything. The Comm. speaking of a 'secret knowledge' rather proves the correctness of this interpretation. May be a double meaning is intended in the expression.

Harmonious: *subhaga*, 'beautiful', as an expression of the correspondence to the cosmic laws.

Khilavidyā: usually it means the supplementary science or texts of the Veda, which could also be applied to the Vāstuveda; or else the word *khila* is used as in the term *khilapañjara*, connoting an open field, a surface on which the line-diagrams are drawn.

II.22. *tattvarūpa* and *rūpatattva* are terms of the philosophy of Art of the VSU, but unfortunately they are hardly explained (even the Nigama Ḍiṇḍima Ṭippaṇī does not elaborate on them). *Tattvarūpāṇi* must be those forms which are corresponding to the principles or the essence of form (*rūpa-tattva*). They are established by the *pañjara*, which seems to be the foundation and guarantee of the *tattvarūpa*, and is formed of *tattvarekhā*-s, acc. to the Comm. on the following Sūtra.

II.23. "Represented image": it is not clear whether *pratirūpa* in this context refers to the secondary images or whether *rūpa* and *pratirūpa* refer to the fundamental conception of form and image (see note on I.2).

rūpātmapratyakṣam of the MSS has to be corrected to *rūpasya ātmā pratyakṣo bhavati.*

Again the comparison of the *āhuti* (sacrificial offering) with the lines (see *trihuta*). The correspondences are:

āhuti – *rūpasaubhaga*
rain – *dhyānabhāva* (Sūtra 23: lines)
food – *laya* (divinisation) (Sūtra 22: forms)

The underlying idea is again that Art is a sacrifice which leads to the highest spiritual state.

II.24. The order of the Comm. on Sūtra 21 and 22 seems to have been confused, but the meaning can be reconstructed from the preceding text. However, the comparison is changed: here the food produced by rain corresponds to the forms brought about by the lines.

II.24–25. The symbolism of fire and water permeates the whole chapter and the conception of the lines.

II.25. *utsuka*: restless, pining, sorrowful, longing; one would rather expect the contrary, that on the horizontal lines resting, quiet figures are represented. In the Nāṭya-Śāstra *autsukya* is one of the *vyabhicāribhāvas* (or *sañcāribhāvas*), transitory moods or states (see VI.18–21, VII.69–70) which is characterised in the following way: "Impatience (*autsukya*) arises from the loss of beloved persons or from remembering them. This is to be represented on the stage by thinking, want of sleep, drowsiness, dullness of the body and desire to lie down and the like." (transl. by Manmohan Ghosh, Calcutta, 1951, Vol. I, p. 136). It is impossible to apply this description to divine images, but none of the MSS gives a better version. Or is *utsuka* a corruption of *supta-* ?

"Feeling of fluidity": the version *ugrabhāva* (fierce mood) of MS क is untenable, we have therefore preferred the reading *ukṣabhāva* of MSS ख and ग.

sthāpakodgītha: unusual term, since *udgītha* usually means the Sāmavedic chanting. It may have become a title without much connection with the Sāmaveda (cf. however VSU I.5 and III.2). The disciples of Pippalāda are also called *udgātāraḥ* (e.g. III.5). The translation of *udgītha* as priest is purposely vague.

III. "preliminary": *prastāvanā*, prelude, prologue. Just as the chanting of the Sāman is preceded by a prelude or introduction, and as a drama starts with a prologue, the work of image-making starts with the drawing of the *khilapañjara*. Like the prelude in the drama, which is the last part of the *pūrvaraṅga* in which the content of the play is mentioned, the *pañjara* contains the image *in nuce*. Cf. Nāṭya-Śāstra V.171 ff.

III.1. The word *bhāva* is so rich that it has to be translated by different terms in different contexts. However, all the connotations should be kept in mind: *bhāva* is a state of being (hence nature or character), then a mental state, an emotion or sentiment which manifests in an outward expression (hence emotional attitude), it is also the inner meaning of a work of art. Art without *bhāva* would be lifeless, merely formalistic. There is a two-way movement of *rasa* (aesthetic emotion) and *bhāva*: the *rasa* of the artist expresses itself in *bhāva* in the creation of art, which in turn evokes *rasa* in the onlooker (listener, etc.). Here both processes are implied, and starting from the *bhāva* of the image, men are led to the experience of the divinity. This theme will be elaborated in Prapāṭhaka V.

saumya and *ugra*: the two aspects of the divinity, a simplified twofold division of the character, expression or sentiment of images (see V), it corresponds to the two ways of performing dance in the Nāṭya-Śāstra (IV.272 ff.), the gentle or graceful (*sukumāra*) and the wild or forceful (*uddhata*) (cf. also *lalita* and *paruṣa* in Kāvyaśāstra). Generally speaking they represent the feminine and the masculine natures (thus Śiva is given as an example of *uddhata* and Pārvatī of *lalita*, cf. Nāṭya-Śāstra IV.322–23). In later aesthetics they correspond to *mādhurya* (sweetness) and *ojas* (strength, vigour).

III.2. *marmajña*: this term, which even in modern Indian languages means a specialist or a person who knows the inner essence of an art or science, has here its original meaning: the *sthāpaka* knows all the forms because he knows the centre-point (*marman*).

III.3. Mantra of dismissal (given in Mantrakhaṇḍa of MS ग):

"May the obstacle go to the auspicious one,
may the disease go to the immortal,
may the stones go back to the mountain, *svāhā* !"

III.4. *nyāsa* generally means composition, arrangement of the forms on the panel. If the Sūtra is not misplaced, it must have a more restricted meaning here.

Parjanya: the god of rain and giver of fertility and nourishment. Cf. AVŚ I.2, IV.15, VI.79, ṚV VII.102.

jaṭāveda: a particular way of recitation of a Vedic text by repeating the words and inverting the order.

"by the rules of the science of *rasa*": *rasavijñātanyāyena* has to be taken as *rasajñāna*. See Sūtra 8 for this science (usually called *rasāyana*).

It appears as if the order has been confused from Sūtra 2 or 4. Sūtras 2 and 3 are only by way of introduction, whereas the actual process of work starts in Sūtra 4. However, the Comm. on Sūtra 3 would better fit after Sūtra 11 which deals with the actual carving.

III.5. The mantra *uttiṣṭha puruṣi...* is found in Vajrapañjara Up. and Vanadurgā Up. (both published in: *Unpublished Upanishads*, ed. by K. Raja, Adyar, Madras, 1933), and also quoted in Śāradātilaka 11.63 ff. (2nd ed., Varanasi, Chowkhamba, 1963, p. 290).

Bṛhaspati: *bṛhaspatergṛhaśālāprakaraṇa*, no such text could be traced so far. Perhaps it refers only to the AV hymns of blessing a house (AVŚ III.12; IX.3), but these are not ascribed to Bṛhaspati. *Vāstūpākhyāna* has been mentioned in some texts, but it could not be identified.

Primitive images: *aparūpāṇi*, which are called *grāmyamūrti* by the Śilparatnakośa, the most inferior among the four types of images (v. 480).

III.7. Again this Sūtra seems to be somewhat out of place, since making the limbs smooth (*snigdha*) would be the last action of the sculptor.

III.8. *ukatsa*: it could not be identified.

Mantra for applying the juice (*rasa*, softening mixture): "The *rasa* to the Lord of *rasa* ! May the particles (of powder) becomes soft (liquid), O *vajra* (instrument for cutting or powdering the stone), soften it, make it as liquid as rain, *svāhā* !" (Mantrakhaṇḍa).

III.9. Lit.: the best science of the instruments.

III.10. *pāṭhāmūlikā*: root of the plant *clypea hernandifolia* ?

Pṛśniparṇī: a medicinal herb (*hemionitis cordifolia* or *uraria lego-podioides*), see AVŚ II.25.

Nirṛti: goddess of destruction.

Kaṇvas: here a class of evil spirits.

III.11. *khodayanti* shows influence of the vernacular.

uḍḍupayanti: lit. make fly, hence remove.

III.13. *gāthānuprāse*: *anuprāsa* does not make sense here, hence the reading *gāthānukrame* of MS घ has been accepted.

Sacred songs: *gāthāḥ*. In these non-Vedic songs the characteristics and deeds of the gods are described, therefore the carving of sacred images is to be accompanied by the singing of these *gāthās*. Cf. Sāyaṇa's definition of *gāthā* as *devatā viṣayākhyānaparā mantraḥ* (on TS VII.5.11.2, *apud* P. Horsch, *Die vedische Gāthā-und Śloka-Literatur*, Bern, Francke, 1966, p. 12, and also for an elaborate exposition of the *gāthā* literature).

hāva-bhāva: this is a technical term in dramaturgy. It is a part of *sāmānya-abhinaya* which combines the three ways of expression by speech (*vāk*), movements (*aṅga*) and subtle emotional expression (*sattva*). *Hāva-bhāva* is especially used for the attractive gestures expressing the feelings of women, mostly related to love. See Nāṭya-Śāstra XXII, Daśarūpaka etc.

"by means of which they do their meditation": *yajñena* is meaningless here, it must be a corruption of *yena* (or *yattena*), see also the Ṭippaṇī note 12 which confirms it. In simpler words: the *bhāva* is attained through meditation on the *rūpa* which itself is related to the *gāthā*.

III.14. Meditation: here the term *dhyāna* in the Sūtra means the visualization of a particular form of divinity.

III.15. Desire: *kāma*, as the Ṭippaṇī rightly suggests, is here not the lower desire, but that love or creative impulse which is at the origin of creation (cf. ṚV X.129.4).

III.16. The implication seems to be, which corresponds to actual practice, that the relief panels (e.g. in cave temples) are meant for meditation, and the full figures for worship.

III.17. The word *apavena* is rare and has Vedic associations (cf. *ven-* to love, desire, *vena*, also as name of a *ṛṣi*). It is a *lectio difficilior* compared to the reading *apidhānena* given in the 1st edition.

III.18. "(The sculptors) obtain perfection by (creating) images with (divine) attributes": *tadguṇāt, guṇa* (quality) refers here to the *saguṇa* aspect of the divinity, hence 'attribute' is here used in its theological meaning.

III.19. *ekāśrayi*: when a limb is set in its entire length on a straight line.

yugalāśrayi: either a bent limb forming an angle, where the two parts lie along different lines, as e.g. the upper and the lower arm, or two corresponding limbs (e.g. a right and left arm) lying on corresponding lines. The definition is not sufficiently clear.

khaṇḍāśrayi: when a limb rests only partly on a line.

sparśī: when a limb only touches a line, as e.g. a hand or an elbow. However, these terms are not sufficiently explained to understand their meaning for the composition, nor could they be found in other Śilpa texts.

III.20. Here the Comm. repeats what has already been said in Sūtra 5.

III.21. mallet: *kuṭumbhaka*, mallet with an iron head for finer chiselwork.

"Process of carving the stone": *śailabhedana-bhraskakrama: bhraska* is a doubtful word, is it related to the root *vraśc*-, to cut (whence *vraścana*, cutting or a chisel)? (cf. *yūpa-vraska*, cutting of a stone Yūpa, VS XXV.29).

IV. The whole introductory passage whose language is very defective wants to stress the continuity between the supreme Brahman-knowledge and the knowledge of form.

"His knowledge is supreme knowledge": read *tasya jñānaṃ vijñānam.*

"whatever they attain through word the same (they can attain also) through form": The language of form conveys the same knowledge as the language of words, or in other words images are a medium for attaining the highest spiritual knowledge, which is equal to the medium of the Vedic Word.

IV.1. Realization: *pratīta*, in continuation of the introductory passage, the realization of Brahman as *nirguṇa* must be meant, which leads to the realization of its *saguṇa* or symbolic aspect. One of the first symbols of Brahman is the Puruṣa of the size of a thumb, a symbol of the inner light of the Self (cf. Kaṭha Up. IV.12–13: "A Person of the measure of a thumb, like a light without smoke"). The material symbol of the Puruṣa and of light is the Yūpa (cf. VSU I.3). The point of the comparison seems to be the upright vertical position of the thumb, the pillar and the flame (one could also add the *liṅga*, although it does not occur in this text). The derivation of the form of the Puruṣa from the Yūpa forms the topic of this chapter. The Ṭippaṇī on VI.20 has been shifted after Sūtra IV.1 because it is a direct commentary on *pratītāt pratīkaḥ*. It may have been wrongly placed by the Ṭippaṇī of Somabhaṭṭa.

IV.2. Puruṣa is the archetype of the human form.

"Where there is duality...": the quotation of the Bṛhad. Up.

II.4.14 is altered to support a contrary philosophic position. Whereas the Up. establishes *advaita* (non-duality), the VSU supports duality (*dvaita*) which is necessary for demonstrating the importance of form and of seeing.

IV.3. "On account of having two aspects": namely *nirguṇa* and *saguṇa* mentioned above. If Brahman were only *nirguṇa* there would be no place for the world of forms.

IV.4. Grid: *koṣṭhaka*, see VSU VI.6 ff. where this topic is developed.

"for sculpture": *grābhārtham*, for stonework (see Note II).

IV.7. "Gestures of the body": *aṅgahāra*, physical movements. Cf. Nāṭya-Śāstra IV.16 ff., 322–3.

IV.10. image-halls: *rūpaśālā* called *mūrtiśālā* in the Saudhikāgama: cave temples with rows of sculptures. An indication of the earliest relief-sculpture in caves.

"No essential difference": lit. no difference regarding the core (*marman*).

IV.11. In the case of the Yūpa the continuity between the Vedic sacrifice and Śilpa is shown.

IV.12. The illustration (Fig. 19) tries to reconstruct this procedure of obtaining the measurement but it is not clear why such a complicated process is needed (according to the Ṭippaṇī it is for obtaining the measure of the flag on top).

IV.13. The pillar may be a reference to the act of creation, by which Indra pillared apart heaven and earth by the mid-space (*antarikṣa*) which stood as a pillar between them both. The whole image is transferred to the human figure, which also stands between earth and heaven. With his feet planted on the earth, Man raises himself from below upwards through all the elements of being: the material, corporeal activity, the vital activity, the life expanding heart-activity, the expression in word, and the spiritual activity located in the head, receiving the light of heaven, seeing and understanding the message of the gods, and thus participating in immortality. The presiding Devatās clearly show the stage of being which is meant, i.e. Bhūmi Devatā for the earth part, Rudra Devatā for the vital part, Prajāpati as the seat of the life-force, the heart, and Savitṛ for the head, the seat of Light, Spirit, illumination. Cf. the fourfold division of the Yūpa in the ŚB II.6.4 and its meaning: "With what is dug in the ground he gains the world of the Fathers, with what is above it upto the girdle rope he gains the world of men, with what is above the girdle upto the top-ring he gains the world of the gods, and what space of two or three fingers breadth is above the top-ring the gods call the 'Blessed' – their world he therewith gains." (Transl. Eggeling).

IV.14. There is some confusion in the terminology, it appears as if only four parts are given with their respective qualities instead of eight. However, if one tries to demarcate eight parts it is strange that the belly should be called *uttamāṅga*, 'the best part', which should apply to the head.

The division into eight parts is also classical (*aṣṭāṅga*, cf. *aṣṭāṅga yoga*).

'invented by him': *upajña* would imply that he did not follow the traditional way but his own invention. The derivation of the form of the Puruṣa from the Yūpa may be Pippalāda's original contribution.

IV.15. Cf. I.4.

IV.17. The Puruṣa (archetypal Man) and the pillar are symbols of the *axis mundi* (cf. AVŚ X.7 and 8).

Ten sacrifices: see Ṭippaṇī, note 8 (Sūtra 24) and D. Bhattacharya, p. 39.

"Prajāpati is verily Vāstoṣpati": this equation is not Vedic, in the Vedas Vāstoṣpati is identified with Indra or Rudra (cf. ṚV X.61.7).

IV.18. The number ten is associated with the Puruṣa since the Puruṣa-Sūkta (ṚV X.90.1, *daśāṅgulam*), see Sūtra 24–25. "The Yūpa and Puruṣa are equated in the VSU. The Brāhmaṇa of the AV equates *prāṇa* and *puruṣa* and enumerates ten *prāṇas*. The ten parts of *puruṣa* are thus inferable. Daśāṅga Yūpa is the next deduction based on the Puruṣa-Yūpa equation. *Daśayajña* seems to be of popular origin, no such Vedic concept exists." (D. Bhattacharya)

IV.20. Three types: see Ṭippaṇī note 6 and Sūtras 21–22.

North-East corner: *aiśāna*, belonging to *iśāna*. The pillar which is erected at the beginning of the construction of a temple is also situated in the North-East corner of the temple.

IV.22. A *vṛṣastambha* is sometimes erected for the dead in the *vṛṣotsarga* ceremony on the 11th day after death, for allowing the soul to pass from its state of *preta* to an abode in heaven (*svarga* or *śivaloka*). A wooden post with a bull carved out at the top is erected near a Śiva temple, next to the Nandī. It is made of *bilva* or *gambhārī* (*gmelina arborea*) wood, the prescribed height is of 5 *hastas*. The ritual is described in Purohita Karmakāṇḍa Part V, by Dayanidhi Khaḍiratna, Cuttack (without date). This ritual is now rarely performed. Four *vṛṣastambhas* (also called *upayūpa*) were found in village Jadupur near Koṇārak, in front of a small Śiva temple, the latest of which was erected in 1993 (see Fig. No. 16).

Mithunastambha: Only few specimen are found nowadays in Orissa, two of them were near the Buddhist site of Ratnagiri, now preserved in the Museum. One was found in village Goruāla near Puri, where it is not a pair of boars, but the copulation of a donkey and a sow which is represented. The villagers have forgotten the meaning and use of this pillar. One of the uses was to erect such pillars on the border of gifted lands or villages to prevent land-grabbing, since the pillars were supposed to paralyse those who transgressed it. The inscription found on the Ratnagiri pillar contains a curse saying that whoever transgresses it, his parents will become a donkey and a sow.

"How the Puruṣa becomes visible in the sections of the grid": Here the term *koṣṭhaka* seems to apply to the vertical divisions of the Yūpa-Puruṣa.

IV.23. The Comm. would be more meaningful after Sūtra 16, giving the reason for proceeding in ascending order. If this is the case, it would be implied that by the very making of the figure from below upwards the *prāṇa* would be infused in it.

IV.24. *Bhāvarūpa*: the terminology does not seem to be identical with the definitions given in the Śilparatnakośa (see note on II.5, *bhāvamūrti*). The Nigama Ḍiṇḍima Ṭippaṇī speaks of the *bhāvarūpa* without giving a clear definition; in any case it refers to the form manifesting or embodying the *bhāva* of the image or divinity.

"As the Puruṣa...": the first one is the inner Puruṣa, the spirit in man, who is identical with the Ātman and ultimately with Brahman, the second is the anthropomorphic form represented in the sculpture. The ten spiritual functions of the Puruṣa (including *vijñānātmā* and *brahma*) are related to the ten actions and to the ten visible parts or limbs. *Daśāṅga* and *daśāṅgula* are taken together in a kind of pun. The Kauṣītaki Up. III.8 speaks of the ten elements of man as the five senses of perception and the five organs of action all of which are directed by *prāṇa* and ultimately by the conscious Self (*prajñātman*): "These ten existential elements (*bhūtamātrā*), verily are with reference to intelligence. The ten intelligential elements (*prajña-mātrā*) are with reference to existence. For truly, if there were no elements of being, there would be no elements of intelligence. Verily, if there were no elements of intelligence, there would be no elements of being. For truly, from either alone no appearance (*rūpa*) whatsoever would be effected." (transl. Hume).

IV.26. Meru: mythical mountain considered to form the central axis of the Jambūdvīpa, the earth, around which all planets, comprising sun and moon, are circulating. The Gaṅgā falls from heaven on its summit and from there flows in four directions into the surrounding worlds. The centre of the world.

brahmāṇḍa and *piṇḍa*: reference to the conception that the macrocosm, the universe consisting of fourteen worlds (*bhuvana*) is symbolically contained within the microcosm of the human body, hence the fourteen divisions. This topic of the *bhuvanakoṣa* is again taken up in V.20.

"As the Atharvavedins...": a tradition of the Atharvavedins of tracing a *maṇḍala* on the earth consisting of ten or fourteen compartments, in which *kuśa* grass or *piṇḍas* (rice-balls) are placed as offerings to the ancestors. Cf. Hemādri, *Caturvargacintāmaṇi*, Khaṇḍa III, Pariśeṣakhaṇḍa, 1st Kalpa, Śrāddhakalpa, ed. Pt. Yogeśvara Smrititīrtha and Pt. Kāmākhyānāth Tarkaratna, Asiatic Society, Calcutta, 1882, p. 1415: *vajreṇa vā kuśairvāpi ullikhettanmahim dvija iti, vajraḥ sphyaḥ, vajro vai sphya iti śruteḥ*. *Vajra* is a wooden sacrificial implement (sword) which is also used for marking lines on the sacrificial ground. See also Devana Bhaṭṭa, *Smṛti Candrikā*, ed. by the Curator, Govt. Oriental Library, Mysore, Government Library Series, Bibliotheka Sanskrita No. 52, Śrāddhakāṇḍa, Mysore 1918, Piṇḍadānavidhi, pp. 365, giving the same information.

While the Śiśuveda Upaniṣad does not find a place in any of the lists of Upaniṣads known so far, there is reference to a text called Śiśuveda in Oriya literature. Further there is an early Oriya language text called Śiśuveda going back to the 14th–15th centuries A.D.

IV.28. In Sūtras 28 and 29 the text comes back from the Yūpa and the human figure to the composition of images on a square (or rectangular) panel, which actually belongs to the description of the *pañjara* at the end of chapter II.

IV.29. "Field made by four lines": *catvara* also means a place where lines cross (such as a cross-road), therefore it can also hint at the *pañjara*.

"The *sthāpakas* make the grid inside the four border lines": the construction is not so clear, since *catasraḥ* is Nom. or Acc.

V. *bhāvasya āropaṇa*: usually *āropaṇa* means assigning, attribution, imposition, but since *bhāva* is not something which is externally and secondarily applied, it has been translated by 'infusion' which is closer to the literal meaning 'making ascend, raise'.

See note on *bhāva* (III.1), cf. also Nāṭya-Śāstra VI and VII on *rasa* and *bhāva*, which apply to all the arts.

V.1–2. "The body is the support of action": the relation between *karma* and *bhāva* is also discussed in the Nāṭya-Śāstra (I.106, 113 etc.). There is no *bhāva* (emotional state) without action, although in sculpture the expression is more limited than in drama. The sequence is thus: body–action–*bhāva–rasa*.

V.3. *Rasa* has been left untranslated. It is the "essence" or "flavour" (taste), the basic sentiment or aesthetic experience. About the mutual relationship between *rasa* and *bhāva* see Nāṭya-Śāstra VI.33-38. From the point of view of the artist *rasa* is first which produces a *bhāva*, from the point of view of the onlooker *bhāva* leads to *rasa* (i.e. the emotion expressed in the work of art produces an aesthetic experience).

In this chapter the terminology is not always consistent and the two terms are often used as synonyms.

V.5. This Sūtra is not found in all MSS, it may be a later interpolation since only eight *rasas* are enumerated. These eight are not identical with the eight of the Nāṭya-Śāstra, *śānta* taking the place of *adbhuta*. The reason may be either that *śānta* is more important in sculpture than *adbhuta*, or that *adbhuta* is produced by different *rasas* such as *vīra* (e.g. the Mahiṣāsuramardinī of Mahabalipuram whose sight brings about the wonder about the heroic deed of the goddess). The explanation of the Ṭippaṇī (note 3) seems to be too narrow, since *adbhuta* is not only associated with fear, but can also be derived from other sentiments as the second part of the explanation suggests: "In Śilpa the sentiment of wonder is to be inferred."

V.6. The example given by the Comm. for *śṛṅgāra* is taken from worldly life in order to demonstrate the erotic emotion. On the basis of this 'common truth' the images of divine couples are made, the so-called erotic images, called 'playful' (additional sentence in MS ख).

V.7. It is not clear in what way horizontal lines are used for expressing *śṛṅgāra*, but the relationship between the lines and the *rasa* is very subtle and not always obvious. *Mithuna* images (playful couples) are mostly on vertical lines.

V.8. In the Nāṭya-Śāstra also *hāsya* follows *śṛṅgāra*, but there it is described as a mimicry of the sentiment of love (VI.39–40). The difference between *hāsa* (Sūtra) and *hāsya* (Comm.) is given in the Nāṭya-Śāstra (VI.48): "The comic (*hāsya*) sentiment has as its basis the Dominant emotion (*sthāyibhāva*) of laughter (*hāsa*)." (Transl. M. Ghosh), and Abhinavagupta says on the same that *hāsa* is a given or accomplished emotion whereas *hāsya*, the sense of humour, has to be achieved.

V.9. This Sūtra and its Comm. seems to imply that all images are meant for worship or meditation (*upāsanā*).

V.10. The psychological derivation of one *rasa* from the preceding one is different from the Nāṭya-Śāstra where they are only given in pairs related as cause and effect (*raudra*, the furious, produces *karuṇa*, VI.39 ff.).

V.11. What is called *raudra* in the context of drama is called *ugra* in sculpture.

V.13. "The fighting between gods and demons": a striking example of such an image is to be seen in Elura, Cave XV, the fight between Narasiṃha and Hiraṇyakaśipu, clashing against each other from both sides of the vertical middle line (cf. its analysis in: Alice Boner, *Principles of Composition in Hindu Sculpture*, Leiden, Brill, 1962, 2nd ed. New Delhi, 1990, pp. 53–59).

V.14. "Different": The difference has to be stressed because it is very close to *vīra*.

V.15. Actually *raudra, vīra* and *bhayaṅkara* are also on diagonal lines, which are not a particularity of *bībhatsa.*

"When desires are given up": *kāmanivṛtti* had to be interpreted differently in Sūtra 7, in order to explain the passage from *śṛṅgāra* to *hāsya.* Here the implication is that all desires leading to the various sentiments have to be given up to attain peace.

V.16. *jīvasya aṣṭavikāra*: cf. the eight *vikāras* of the body as manifestations of *bhakti* in Vaiṣṇava literature which may be related to the *bhāvas* and *rasa.*

V.17. "Inactive": the reading *ālasya* (MS घ) has been preferred to *alāsya* (MS क). It is difficult to conceive a clearcut division of all the *rasas* into four categories or types of lines, especially the distinction between diagonal and (other) oblique lines, since all dynamic *rasas* (*raudra, vīra, bhayaṅkara* and *bībhatsa*) can be represented on either of them. Ultimately it can be reduced to a twofold division which corresponds to the two aspects of the gods: peaceful (*saumya*, gentle) and fierce (*ugra*). The first would include the vertical and horizontal lines (representing stability), the second the diagonal and oblique lines (representing dynamism).

V.18. *vṛtti* has a double meaning: it is at the same time the mental modification or state of mind which gives rise to the conception of these beings, and their attitude or mode of activity. See also Sūtra 19 and VI.2 on the same subject.

"The inimical mood constitutes their connection": *aribhāva*. There is a constant struggle between these classes of beings which express various feelings (*bhāvas*) and the religious activity of man aims at overcoming the evil forces and propitiating the good powers (*devas*). Caste etc. determines the religious actions of men. Thus all living beings, including the gods, are interconnected and interact.

"Just as *brāhmaṇas*...": this passage seems to indicate that image-worship was propagated by non-*brāhmaṇas* and that there was some resistance from the priestly caste against it.

"Through *bhāva* they are released": i.e. *bhāva* or emotions evoked by image-worship; or else it means: they are released from becoming (*bhāva*).

āropaṇa: translated here as "(spiritual) ascent" could also refer to Sūtra 1 in which case the translation would be: "In this way form is to be considered in relation to the infusion (of *bhāva*)".

V.19. On *vṛtti* see above. All sentiments and their external projections depend upon the mind and its various states.

"Inactive and active": if all the *bhāvas* are divided into these two categories, only *śānta* can be *niṣkala*, all others have to be *sakala*.

"Become *brāhmaṇas*": as image-worship is frequently identified with Vedic sacrifice, the image-worshippers are also elevated to the rank of *brāhmaṇas*.

V.20. It appears that a *vikalpa* has been lost between the Sūtra and the Comm. because of haplography. The reconstruction is as follows: Sūtra 20 *saṅkalpād vikalpaḥ*. Comm. *vikalpa iti viśeṣaḥ. yathā saṅkalpād...* When reconstructed in this way, emending the haplographical error, the meaning of both Sūtra and Comm. becomes clear, i.e. that the desire (the intention) to worship is the cause for the imagination of particular forms of God. This is a common post-Vedic idea (cf. *upāsakānāṃ kāryārthaṃ brahmaṇo rūpakalpanam*, cited by Rāghava Bhaṭṭa in his Comm. on Śāradātilaka) (suggestion by D. Bhattacharya).

"cycle of the senses": *indriyacakra*, in worldly behaviour the relation between a particular desire and its effect leads to bondage whereas in the case of religious desire (*saṅkalpa*) it leads to faith and realization.

V.21. "arrangement of the (fourteen) worlds (stages)": *bhuvanakoṣa,* actually the sphere of the world, because of the Purāṇic conception of the universe as consisting of fourteen worlds (*bhuvana*), it is taken in the meaning of the number fourteen (Ṭippaṇī, note 6). But this passage also represents a popular understanding of the idea of the macro-microcosmic relations, corresponding to elements of the ritual and to the body. Cf. also Bṛhad. Up. II.5 where fourteen elements are related to fourteen human powers, namely: *pṛthivī* to *śarīra, āpas* to *retas, agni* to *vāc, vāyu* to *prāṇa*, Āditya to *cakṣu, diśaḥ* to *śrotram, candra* to *manas, vidyut* to *tejas, stanayitnu* to *śabda* or *svara, ākāśa* to *hṛdākāśa*, the last four being *dharma, satya, mānuṣa* and *ātman* (some of them are related to the Puruṣa-Sūkta, ṚV X.90). Since in this context *bhuvanakoṣa* does not mean a static arrangement of worlds but rather stages in the development of worship or religious action, it has subsequently been translated by 'fourteen stages'. These stages, representing the process by which the Ṛṣis realised the forms of divinities, are sacrifice (*yajña*), *dhvani* (mantra, or rather the subtle aspect or inner meaning of the mantra, 'sound', in later poetics the suggestive power of poetry, hence left untranslated), attribute (*lakṣaṇa* characteristic, sign), archetype (*rūpa* in the subtle aspect, not the manifest form which comes later), nature (*bhāva*, again in the fundamental sense of being), quality (*guṇa*), action (*kriyā*), practice (*ācāra*), method (*upāya*), ritual performance (*ceṣṭā*, religious effort), way (*mārga*, also in the sense of a particular tradition or *sampradāya*), forms (*rūpāṇi*, the plural indicating the concreteness of divine forms), derived forms (*pratirūpāṇi*, representations of divine images, probably not in the sense of *upadaivata* given in VI.21), and finally image-making as the science which is the end-product of this whole development.

As said above, where *lakṣaṇa* (attribute, characteristic, feature) is identified with *ṛta* (cosmic order) the created forms are in full accordance with this cosmic order. Curiously, the word *dharma* is not included in the list of the 14 stages. However, the freedom of the creators of form (called Ṛṣis) is shown by the verb *vṛṇute* to choose (cf. *kāmacāraḥ* at the end of chapter I).

The note 8 of the Ṭippaṇī relating to *lakṣaṇa* is totally wrong, since the AV quotation concerns the marks (*lakṣma*) in the ears of the cow, and has nothing to do with the features of gods as revealed to the seers for creating divine images.

The mantra "*Oṃ rudraśatakeśāya...*" is not found in the AV, nor does it belong to the Śaiva Āgamas as far as we know. There may be some connection between the *Śatarudriya* of the VS XVI, a hymn and a *homa* (called *śataśīrṣarudrāśamanīya*) for appeasing the terrible form of Rudra who has come out of Prajāpati and his wrath (according to a legend of the ŚB IX.1.1). He is hundred-headed etc., but is not the same as *śatakeśī vṛṣa* who seems to belong to a local tradition of Orissa (see note on II.3).

V.22. As an illustration of this process leading from the formless to form the development of the worship of Āditya (the Sun) is given in fourteen stages.

"The archetype": from the example given (rays and chariot) one could also infer that *rūpa* here means 'symbol'.

"Thus the space-directions are responsible for creating forms": *etadarthaṃ rūpārthaṃ diśaḥ, arūpād rūpaṃ tasya phalam.* The whole passage wants to show not only that there is a formless and a concrete aspect of God (*arūpa* and *rūpa*), as many Upaniṣads affirm (cf. Praśna Up. I.5–6; Maitrī Up. 3, etc.), but what is the process leading from the one to the other. The way in which space-directions mediate can be explained in the following way: in the Praśna Up. *prāṇa* (breath, energy) is formless and *rayi* (matter) is concrete (*amūrta* and *mūrta*). Āditya, the Sun is identified with *prāṇa*, but its heating quality becomes concrete only when its rays enter the quarters of space and it becomes the bodily fire. Thus the transition from *prāṇa* to *rayi* is effected by way of the quarters. Even in an abstract sense no form would be possible in this world without the space-directions creating space (see Sūtra 23).

V.23. The concrete application of space-directions to divine forms is given in their personification as the guardians of the quarters (*āśāpālāḥ*).

daśapracetasaḥ: probably refers to Ādityas and the guardians of the quarters mentioned in the same sentence; the Ṭippaṇī explains them as the stars and other divinities.

V.24. "different ways": the *sampradāyas* or sects, which have a different iconography.

"These are not natural...": *aprākṛtam nānṛtaṃ ca*, these three words contain a whole philosophy of Art. The images, though derived from natural forms, are not simply imitations of nature (e.g. many arms etc.), and yet they are "true to cosmic order", they are not false (*anṛta*). In Vaiṣṇava literature *aprākṛta* means supernatural.

Īḍā (Iḷā): Vedic goddess, personification of the sacrificial food and of praise, daughter of Manu, often invoked together with Bhāratī and Sarasvatī (cf. ṚV VII.2.8; IX.5.8). However, no such sect as the Aiḍas is known to us.

"They worship...freely": *kāmacāraḥ*, see I.10.

VI.1. "conception": *dhāraṇā*, holding firmly, also concentration.

The link between the quotation from the Praśna Up. and the following text seems to be again the idea of the creation of form: the way in which the spiritual (formless, *prāṇa*) becomes material (form, *rayi*). The creator of forms or artist is compared to Prajāpati who brings forth beings out of his desire by practising *tapas* (concentrated spiritual energy). (See above note on V.21).

VI.2. "mental modification": *vṛtti*, a state of mind as the source of differentiation.

"twofold": it is not very clear what are these two, it could be *avyakta* (*amūrta*) and *vyakta* (*mūrta*).

"perfect Puruṣa": *ṣoḍaśakala*, lit. sixteenfold Puruṣa, see Praśna Up. VI, 2. The number sixteen indicates completeness. In Bṛhad. Up. I.5, 14 the year is identified with Prajāpati and is explained as having sixteen parts. The person who understands this connection becomes similarly characterised. The correspondence between the "Lord of creation" and the human person, both being sixteenfold, shows the divine-cosmic-human relationship so characteristic of the Upaniṣads. Here this designation is meant to exalt the Ṛṣi Pippalāda, equating him with the Puruṣa in the fullness of Being.

VI.4. This Sūtra gives a table of contents of Prapāṭhaka VI. "attitude of the god": *daivabhāva*, or "divine nature" (but this latter word has been reserved for translating *prakṛti*).

VI.6. The *koṣṭhaka* consisting of sixteen compartments is different from the *pañjara*. Again the symbolism of the sixteenfold Puruṣa indicates completeness.

VI.7. "fixing the centre": *marman*, the symbolism of the *bindu* and the circle has been fully explained in Prapāṭhaka II.

"manifestation of Brahman": *ābhāsa*, his splendour, radiance; cf. A.K. Coomaraswamy, *The Transformation of Nature in Art*, Cambridge, Mass. (Harvard University Press), 1935, p. 141.

VI.8. *aṅgabhāva*: or "the attitude of the body (figure)". It should be *aṅgāṅgibhāva*, the correlation of body and limbs.

VI.10. The reference to the *mūrtitāraka* and *amūrtitāraka* of the Advayatāraka Up. is given to support the upper division of the figure. In the quotation a yogic division of the human body is given: up to the eyebrows *tāraka* (the divine saviour) is perceptible (incarnate) but beyond the eyebrows he is formless (disincarnate, spiritual). In the VSU the third division (all three being with form) reaches upto the neck where the lightpart starts. Again the human body, and hence the image, is a microcosm: the earth below, the heavenly light at the top. In the same way the divisions of the Yūpa are described in Prapāṭhaka IV, where the gross and the subtle, the material and the spiritual elements of the Puruṣa are embodied in the different layers, one above the other. In the Nigama Ḍiṇḍima Ṭippaṇī the layers of the image are described as being determined by the three *guṇas*, from below upwards: *tamas, rajas, sattva.*

VI.12. Brahman and *satya*, symbolised by the two *bindus*, are established as two fundamental principles.

"created from the navel": cf. the creation of Brahmā out of Viṣṇu's navel.

The correspondence between the elements of the *pañjara* and the human body is more elaborated in the Nigama Ḍiṇḍima Ṭippaṇī IV: "As the semen (is the origin) of the formation of the body of an embryo, in the same way the (central) point (*bindu*) (is the origin) of the panel with the line-diagram in the *pañjara*. The central vertical line (*madhyarekhā*) corresponds to the spine in the body. As in the body there are three *nāḍīs*: *iḍā, piṅgalā* and *suṣumnā*, the arteries and veins, so there are the crosswise lines. Thus, as (it is) in the (cosmic) Puruṣa, so in the divine image (*daiva*) and equally in the (human) body." Cf. also the Vaiśravaṇa Śilpācāra: "As are the bones in the skeleton in the human body, thus in the work of form these three, the painter, the architect and the sculptor trace the lines. As the yogis consider the skin as the outer envelope of the body, thus these three consider the outline of the field as the outer envelope. Inside the skin the blood is flowing. That is the circle. Inside blood and flesh there are the bones considered by these three (artists) as lines. As the supporting bones are joined in a knot (=joints), thus all consider the points where the lines cross each other. As inside the bones the marrow (*bindurasa*) gives strength to the human body, thus the *bindu* made in the centre is the *marman*, the life-breath of the form."

VI.13. To the *brahma-bindu* which is the creative centre of the image, another *bindu* is added (*satyabindu*) which represents the spiritual centre of the image. The Comm. gives a yogic interpretation of the two *bindus*: they correspond to different *cakras* or nerve-centres in the body. The *brahmabindu* or *marman* may correspond to the navel or heart centre, the *satyabindu* is the *ājñā cakra* between the eye-brows.

"in a golden vessel": *hiraṇmayena pātreṇa*. Cf. Īśa Up. 15 where it refers to the Sun. Here the yogic-tantric conception of the nectar contained in a cavity of the centre between the eye-brows is implied.

"glory of the limbs": *rūpāṅga-vaibhava*, the greatness, expansion of the figure.

That for female divinities the *bindu* should be placed somewhat lower most probably simply accounts for their figures being generally of a smaller size.

"(the image) bestows perfection": can mean that either the image itself becomes powerful or that it bestows power on the worshipper, both are interrelated. The power depends mainly on the two central *bindus*, or on the relation of the composition to the *marman*.

VI.14. In the Introduction it has been discussed how ornaments have not only the function of embellishing images and making them more pleasing to the eye, but also enhance their transcendent significance.

VI.15. This Sūtra shows the effect of the ornaments: at first they attract the senses, then they arouse delight, from which comes vision which ultimately leads to spiritual realization. This is an example that there is no break in the ascent from the aesthetic to the spiritual experience.

VI.16. The *mudrās* are derived from those used in the Vedic ritual.

"Five are the principal *mudrās*": in the MS it is not clear whether *mudrāpañcakaṃ śreṣṭham* is a Sūtra or part of the Comm.

VI.17. *bādhra*: the derivation of this word is not clear. As indicated by the Comm. it is a technical term for *āyudha*. Since this word occurs in all the MSS, it has been retained. Not all the attributes are weapons since other attributes are also called *āyudha* because they represent the particular power of the god.

VI.18. The Sūtra is placed in the MS after "are represented in stone sculpture", but it has been restored to its original place before the subject of *āsana* starts, following the general logic of Sūtra and Comm. in this Prapāṭhaka.

"the emotional state embodied in the action of the image": *rūpasya kṛtyabhāva*, cf. *karmabhāva* in V.1. Among all the nine elements of the image it is the *āsana* which reveals the action of the whole figure. The *mudrā* manifests a particular *bhāva*.

VI.20. "nature": *prakṛti*, the *vāhanas* represent the connection of the god with nature (animal form).

Airāvata: Indra's mount is the elephant, representing rainclouds.

"when the figure of the *brahmakṣetra* is in depression...": according to this interpretation the sentence refers to the depth of the carving (*nimna*) i.e. when the main figure is carved out more deeply the figure below (*vāhana* etc.) serves as a support. Or, it could simply mean "*vāhanas* are to be made in the *jaivakṣetra* of the sixteenfold grid, below the *brahmakṣetra*, and also other figures (such as enemies, see Sūtra 23–24) are good below."

VI.21. About the meanings of *pratirūpa* see note on I.2. The secondary or attendant divinities are here limited to the Śaktis (female energies).

"forms embodying the sentiment": *bhāvarūpa* is difficult to translate, and it appears to have different meanings. The Nigama Ḍiṇḍima Ṭippaṇī VI uses this term without giving any explanation. It gives the derivation of images in four stages: *prakṛti* (nature), *bhāvarūpa, tattvarūpa* (essential form or archetype, corresponding to the inner visualization), *pratirūpa* (representation, material image). Although the sequence is different there is yet a certain correspondence with the four stages of *vāk* (speech, word) in the philosophy of language (cf. Bhartṛhari) and in Kashmir Śaivism (cf. Abhinavagupta) where the material, spoken word is only the outer manifestation of the subtler levels of the word (*parā, paśyantī, madhyamā, vaikharī*).

Ākūti: wrongly written as Ākuti, intention, purpose, personified as a goddess in the AV (cf. AVŚ VI.131.2):

> "In front I set Intention (Ākūti), blessed Goddess, Mother of thought,
> May she be prompt to hear us.
> Mine and mine only be the hope I fashion. May I gain this that has possessed my spirit.
>
> With Purpose (Ākūti), O Bṛhaspati, with Purpose come thou near to us,
> Bestow on us a share of luck and so be swift to hear our call."
>
> AVŚ XIX.4.2–3 (Griffith)

"the golden-coloured Hariṇī": =Lakṣmī, cf. Śrīsūkta 1.

Gāyatrī (worshipped in the morning), Sāvitrī (at noon) and Sarasvatī (in the evening): these three Devīs are represented in the three parts of the Mahāgāyatrī temple dedicated to the Śaktis of Mahābhāskara, the Sungod, in Koṇārka. Gāyatrī in the *garbhagṛha*, Sāvitrī the *mukhaśālā* and Sarasvatī with Gaṇeśa in the portico. Cf. Alice Boner–Sadasiva Rath Sarma–Rajendra Prasad Das, *New Light on the Sun-temple of Koṇārka*, Varanasi (Chowkhamba), 1972, pp. 37ff.

"what are the Śaktis?": *hetayaḥ* would normally mean "instruments", but in this context it does not make sense. None of the MSS has a better version, hence the meaning given by the lexicographers of *heti* as *śakti* has been taken (the Śaktis are instruments of the gods).

In the explanation which follows the different divinities are related to Time. Again the same Śaktis are enumerated with a reference to their meaning.

"(*devayāna*) which is day": read *divam* instead of *divyam*.

Aryaman: He is one of the oldest Vedic gods closely related to Mitra, the chief of the forefathers, and also the arranger of marriages and protector of fertility and birth.

"five generations of Fathers": *pañcapāda-pitaraḥ*, or "the five-footed Fathers"; the translation follows the Ṭippaṇī. Cf. ṚV I.164.12 (*pañcapādaṃ pitaram*), where the Father is the year or the Sun, and the five feet are the five seasons.

"twelve divine forms": cf ṚV I.164.12, where it means the twelve months of the year. Since the whole passage is related to Time, the "twelvefold" Brahman is again the year (identified with Prajāpati).

The superficial knowledge of the author of the Ṭippaṇī is obvious here since he does not even quote the ṚV.

"Where there are many qualities": *guṇāḥ*, since the secondary figures represent the various qualities of the divinity, there is no end to the Śaktis. The example of Agni Vaiśvānara is taken form Muṇḍ. Up. I.2.4–5.

Bhāratī: in the ṚV connected with the goddesses Iḷā and Sarasvatī (cf. ṚV VII.2.8; IX.5.8), she is daughter of Āditya, later identified with Sarasvatī, being the embodiment of Word, speech, eloquence, wisdom, related to poetry (*kāvya*).

śrutermahatī mahīyasī sarasvatī...: cf. the last verse of Kālidāsa's Abhijñāna-Śākuntala: *sarasvatī śrutamahatāṃ*, "may the speech of those who stand high in their knowledge of the Veda be honoured."

Devahūti: invocation of the gods, here one of the Śaktis of Lakṣmī.

VI.22. "magic powers": *bhūtavidyāḥ*, since the knowledge of evil beings amounts to power (cf. Chānd. Up. VII.1.2; VII.7.1). The connection with the Sūtra is not clear, it may be in the wrong place.

VI.24. "condition (of the mind)": *vṛtti*, state, attitude; as much as it is the mind which created the forms (cf. VI.2), the forms in turn transform the mind. The Comm. does not speak of the influence of images on the minds of devotees, but on the real transformation, starting from the creation of mind.

sadasadvidyā: sadvidyā (or *parā vidyā*) is related to truth (*ṛta*), to divine action, hence to the gods; *asadvidyā* (or *aparā vidyā*) is related to untruth (*anṛta*, "dis-order"), to godless action (*adaivā*) and hence to the Asuras (instead of *aparājñād-* read *aparajñānād-*). Cf. *sadvidyā* and *asadvidyā* in the Śaivāgamas.

The description of the demons is related to Sūtra 23, the adversaries.

Nikandins, Kaṇvajambhas, Yātudhāna: are supposed to be kinds of demons. Pṛśniparṇī is actually a medicinal herb, wrongly included in the list of evil beings, probably because it is invoked in the AV for destroying evil powers (cf. AVŚ II.25).

kimpuruṣas: mythological beings, half animal and half man.

"For this purpose some gods meditate on the Ṛṣis": In V.17 (*aribhāvas teṣāṃ sandhāḥ*) evil beings were said to constitute the connection between gods and men. The evil beings overpower men who worship gods for release from their clutches. The present Sūtra shows the other way of operation through the same relation, the way in which gods depend upon men in order to get release from the influence of evil beings.

The context of the passage under discussion mentions that evil beings cause trouble for the gods and that they are saved because of sacrifices. In V.20 it was said that divine attributes are visioned by the *brāhmaṇas* called Ṛṣis (seers) performing sacrifice. It is for this reason that the gods meditate upon the Ṛṣis in order to get sacrifices performed by them and then to get release from the influence of the evil beings. (D. Bhattacharya).

"with devotion": *daivabhāvena*.

"Ṛṣis become singers of praises": this sentence leads from the subject of adversaries to the last category of beings represented on the panel, the worshippers.

VI.25. "beautiful": *subhaga*, or auspicious, glorious.

"sound": because the praisers represent the aspect of sound (music) in worship and in the image.

The celestial worshippers are represented in the two upper corner-fields, the human worshippers in the two lower corner-fields.

VI.26. *vāstūpākhyānam* must be a scribal error for *vāstuvyākhyānam*, as is clear from the Comm.

In spite of the imperfect expression, this Sūtra wants to lead back to the importance of knowledge as a way to liberation, given in the first Prapāṭhaka (I.1 and I.5).

VĀSTUSŪTRA UPANIṢAD

SANSKRIT TEXT

ओं वास्तुसूत्रोपनिषद्

ॐ भद्रं कर्णेभिः शृणुयाम देवा
भद्रं पश्येमाक्षभिर्यजत्राः ।
स्थिरैरङ्गैस्तुष्टुवां सस्तनूभि-
र्व्यशेम देवहितं यदायुः ॥
स्वस्ति न इन्द्रो वृद्धश्रवाः
स्वस्ति नः पूषा विश्ववेदाः ।
स्वस्ति नस्तार्क्ष्यो अरिष्टनेमिः
स्वस्ति नो बृहस्पतिर्दधातु ॥

॥ ॐ शान्तिः ॐ शान्तिः ॐ शान्तिः ॥

अथ अथर्ववेदीय वास्तुसूत्रोपनिषद्

प्रथमः प्रपाठकः

षट्शिल्पविचारः

आथर्वणाङ्गिरस[1] - शिल्पकाश्यपो[2] होवाच पिप्पलादमहामतिम् । षोडशतापिनी[3]मध्ये वास्तुस्थापकविद्येयम्[4] । य एनां वेद । आथर्वणीये होतोद्गातृभिः शिल्पश्रोतृभिः

वास्तोष्पतिर्ज्ञेय[5] इति ॥ १ ॥

स विश्वकर्मा देवता । तस्य विद्या षट्शिल्पविचारः[6] ।

केषां शिल्पकारा उपपादयन्ति केषां शिल्पकर्मादय उपजायन्ते, कतिविधानीति तान् ह स आङ्गिरसादीन् निरीक्षमाणान्[a] पिप्पलादो वव्रे । स ह कुवित्सोवलभुजोत्तोलकः,[7] शिल्पकाश्यपः प्रणिधाय यथाकामं पृच्छामीति । को वास्तोष्पतिर्विश्वकर्मा[8], तस्मै होवाच, मन्ये वयं वेदसदस्या ज्ञापयिष्यसीति[b] ।

पिप्पलादो होवाच - ये वै के चास्मिंल्लोके प्रयान्ति ज्ञानमेव ते सर्वे कामयन्ते ।

---

[1]अथर्व० ११.४.१६ मण्डलोक्तऋषिविशेषः । १९ काण्डे पञ्चमानुवाकस्य प्रवर्तक ऋषिः अङ्गिराः ।

[2]काश्यपशिल्पसूत्रकारः शिल्पकाश्यपनामा ऋषिः ।

[3]आथर्वणीय-षोडशविध-तापिनीग्रन्थाः-अवधूततापिनी, त्रिपुरातापिनी, नृसिंहतापिनी, पुरुषतापिनी, वृषतापिनी, इत्यादयः सर्वे आथर्वणीयाः ।

[4]वास्तुविषयकसूत्राणि ।

[5]वास्तुदैवतं वास्तोष्पतिरित्यर्थः ।

[6]काश्यपशिल्पसूत्रस्य
दैवशिल्प-प्रासादशिल्प-नगरशिल्प-दुर्गशिल्प-धातुकरणलेखविचारादि विषयाः ।

[7]रूपशिलास्थापनार्थं शुभयोगे दर्भोत्पाटक आथर्वणब्राह्मणविशेषः ।

[8]शिल्पाधिदैवतम्, अथर्ववेदसंहितायामुक्तम् । विश्वकर्माणं ते सप्तऋषिवन्तमृच्छन्तु, अथर्व० १९.१८.७

---

[a]निर्यक्ष्यमाणान्, ख, ग, घ ।

[b]ज्ञापयिष्यामो, ग ।

षट्शिल्पाङ्गप्रयोगेण प्रजनयन्ति रूपाणि[9] ॥ २ ॥

रूपं शैलेन[10] खादिरेण, एवं रूपज्ञानञ्च लोके । वेदे रूपं रूपं प्रतिरूपं भवतीति विशेषः । तज्ज्ञानं दिव्यज्ञानञ्च ।

यूप[11] इदं ज्योतिः ॥ ३ ॥

स हि यूपः खादिरेण शैलेन वा वैताने[12] उक्तम् । वृत्तं हि यूपमूर्धन्यं स विश्वमिति यूपदण्डादौ । कर्माणि समरूपाणि समरेखायां स यूपस्तम्भो यूपदण्डः[a] । तत् संयोगेन यूपो भवति तज्ज्ञानं विज्ञापयति य एवं वेद स हि विश्वकर्मा शिल्पाधिदैवतम्[13] । य एवं जानाति स पुरश्रेष्ठः ।

वृत्तज्ञानं रेखाज्ञानं च यो जानाति स स्थापकः ॥ ४ ॥

खादिरदण्डहस्तो दर्भरज्जुकरः, तद् रज्जुवलयवेष्टितमिदं तस्य रूपं तज्ज्ञानञ्च शिल्पज्ञानम् । तद्ज्ञानाद्[b] दिव्यज्ञानं भवति[c], तद्ज्ञानान् मोक्षः, स हि मधुः[14], य एवं वेद ।

शिल्पात् प्रतिमा[15] जायन्ते ॥ ५ ॥

प्रतिमायाः श्रद्धा सञ्चरति, श्रद्धातो निष्ठा, ततश्च ज्ञानम्, तस्मान्मोक्षो भवतीति पञ्च वास्तुसोपानानि, य एवं वेद । आथर्वणीये सर्वानुभूतिरित्यनुशासनम् । अथ शिल्पकाश्यपाथर्वणाङ्गिरसकुवित्सा[16]

---

[9]पैप्पलादसंहितायां प्रथमकाण्डे उक्तम् – श्यामा सरूपंकरणी पृथिव्या अध्युद्भृता ।
इदमू षु प्र साधय पुना रूपाणि कल्पय ॥१.२६.५ (शौ० १.२४.४)

[10]मूर्तिश्चतुर्विधा प्रोक्ता मृण्मयी शैली एव च । धातवी दारवी चैव पूजनार्थे विशेषतः (घ) ॥

[11]आदित्यो यूप इति ऐतरेये उक्तं तथा तैत्तिरीये च ।

[12]अथर्ववेदे वैतानसूत्रमिति । अथर्ववेदे १३.१.४७ उक्तम् । पुनः यूपमुग्रा मरुतः स्कम्भहिमं घ्रंसं चाधाय यूपान् कृत्वा पर्वतान् । इन्द्रेण मन्त्रे उक्तम् पुनः अथर्ववेदे यूप स्कम्भरूपेण उक्तश्च दशमकाण्डे चतुर्थानुवाके दैवतरूपेण ।

[13]गृह्यसूत्रे च अथर्ववेदे ७ काण्डे नवमानुवाके ३ सूत्रे उक्तम् । शतपथब्राह्मणे । वास्तु हि तद् यज्ञस्य यद् घृतेषु हविषु इति उक्तम्, तद् देवता वास्तुपुरुषः शिखिन्यादि इति ।

[14]ब्रह्मसुखं हि मधु इति अथर्ववेदे १.३४.१ उक्तम्–
इयं वीरुन्मधुजाता मधुना त्वा खनामसि ।
मधोरधि प्रजातासि सा नो मधुमतस्कृधि ॥

[15]प्रतिमा – अथर्ववेदे ९.४.२ उक्तम् – अपां यो अग्रे प्रतिमा बभूव प्रभूः सर्वस्मै पृथिवीव देवी इति । वाजसनेयिसंहितायामुक्तम् – असौ वै लोकः प्रतिमेषा ह्यन्तरिक्षलोके प्रतिमा इव इति ।

[16]ऋत्विग्विशेषाः आथर्वणपुरोहिताः ।

---

[a]इत्यधिकपाठः, क ।

[b]तच्छिल्पज्ञानाद्, ग ।

[c]प्रभवति, ख ।

दयो होद्गीथे[17] कुशला बभूवुः । वास्तुषडङ्गकथां यथामति ब्रूहीति प्रोचुः पिप्पलादमिति । तथेति समुपदिदिक्षुः ।

स प्रवहणः शिल्पसूत्राध्यायं स्थापकविद्यां चावदत् ॥ ६ ॥

सा विद्या श्रेष्ठा, प्रजापतेश्चाग्रा । प्रजापतेर्नारदः, नारदान्मयः, मयाद् वैश्रवणः[18], वैश्रवणात् पिप्पलादः । श्रोष्यामीति । एषामुन्मेषः सत्यम् ।

होवाचाङ्गिरसस्त्वां पृच्छामीति । पृच्छेति होवाच । केन प्रतिमा सम्भवति । कथं रूपं रूपं प्रतिरूपाणि लोके सम्भवन्ति । नाहं प्रभो पश्यामीति ।[a] स प्राजापत्यमार्गेण पिप्पलाद उवाच । भव त्वं शान्तहृदयः आङ्गिरस, मर्त्यै वा इदं सदासीत् श्रेष्ठयजने ।

> अपां यो अग्रे प्रतिमा बभूव प्रभूः सर्वस्मै पृथिवीव देवी ।
> पिता वत्सानां पतिरघ्न्यानां साहस्रे पोषे अपि नः कृणोतु ॥

इति मन्त्रेण[19] तृस्यर्थमुपासत[b] इति भावः ।

यजनोपासने च ।

शरीरमूर्तिरहिते मन आवेश्य विशेषेण विकल्पिदोषयुक्तं भवति ॥ ७ ॥

इति । रूपात् क्रमेण [प्रतिमा], प्रतिमायास्तत्त्वबोधो जायते । तत्त्वबोधाद् धारणेति । धारणाया गाथा, कथा प्रसरति लोके । गाथाया रूपाण्युत्पादयन्ति स्थापकाः । तस्मै होवाच रूपकलनार्थं कारुसाधनार्थं विशेषः ।

वास्तु षडङ्गमिति श्रेष्ठम् ॥ ८ ॥

शैलं खिलपञ्जरं[20] कीलेन पञ्जराकृतिकोष्ठका[c] रेखावासः[d] तदा रूपाङ्गानि मर्माण्याश्रयन्ते तच्छैलभेदनम् । अङ्गप्रयोगः; न्यासभावना[e]सम्बन्ध-प्रबोधनम् इति । होवाच आङ्गिरसः–

---

[17]अथर्ववेदे २.८.१ काण्डे उक्तम् – उदगातां भगवती विचृतौ नाम तारके । इति ॥
[18]पौलस्त्यस्य अपत्यं विश्रवापुत्रः रावणः ।
[19]अथर्व० ९.४.२
[20]प्रयोगात्मकसूत्रमिति खिलम् ।

---

[a]नाहमत्र भोग्यं पश्यामीति, ग ।
[b]०मुपासयन्ति, ग ।
[c]कोष्ठकाणि यदा रूपाङ्गाणि आश्रयन्ति, ग ।
[d]कीर्त्त्यावासः, ग ।
[e]भावनान्यास, ख ।

कथं विकाशेन रूपवास्तुषडङ्गं शिल्पं संसिद्धं भवति । भगवतस्तस्यैव मे कामं ब्रूयात् । श्रुत्वाह, येनैवं मे स्थापकविद्या प्रपातिनी समावर्त्तते[a] । स हि षडङ्गक्रममाह ।

[शैलम्]

षड्धा शैलं ज्ञेयम् ॥ ९ ॥

शिला तद्देशे लोकज्ञाने षड्धा प्रथिता । हिरण्यरेखिका, समवर्णा, ताम्रा, धातुपुटिता, बज्रलब्धा, सैकतालिकेति । यदा हिरण्यरेखा कुटिला सोऽवलक्षणः । सा प्रतिमार्थं हीना विरूपं प्रददाति । तद्दर्शनेन विकल्पभावो प्रभवति । दर्शनादेता अर्थहीना उच्यन्ते, वदन्ति, भवन्तीति ।

एतदर्थं प्रतिमावैलक्षण्यं भवति । यदा पूर्णशैलमेकवर्णं कृष्णं कृष्णपिङ्गलं हारिद्रं वा मुख्यप्रतिमार्थं ध्येयं सा समवर्णा । कठिनतमगाढपिङ्गलशिला न ध्येया ।

यदा शैलं भित्त्याकृतेरपृथक् प्रतिमाशालार्थं[21] तद् ध्येयम् । शैलं पृथक्त्वेन हीनं भवति ।

यत्र केवलं लीलाविग्रहा निवसन्ति भित्त्यङ्के, इति । शिला धातुपुटिता धूमवर्णा व्रणोपेतारूपार्थं घोरेति । शैलान्तरे स्तराभ्यन्तरे कोमलरसबद्धा रेखाः सन्ति याः पीतप्रभाः सदाऽधमा भवन्ति श्रेष्ठैः शिल्पकारैः ।

सैकतालिकशिला यूपयोनिमिथुनस्तम्भ[22] वृषस्तम्भकुण्डार्थं विशिष्टा, न रूपार्थं ग्राह्या, तज्ज्ञानलब्धस्थापकाः[b] समुपतिष्ठन्ति जनलोके सम्पन्ना महीयन्ते ।

शैलादङ्गरागज्ञानं प्रसरति ॥ १० ॥

सर्वेषु लोकेषु कामचारो भवति ।

इति आथर्वणीये वाङ्कायमनोमार्गेण पिप्पलादकल्पे वास्तुसूत्रसम्प्रदान-मिति चर्चाक्षेण मुनिहोतारोपनिधानेन शैलषडङ्गज्ञाननाम प्रथमप्रपाठकः ।

---

[21]भीत्त्याकारे महाशैले दैवलीलादयो यथा । रूपशाला तपस्विनां मोदार्थमभिखोदिता । इति काश्यपवचनम् ।

[22]स्तम्भ इति यूपः यूपः वै स्तम्भ (स्कम्भ) इति अथर्ववेदे १०.७ उक्तम् ॥ प्रयोगभेदे स्कम्भत्रयं ब्रह्मयजने स्कम्भो वै यूपः, पितृयजने वृषस्तम्भः, कामयजने मिथुनस्कम्भ इति भेदः ।

---

[a]समावर्तने, ख, ग ।

[b]ग्राह्या सज्ञान वा स्थापकाः, ख । तल्लब्धज्ञानस्थापकाः, ग ।

द्वितीयः प्रपाठकः

खिलपञ्जरज्ञानम्

अथ खिलपञ्जरज्ञानं[1] घटनमिति ब्रूमः । तेन आचेष्टो भव आङ्गिरस[2] ग्राभकार इव ।

निर्दिष्टार्थकप्रतिमा[3] ग्राह्या ॥ १ ॥

अनुकूल[a]शिला अभिजिति[4] संप्राप्ते दर्भेण पातयेत् कारुशालायाम् । ततः उदुम्बरकीलेन शिलां रोधयेत् ।

पातनं प्रथमा क्रिया ॥ २ ॥

पातनान्ते उत्ताडनञ्च, पिच्छिलकरणार्थं होताऽध्वर्युः स्थापकैः सह रूपशिलां मर्दयेत् ।

मर्दनं द्वितीया क्रिया ॥ ३ ॥

आदौ ओं–

दधिक्राव्णो अकारिषं जिष्णोरश्वस्य वाजिनः ।
सुरभि नो मुखा करत्प्र ण आयूंषि तारिषत् ॥

[इति] मन्त्रेण[5] ततः महीलुक[6]पयसा शिलां क्षालयेत्[b], एतत सर्वं कुम्भीका[7]मोचनार्थम्[c] । तत आपादशीर्षं शतकेशिवृषं[8] चिन्तयेत्[d] प्रार्थयेच्च ।

---

[1]यद्गुह्यम् अधिकोपायेन विग्रहप्रामाण्यं भवति । सा खिलपञ्जरविद्या, असाधारणी इत्यर्थः, गुह्यं रेखाज्ञानमिति ।

[2]उद्गीथमुपासाञ्चक्रे । एतमेवाङ्गिरसं मन्ये । अङ्गानां यद्रसः । आत्मज्ञऋषिविशेषः ।

[3]सपर्योपयोगिनी प्रतिमा ।

[4]तैत्तिरीयब्राह्मणोक्तः नक्षत्रविशेषः यः शुभदायकः, अभिजिन्नाम नक्षत्रमुपरिष्टादिति वाक्यम् ।

[5]अथर्व० २०.१३७.३ ।

[6]एकवर्णा कपिला गौः, पुरुरूपा गौरिति भावः । दैवतन्त्रे शक्तिप्राप्ता गाव । अथर्ववेदे १०.१०.६ उक्तं 'स्वधाप्राणा महीलुका' इति ।

[7]कुम्भीकामोचनार्थम् अथर्ववेदे १६.६.८ उक्तम्–ॐ कुम्भीका दूषीकाः पीयकान् । इति ।

[8]शतकेशी रुद्ररूपो महावृषः । अथर्ववेदे ५.२२.८ उक्तः । यथा–
महावृषान् मूजवतो बन्ध्वद्धि परेत्य । प्रैतानि तक्मने ब्रूमो अन्यक्षेत्राणि वा इमा ॥ इति ।

[a]प्रतिमानुकूल, ख, ग, घ ।

[b]मर्दयेत्, ग, घ ।

[c]वर्जनार्थं, ग, घ ।

[d]हिरण्मयं सवितारं चिन्तयन् प्रभमानं प्रार्थयेत् शतकेशीवृष रक्ष मामिति ब्रूयात्, ख ।

ॐ शतकेशाय महर्षभाय मे रक्ष रक्ष स्वाहा इति ब्रूयात् । महर्षभ तस्य नव नभस्ततो वाश्रा आपपृथिवी तर्पयतु ।[a]

एतेन जङ्गिडादयः[9] पलायन्ते । एवं शुभं भवति, मनः प्रमोदं भवति, सोऽमृतो भवतीति[b]। ततो मण्डलकरणम् वलयकीलसंयुतयुजुव[10]दण्डेन रज्जुसंयोगेन मण्डलैकं रचयन्–

पुनन्तु मा देवजनाः पुनन्तु मनवो धिया ।
पुनन्तु विश्वा भूतानि पवमानः पुनातु मा ॥[11]
इत्यनेन मन्त्रेण विलं निर्धारयेत् ।

विलमिति मर्म[c] ज्ञेयम् ॥ ४ ॥

एषा तृतीया क्रिया[12] । विलस्योभयपार्श्वगं पृथग्बिन्दुमवलम्ब्य मण्डलद्वयं रचयन्ति स्थापकाः । तद्देशे शिलाक्षेत्रे रेखायां प्रकृतिपुरुषन्यायेन संलग्नेन वृत्तयुग्ममाचरन्ति । तद् यामलमण्डलमिति । एकेन,[d] द्वौ एकरेखायामिति ध्येयम् ।

शिल्पश्रोतारः[e] शृणुत, केनोपायेन वज्रेण[13] रेखाः कर्त्तव्याः । ततः कीर्त्त्यावासः[14] प्रजायते ।

न कृत्यरूपार्थं[15] रेखाकरणं कर्त्तव्यम् ॥ ५ ॥

आदौ वृत्तं वृत्तम्[16] इति विश्वम् ॥ ६ ॥

तद्रूपे प्राणः, यथा पुरुषस्य मनः, तद्वृत्तं कालः, एष वास्तुवेदे । वृत्तस्य गतिरवधारिता[f], यथा चित्तवृत्तिः । वृत्तस्याधारोऽमृतम् बिन्दुस्तस्य

[9]तापवर्गप्रदयोनिविशेषाः तथा च–अथर्ववेदे १९.३५.२ उक्तम्–स नो रक्षतु जङ्गिडो धनपालो धनेव इति ।

[10]काश्यपसंहिताशिल्पशास्त्रे प्रथमाध्याये उक्तम्–युजुवदण्डसंयुक्तं वलयं वेष्टितं तथा । रज्जुद्विमुष्टि यस्याग्रेऽप्ययःकीलसघूर्णिका इति ।

[11]अथर्ववेदे ६.१९.१ अयं मन्त्रः । मर्मनिर्धारणे उपाध्यायाः पवमानसूक्तं पठन्ति इत्याचारः ।

[12]पातनं मर्दनं चैवमङ्कनं सा त्रिधा क्रिया । खोदनोत्तरकर्माणि स्थापकः संस्मरेत् सदा ॥ काश्यपसंहिता अ. १, श्लो १४ (ङ)

[13]शुक्लशिलाचूर्णमिति वज्ररेखाङ्कनस्योपादानम् ।

[14]कीर्त्तिरिति रूपं सा प्रतिमा, तस्याऽऽधारः रेखापञ्जर इति ।

[15]न मृण्मयप्रतिमार्थं रेखान्यासस्य प्रयोजनम् ।

[16]वृत्तबिन्दुविषयाणि विशदरूपेण पिप्पलादीयप्रणवतारके ध्येयानि (घ)

[a]Additional sentence in MS क, meaning not clear.

[b]इति अधिकपाठः, क ।

[c]दण्डविल इति मर्म, ख ।

[d]एको वा द्वौ एकेण रेखा रचनं ध्येयमिति, ख ।

[e]०होतारः, ख, ग ।

[f]वृत्तस्य स्थितिरवधारितः, क ।

स्थितिः[a], यथाऽऽत्मा । बिन्दुं समारभ्य तद्बिन्दुमिलितेन परिभू[b] परिधिः सञ्जायते । तद् हि वृत्तं परमेष्ठी, तद् द्रष्टा, तद् योगः । तत् क्रतुः, तत् सत्यं । य एवं वेद ।

एकैकस्य संयोगे एकीभवति इति तस्य भावः । वृत्तं हि पूर्णम् ॥ ७ ॥

बिन्दुस्तस्याधारः, आहुतिरिव[c] जगन्मयः प्राणः[d]। सा स्थितिः, यथा गायत्री वेदपदं । तस्यैव शैलस्योपरि मण्डलम्, मण्डलकरणे वास्तुगायत्रीम्[17] अथवा अष्टाक्षरीमन्त्रं[18] जपेत् । इति कृत्यम् वृत्तमभ्यन्तरे क्षेत्रस्याधारं मन्ये, यथा[e]सर्वाणि भूतानि भ्रमन्ति तथा नानारूपाणि जायन्ते । स वै प्राणः क्षेत्रविभाजनं प्रतिमाङ्गोपलब्धये, तस्मात्–

रेखान्वये सर्वाङ्गानि न्यासय[f] ॥ ८ ॥

इति भेदनक्रिया । एवं वज्रेण शिलायां रेखाङ्कनकरणं ध्येयम्, न भूमौ न वा इष्टके[19] । अथासौ आङ्गिरसो होवाच – ब्राह्मणं भगवन्तं पिप्पलादं द्वौ प्रश्नौ पृच्छामि, तौ चेन्मे वक्ष्यति । का रेखा, कस्तस्या भावः, कति भेदाः, ब्रूहि पिप्पलादेति ।

तान् ह स ऋषिरुवाच–आङ्गिरस, शिल्पकाश्यप शृणु रेखाव्याख्यानम् । तथा तासां भावञ्च । रेखा न्यासस्याधारः सा धारेव[g]। सा कर्मप्रतीतेरधिभूतमधिदैवतञ्च ।

तेजांसि सरलरेखाः ॥ ९ ॥

तद्रेखेण मण्डलं भिन्दन्ति, यथा कर्त्तारः कर्मणा विश्वं परिभिन्दन्ति, तेभ्यः तद्रूपेण रूपार्थं चाक्षुषत्वेन[20] देशकथानुमतं[21] सर्वाणि रूपाङ्गानि प्रभवन्तीति[h] अङ्गसाम्यं प्रभवतीति ।

---

[17]ॐ विश्वकर्माय (विश्वकर्मणे) विद्महे कारुकाराय धीमहि तन्नो शिल्पी प्रचोदयात् ।

[18]ॐ विश्वकर्माय (विश्वकर्मणे) नमः, इति तस्याष्टाक्षरो मन्त्र इति ।

[19]न यज्ञशुल्वप्रयोगे विश्वज्योतिरित्यादिनिर्माणे प्रयोजनम् ।

[20]दृश्यरूपेण शिलोपरि इति भावः ।

[21]यस्मिन् देशे यथाकारे दैवलीला प्रवर्त्तते ।

---

[a]विन्दुसमुच्चयस्य समष्टिः वृत्तम्, ख ।

[b]०भुवत्, क ।

[c]हुत्वामेक, ग ।

[d]इति अधिकपाठः ।

[e]यत्र, ख, ग ।

[f]आचर, ग ।

[g]स हि धारा, ग; गति हि धारा, ख ।

[h]आतप्यन्ते, क ।

नाभौ रूपकर्म[a] प्रारभ्यते ॥१० ॥

समतार्धं सर्वाण्यङ्गानि निर्णयेत् । एवं ब्रह्मविकल्पः । यथा ब्रह्मविद्या तथा रूपप्रज्ञा । तद् विज्ञाय कारुज्ञा वक्रतः रूपकर्मणि ब्रह्म प्रतिपादयन्ति । रमन्ते यथापूर्वपूर्वप्रज्ञायाम् । यथा ब्रह्मविद्या तथा रेखान्वये रूपाङ्गन्यासो महीयते । यज्ज्ञात्वा स्थापकाः प्राज्ञा महीयन्ते । य एवं वेद । तज्ज्ञानेन स्थापका रूपज्ञा भवन्ति[22] । ते विद्वांसः, ते विज्ञातारः कारुकर्मणि ब्रह्मानुभूतिं लभन्ते । यथा विश्वसृष्टौ पञ्चमहाभूतानि[23] प्रजायन्ते, तथा वृत्ताधारे शिल्पकाश्यपादयो वास्तुहोतारो भूत[b]महाभूतलक्षणानि कल्पयन्ति प्रज्ञापनेनेति ।

प्राजापत्यरीत्या वृत्तं हि तेजस्तदाऽपांभासे चतुरस्रम् ॥११ ॥

चतुरेखाबद्धक्षेत्रमिति । यथा सरित्कुण्डे तथा रूपक्षेत्रे चतुरस्रं[24] सर्वमापादविश्वं प्राजापत्यमार्गेण श्रुतिर्दर्शयति[25] । तथा हि रूपक्षेत्रे तद्रूपस्याधारः । भूयस्त्वाद् वास्तुश्रोतार एनं गृह्णन्ति भूयो वृत्तमध्ये ।

कर्णद्वयं मरुद्भावेन आचरन्ति ॥१२ ॥

यथा मरुदप्संयोगात् फेनो भवति । पुनः फेनाद् बुद्बुदः सम्भवति, तथा चतुरस्रं कर्णरेखायुग्मसंयोगाद्रूपक्षेत्रं सक्रियं भवतीति । सा मारुतकीलस्य क्रियाप्रतीतिः ।

धरेव कर्णिकक्षेत्रमाकर्षयन्ति स्थापकाः ॥१३ ॥

ततः स्थापका मध्यमारुह्य[26] कर्णिकक्षेत्रमाचरन्ति । मण्डलमध्ये द्वे मध्यरेखे लिखन्ति मध्यरेखा मध्यप्रस्थरेखा भवति । सममानेन तत्रोपलभन्ते चतुष्खण्डक्षेत्राणि चतुर्द्वीपां पृथिवीमिव, एषा भूमिक्षेत्रस्य भावना । तत्र मध्ये–

लब्धबिन्दुः रसायाः प्राणः ॥१४ ॥

मर्म वदन्ति शिल्पकाराः । तस्य भावं शृण्वन्तु सर्वेऽमृतस्य पुत्राः

---

[22]तालांशज्ञानसम्प्राप्ते शिल्पी स्थापक उच्यते । रेखान्यासं यो जानाति स रूपज्ञो भवेत् तथा । शिल्परहस्यागमे ४, २ उक्तम् ।

[23]प्रजापतिरेते सर्वे देवा इमानि च पञ्चमहाभूतानि वायुराकाश आपो ज्योतिरित्येतानीमानि च क्षुद्रमिश्राणि ऐतरेये पञ्चमखण्डे उक्तम्–तथा हि वास्तुवेदे सम्यक् भिन्नता जायते, दृश्यते ।

[24]सर्वरूपशैलस्य आधारः चतुरस्रम् ।

[25]अश्मना ह्यापः प्रभवन्ति । शतपथब्राह्मणे नवमाध्याये उक्तम् ।

[26]मध्यदैर्घ्यमध्यप्रस्थयोर्मध्यबिन्दुमवलम्ब्य ।

---

[a]०क्रिया, ख ।

[b]पञ्च, ग ।

शिष्याश्च । अप्पृथिवीसंयोगात् यथा द्यौः[27] सम्भवति यथा श्रुतौ उक्तं[28] तदाकाशे सविता द्युरूपेण भ्रमति । स सविता व्योमचरो, यस्य गतिरखण्डा । तथा हि मारुतस्य तिर्यग् गतिः। तत्र खण्डितरेखान् नीत्वा शिल्पसम्बन्धार्थमाकल्प्य लब्धस्थापकाः[a] शिल्पसम्भारेण द्विधा बहुधा बिन्दून् कल्पयन्ति प्रजनयन्ति बिन्दून् । तद्विज्ञातारो वृत्तालये अधोर्ध्वे द्विधाकरणन्यायेन वह्निवत् क्षेत्रमाचरन्ति[29] कारुकाराः । वृत्तमध्ये कदाचित् सम्प्रतिष्ठति तत्[b]त्रिहुतम्[30] ।

त्रिहुताग्निः स्मर्यतेऽपि च लोके ॥१५ ॥

निम्नगास्त्रिहुता आप इति ॥१६ ॥

तदुभयस्य संयोगान् मिथुनभावो भवति । ये जानन्ति ते सम्पन्ना भवन्ति । स उन्मेषभावः । अग्निरापः संयोगाद् दिव्यं[c31] भवतीति । तन्महच्छन्दो[d] होतारो जानन्ति यज्ञे प्रयोजयन्ति कुण्डे स्थण्डिले लिखन्ति, तेन देवलोकाः पितृलोका आहुत्या तृप्यन्ति[32] । मनुष्याणां तत् सायुज्यं प्रददाति । एवं बहुधा श्रूयते, सर्वे रूपकारा ब्रह्मज्ञा वृत्ताभ्यन्तरेण क्षेत्रमध्ये समान्तरालषड्बिन्दुमारुह्यरेखाः रेखां रोधयन्ति ।

षट्कोणको हि आकर्षणीविद्या[33] विशेषः ॥१७ ॥

तन्मिथुनच्छन्दोयोगेन यातुधानाः[34] प्रतिघातयन्ति । माण्डव्यादयो[35] बहुधा देवान् पूजयन्ति । आकर्षयन्ति रुद्रानादित्यान् वसून् । साऽऽकर्षणी

[27]व्योम इति भावः ।

[28]द्यावा-पृथिवीं संजानीथ, अथ वर्षति, शतपथे उक्तम् । अथर्व १२.१ उक्तम् अर्णवभूम्यात् परम व्योम जायते इति भावः ।

[29]अग्निरूपं त्रिभुजक्षेत्रम् ।

[30]हुतमिति रेखा, त्रिरेखेण यत् क्षेत्रं तत् त्रिहुतं भवति ।

[31]दिव्यं दैवीभावः । अथर्वसंहितायामुक्तम् २.१२.४. - पितॄणामामुं ददे हरसा दैव्येन इति ।

[32]गुह्योक्तविधिना अग्निस्थापने ब्रह्मोपदेशने स्थण्डिले षट्कोणलिखनानन्तरं विष्टरद्वयं स्थापयन्ति । तदुपरि अग्निं स्थापयन्ति, इति अग्निसन्धानविधिः ।

[33]तन्त्रे तथा कालिकोपनिषदि उक्तम्–कूर्चबीजं व्योमषष्ठस्वरां बिन्दुमेलनरूपां, तद्वयं मायाद्वयं दक्षिणे कालिकेति ।

[34]यातुधानः निर्ऋतेरादिवाक्यात् तापवर्गप्रदो योनिविशेष इति अथर्ववेदे उक्तम् ।

[35]मण्डुवंशजातः कौत्सस्य शिष्यः ऋषिविशेष इति बृहदारण्यके उक्तम् ।

[a]लब्धज्ञानस्थापका इति युक्तम्, ख ।

[b]स कारुकाराः त्रिभुजं वदन्ति, ख, ङ ।

[c]द्यौः, ख, ग ।

[d]स महान् शब्दः, ग ।

वास्तुवेदीयरेखाङ्कने श्रेयसी[a]भावव्यक्तोपायेति ।

यथा रूपे तथा यूपेऽनुच्छेदान्ता ग्राह्याः ॥ १८ ॥

याज्ञिका यूपे स्थापका रूपे समानाश्चरन्ति[36] ।

खनित्रप्रकारो ध्येयः ॥ १९ ॥

एतद् ब्रह्ममण्डले[b] खनित्रकाराणां[c] कलाषोडशीन्यायेन तत्क्षेत्रं षोडशांशेन छेदयन्ति[37] । सौम्ययूपस्य[38]दण्डो यदाऽष्टांशः स यजमानाय प्रीतिकामार्थः । कदाचित् तत्कलांशेनांशान् छिन्दन्ति सोऽपराविद्यायां वृषस्तम्भः । अग्निस्तम्भो भवति काम्यानुसारतः शिलायां वा उदुम्बरदारवीयः । शिलायूपो ध्रुवेति शिल्पकाश्यप ज्ञेयम् । यज्ञार्थं सौम्ययूपो, विष्णुयज्ञार्थमष्टांशयूपः, काम्यकर्मार्थं षोडशांश इति ध्येयम्[39] ।

सूत्रायने[40] रेखाः सुभगा भवन्ति ॥ २० ॥

भावं प्रददति । एतज्ज्ञानम् गुह्यज्ञानम् । एषा खिलविद्या, रेखाकरणं तत् ।

खिलपञ्जरज्ञानं श्रेष्ठम् ॥ २१ ॥

ये जानन्ति ते रूपज्ञास्तत्त्वरूपाणि घटयन्ति । रूपतत्त्वे विना रेखाकरणं रूपं हीनमिति ध्येयम् ।

उत्थितरेखा[41] अग्निरूपाः, पार्श्वगा[42] अब्रूपाः, तिर्यग्रेखा मरुद्रूपा इति ॥ २२ ॥

रेखाप्रभेदे भावभेदा उपजायन्ते । रेखानुसृतं रूपं विभाति । रूपं सुरूपं

[36]प्रयोगरूपेणैतत् षड्धाङ्कनोपादानम्, व्योमाभासे मण्डलञ्च चतुरस्रोपसंज्ञकः कोणरेखाः वायुश्च कर्णिकापृथिवी तथा त्रिभुजमग्निरूपञ्च षट्कोणं दैवमन्दिरम् । काश्यपवचनम् ।

[37]रूपक्षेत्रे खनित्रेणाविशन्ति, सितवज्ररेखायां ततः अयसा खोदयन्ति मूलम् ।

[38]वास्तुयागे शिलानिर्मितसौम्ययूपः, विष्णुयज्ञे षोडशांशविशिष्टशिलायूपः विधेयः, पितृयज्ञे दारवी वृषयूपस्य प्रयोजनं भवति ।

[39]इन्द्रे लोका इन्द्रे तप इन्द्रेऽध्यृतमाहितम् । इन्द्रं त्वा वेद प्रत्यक्षं स्कम्भे (यूपे) सर्वं प्रतिष्ठितम् ॥ (१०.७.३०) अथर्ववेदे एवं बहुधा उक्तम् ।

[40]सममानेन सूत्रपातनेन रेखाः सौम्या भवन्ति ।

[41]दैर्घ्यरेखाः ।

[42]प्रस्थरेखाः ।

[a]श्रेयः, ग ।

[b]ब्रह्मक्षेत्रे, घ ।

[c]खनित्रकाराः, ख, ग ।

भवतीति[43]। तत्त्वरेखावलम्बने रूपात्मप्रत्यक्षं भवंति प्रतिरूपे च । यथाऽऽहुत्या वृष्टिर्भवति तथा रूपसौभगाद् ध्यानभावः सम्प्रतिष्ठते । यथा पर्जन्यादन्नं सम्भवति तथा ध्यानाल्लय उपजायते । लयान्मनुजा दिव्या भवन्ति । यथाऽन्नात् प्राणः सञ्चरति तथा लयात्तद्भावमनुभवन्ति, मनो निश्चलं भवति । तेषां न पुनरावृत्तिः, एतदर्थं रूपं कल्पयन्ति ऋषयो लोके । रूपे रेखा आहुतय इव ।

रूपसौभगाद् ध्यानभावो जायते ॥ २३ ॥

सा हि वृष्टिः । सा ऋतस्य धारा यथा पर्जन्याद् बहुधाऽन्नानि सम्भवन्ति[44] तथा रेखाया रूपाणि ।

अग्निरेखायामुत्तुङ्गरूपाणि जायन्ते ॥ २४ ॥

तानि सर्वाण्युदारभावप्रदायकानि सौम्योत्थिताकृतीनीति ।

अब्रेखायामुत्सुकरूपाणि जायन्ते ॥ २५ ॥

तान्युग्रभावप्रदायकानि[a]।

मारुतरेखायां तैजसरूपाणि ॥ २६ ॥

तीक्ष्णभावप्रदायकानि योधरूपाण्युपजायन्ते । तानि सर्वाणि भीषण-रूपार्थम् । कर्णजा रेखा ग्राह्या इत्थं रूपकर्मार्थम् ।

रेखाज्ञानं सर्वमिति ज्ञेयम् ॥ २७ ॥

ये जानन्ति सर्वं ते स्थापकोद्गीथरूपेण[45] ख्याता भवन्ति ।

इति पैप्पलादीयवास्तुसूत्रे वाक्कायमनोमार्गेण सम्प्रदानमिति चर्चा-क्षेण मुनिश्रोतॄणामुपनिधानेन खिलपञ्जराकर्षणज्ञानमिति वास्तुसूत्रस्य द्वितीयप्रपाठकः ।

---

[43]पैप्पलादसंहितायां प्रथमखण्डे रूपस्य स्वरूपविषये उक्तम् – रूपं रूपवयोवस्तेन त्वां परिदध्मसि, इति रूपभावस्य धारणा ।

[44]अन्नाद् भवन्ति भूतानि पर्जन्यादन्नसम्भवः इति गीतायाः ३.१४, तैत्तिरीयोपनिषदि २.२ अपि च प्रश्नोपनिषदि षष्ठप्रश्ने उक्तम् ।

[45]मूर्तिकारा हि स्थापकाः, ते स्थापकोद्गीथा इति ।

---

[a]उक्षभावप्रदायक उग्ररूपाणि पार्श्वगः, ग ।

तृतीयः प्रपाठकः

शैलभेदनम्

शिल्पव्याख्यानम् आश्रृणुतेदम् । वास्तुषडङ्गमध्ये एते शैलभेदनोपायाः तथेति समुपविशन्ति ते । आथर्वणाङ्गिरसशिल्पकाश्यप उवाच भगवन्तं पिप्पलादम्, अस्मान् वदन्तु शिल्पाचारे भेदनार्थं यद् यद् श्रेय इति । यत् कतिधा अलभ्यमुवाच त्वां पृच्छामीति, पृच्छेति होवाच । का शैलभेदनस्य गतिः, के प्रयोजयन्ति । प्रस्तावनाक्रमेण प्रस्तरे खिलपञ्जरार्थं रेखाकरणे किं वा प्रयोजनम्,

पिप्पलादो होवाचः-

रेखानुक्रमेण रूपाङ्गान्याचरन्ति ।

रूपस्य भावो मुख्यः ॥ १ ॥

भावात् प्रेरणा[1] प्रसरति, प्रेरणया दिव्यबोधः सञ्जायते । तत्क्रिया हि भेदनविद्या । यथा पराविद्याया दिव्यत्वं जायते तथा सुरूपाद् दिव्यत्वमुपलभन्ते मनुष्याः । तेषां मनोवृत्त्यां रूपस्य भावज्ञापनार्थं रूपकर्माणि सावधानेन स्थापका आचरन्ति । रूपमध्ये किञ्चित् सौम्यं किञ्चिदुग्रं च ।

भावानुसारतो रेखाविधानमिति ज्ञेयम् ॥ २ ॥

एतद् यो जानाति स मर्मज्ञः[2] । स लोके मान्यो भवति ग्रामे वास्तूद्गीथरूपेण ख्यातो भवति । नृपे चाक्र[3] रूपेण ।

तेषां बहुधाकृत्यं श्रेयः ॥ ३ ॥

ते शैलं छिन्दन्ति, रूपाण्युत्खोदयन्ति । रूपाङ्गानि रेखानुपाते पातयन्ति । अङ्गयोर्मध्ये क्षीणकूटाङ्गानि भिन्दन्ति । कूटाद् यत्त्यक्तशिला उद्धृतास्तच्छिलाः निक्षिपन्ति समन्त्रेणेति त्यागः । अङ्गान्युत्थितकूटानि[a] नीचानि, एतन्न्यासबोधः ।

न्यासार्थं कालबोधो ध्येय इति ॥ ४ ॥

---

[1]मूर्तिदर्शनमात्रेण यद्भावो मनसि जायते सा रूपप्रेरणा ।

[2]रूपमध्ये यथाकीलं कीलाभासे यदङ्कः । यो जानाति इमं भावं मर्मज्ञः स इति स्मृतः ॥ शिल्परत्नकोषे द्वितीयसर्गे १८ श्लोके उक्तम् ॥

[3]चाक्रः स्थपति-श्रेष्ठ इति पाटवचाक्रशतपथे उक्तम् ।

---

[a]उत्थितानि कूटानि, ग ।

न रात्रौ, न दर्शे, न सूर्यसोमयोः सङ्गमे, न सन्ध्यायां वा उषायां चरन्ति श्रेष्ठरूपकाराः । तेऽभिधृतार्थमुदुम्बरद्विपक्षान्[4] निखाय रूपशिलामवरोधयन्ति । तद् रोधनम् । रोधनकाले पर्जन्यपूजने जटावेदं[5] पठेदिति पठनोपासनेन रसविज्ञातन्यायेन[a] ऋषयः शैलाचार्या भिन्दन्ति शैलम् ।

तद्भेदनेऽभिमन्त्रयन्ति खनित्राणि[b] ॥ ५ ॥

ॐ उत्तिष्ठ पुरुषि किं स्वपिषि भयं मे समुपस्थितम् ।
यदि शक्यमशक्यं हूँ (दुर्गे) भगवति शमय स्वाहा ॥

इति खनित्रप्रयोगमन्त्रः । मन्त्रात् कालो विनश्यति, भयं व्यपोहति । एतज्ज्ञानेन अग्निहोत्रं चरन्ति वैश्वानरे जुह्वति । यथाऽङ्गारेषु भस्मार्थं जुहुयात् पापानां[c] तथा शिल्पकारा रूपार्थमग्निहोत्रमाचरन्ति वैश्वानरे जुह्वतीति ।

वास्तुयज्ञात् खनित्रबाधो व्यपोहति । कुशङ्का विनश्यन्ति । खनित्रप्रयोगे दौर्बल्यबोधे मन्त्रं मनसि ध्यायन्ति ।

मन्त्रः- ॐ चक्षुरसि चक्षुर्मे दाः स्वाहा ।
परिपाणमसि परिपाणं मे दाः स्वाहेति ॥ (अथर्ववेद २.१७.६ - ७)

एषा क्रिया ध्येया, य एवं वेद ।
अथाङ्गिरसादय उद्गातारः पप्रच्छुः कश्च खनित्रप्रकार इति ।

खनित्रपञ्चकं श्रेष्ठम् ॥ ६ ॥

शृणुत, केनोपायेन शिल्पोद्गातारो भेदनकर्त्तनाद्याचरन्ति । खनित्रकर्म न वै रूपे सोमशालायां स्थण्डिलकरणे होतारः प्रयोजयन्ति । यथा बृहस्पतेर्गृहशालाप्रकरणे लोकवास्तूपाख्याने पूर्वं वेदे उक्तम्[6] । खनित्रापप्रयोगे रूपाण्यपरूपाणि भवन्ति । कुक्कुटिका[7] अपरूपाणि पूजयन्ति न ब्राह्मणाः । तत् खनित्रप्रयोगे श्रेष्ठान् तद्भेदान् वदामि ।

---

[4]दारवी मुष्टिमानेन कीलान् सङ्गृह्य यत्नतः । चतुःपार्श्वे यदा शिला तदा तु अवरोधनम् । इति शिल्परत्नकोषे रोधनक्रिया ।

[5]गाथां गायन्ति गाथिनः यथा कुन्तापसूक्तानि अथर्ववेदे (२०.१२७.१) उक्तानि 'इदं जना उप श्रुत नराशंस स्तविष्यते' इत्यादिजटाक्रमेण पठन्ति गाथिनः ।

[6]अथर्वसंहितायां ३.१२: शालाया ध्रुवा-स्तम्भः अश्वावती-भित्तिः; स्थूणा-वंशस्तम्भः; कुम्भ- धारककाष्ठानि; निर्माणेऽपि खनित्रप्रयोजनं भवति ।

[7]वनवासिनः ।

---

[a]अभिज्ञानन्यायेण, ग ।

[b]पञ्चखनित्राणि श्रेष्टांश्च, क; पञ्चखनित्र, ग ।

[c]पापाः, ग ।

भेदास्तु लाङ्गी, लाङ्गली, गृध्रदन्ती, सूचीमुखा, वज्रा इति । सर्वे आयसा द्विविधा भवन्ति क्षीणाः प्रशस्ताश्च । मुषलधरुभे मुषलदण्डेन खनित्रं घातयन्ति प्रयोजयन्ति शिलाभेदने तत् । सर्वास्त्राणि तीक्ष्णानि, गवाम्बुपुटितानि । ततः इङ्गिडलेपितानि चर्मशाणितानि च ।

रूपप्रकर्षार्थं रूपाङ्गं स्निग्धमिति[a] ॥ ७ ॥

सौम्येन छेदयन्ति ये ते शस्त्रिणः । शस्त्रं द्विमुखी घूर्णिकेति[8], अयोमुखास्त्राणि पालाशशलाकां वहन्ति[b], इदं तेषां रूपम् । अथ, आङ्गिरसः पप्रच्छ भगवन्तं पिप्पलादं, केन वज्रमिव कठिनशिलां खनित्रेण भिन्दन्ति वास्तुकाराः । तं होवाच वक्ता–

शिल्पकाराः प्रलेपयन्ति द्रावकरसम् ॥ ८ ॥

शङ्खद्राव-कुष्ठरस-सैन्धवखर्पर-उकत्सवल्कलचूर्णेन[9]सहितं शिलाद्रवणार्थमेवं रसचतुष्टयम्, अनेन मन्त्रेण दशाह[c]मर्दनान्ते वैताने खनित्रं प्रयोजयन्ति, खननमाचरन्ति भद्रेण[10] स्थापकाः ।

एषा हेतिविद्या श्रेष्ठा ॥ ९ ॥

रक्षार्थं पर्णमणिः परिधेयः ॥ १० ॥

खनित्रकर्मणि रक्षार्थं पाठामूलिकां धारयन्तीति स कवचः । मन्त्रेण सह धारयन्ति पर्णमणिम् । अनेन मन्त्रेण–

ॐ शं नो देवी पृश्निपर्ण्यशं निर्ऋत्या अकः ।
उग्रा हि कण्वजम्भनी तामभक्षि सहस्वतीम् ।

(अथर्ववेद २.२५.१)

भेदनादङ्गसौभगं[11] प्रभवति ॥ ११ ॥

यथा देहे तथा दैवाङ्गे गुल्फवलयकुक्ष्यादयः, उष्णीषमेखलादयः खोदयन्ति सौभगेन, उड्डुपयन्ति कुक्षशिलाः, विसृजन्ति तच्छिलामिति ।

---

[8]मण्डलकरणार्थं सूचीमुखाकृति (रज्ज्वे) शोणप्रस्तरन्यासितशस्त्रविशेषः ।
[9]प्रस्तरभेदिवृक्षस्य वल्कलं माहेन्द्रपर्वतारण्ये उपलब्धम् इति ।
[10]यथाविहित–लक्षणानुपातेन इति भद्रोपायः ।
[11]ग्रन्थिरेखा वलिः पर्वाण्यङ्गरागं यथोचितम् । प्रकृत्यानुसृतेः कुर्यात्तदङ्गसौभगं स्मृतम् । शिल्पागमे तृतीयाध्याये १४ श्लोके उक्तम् ।

[a]स्निग्धेन, क । प्रबोधार्थं सौम्येण छेदन्ति, ख, ग ।
[b]पालासदण्ड शलाकहस्त इति । ख ।
[c]पञ्चाहोरात्र, ग ।

रेखानुपातेनाङ्गानि निधेयानीति श्रेष्ठकृत्यम् ॥१२ ॥

एतेन वास्तुवेदविधानेन रेखानुपातेऽङ्गन्यासो विधेयः ।

गाथानुप्रासे[a] लक्षणं व्यक्तं भवति ॥१३ ॥

यथा गाथायाः कथास्तथा रूपलक्षणान्याचरन्ति रूपकार-रूपज्ञाः, तथा व्यक्तरूपं सम्भवति । यद् रूपस्य हावभावादि प्रत्यक्षं तद् व्यक्तरूपम् । रूपादुपासका भावसिद्धिमुपलब्धयन्ति[b] यत्नेन ध्यानमिति प्रयोगः[12] ।

ध्यानप्रयोगे रूपसौष्ठवं स्पष्टं भवति ॥१४ ॥

तथा हि ध्यानरूपं कथयन्ति वास्तुकाराः ।

यथा प्रकृतिस्तथा रूपलक्षणम् ॥१५ ॥

रूपस्य स्वभावानुक्रमेण रूपाणि भवन्ति । तेषां तत्तद्गुणाः प्रभवन्ति कामचारीणां हृदये इति ।कामो[13] जनानां ध्रुवावृत्तिरिति ।

अङ्गानि अर्धाकले[14] सुषमं[15] ध्येयानि ॥१६ ॥

अर्चायां श्रेष्ठं पूर्णाकलं वर्त्तुलाङ्गं, न श्रेष्ठमितिभित्ये-

हर्सावधि उभयदिशि चोर्ध्वे न वर्धयेत् ॥१७ ॥

उष्णीषमेखलादि अपवृजिनेन रेखाकारे उत्थिते दर्शयन्, भेदनकाले रूपशिलोपरि शङ्खद्रावं सिञ्चयन्, अपवेनात् संरक्षयेदिति क्रमः ।

रक्षाविधानेन विघ्नघातयः ॥१८ ॥

रक्षाविधानेन विघ्ना विनश्यन्ति ।खोदनारम्भे 'ॐ होजा होजा शतकेशि वृष मे संरक्षय' इति ब्रूयात् स्थापकः ।अविघ्नेन कररेखादि गात्रलक्षणानि दृषदि दैवभावेन[c] कर्तव्यम् । तद्गुणात् सिद्धिं प्राप्नुवन्ति काम्येन वा, अकाम्येन सायुज्यं प्रददाति एतदर्थं भेदनकारुकर्म श्रेष्ठम् ।

---

[12]ध्यानानुसृतं यद्रूपं तद्रूपो ध्यानविग्रहः, शिल्परत्नकोशे ४५५ तमे श्लोके ।
[13]कामस्तदग्रे समवर्त्तताधि मनसो रेतः प्रथमं यदासीत् ।इति नासदीये ।
[14]शिलाया अपृथक् संलग्नरूपेण सर्वाङ्गं यत्र सुषमं तदर्धाकलम् ।
[15]सदा यौवनसम्पन्नं पेशिग्रन्थिविवर्जितम् ।दैवलक्षणसंयुक्तं रूपं सुषममुच्यते ।शिल्पागमे ।

---

[a]अनुक्रमे, घ ।
[b]उपलभन्ते इति युक्तम्, घ ।
[c]वृषिते इत्यधिकपाठः ङ ।

रेखान्वितमङ्गपातनं भेदने मुख्यम् ।

रेखाक्रमेण भेदनं चतुर्धा ज्ञेयम् ॥ १९ ॥

न्यासविधानेन तदेकाश्रयि, युगलाश्रयि, खण्डाश्रयि, स्पर्शीतेति । यदा पूर्णरेखायां रूपाङ्गं निपतति तदेकाश्रयि । यदा रूपस्य प्रभवाङ्गं सम्मुखाङ्गं वा भिन्नरेखामाश्रयति तद् युगलाश्रयि । यदा तत् पृथगङ्गं भिन्नरेखायां वा मूलरेखायां केवलमङ्गाङ्गं निपतति, अध ऊर्ध्वे च तत् खण्डाश्रयि । यदाऽङ्गांशः केवलं किञ्चिद् रेखाचुम्बितस्तत् स्पर्शिता हीनम्[16]। नेम्यवलम्बिताङ्गं कदा श्रेष्ठं भवति ।

नेम्योत्तरे रूपाङ्गं न वर्धयेत् ॥ २० ॥

इति पातनानुशासनम् । भेदनकालेऽवाग् भवेत् । गाथाकथाः सततं स्मरेत् । रूपप्रारम्भे खनित्राणि प्रोक्षयेत् प्रोक्षणमन्त्रेण । तत्प्रभावेन दोषा अरिष्टा विनश्यन्ति ।

खनित्रचालनविधिर्ध्येयविशेषः ॥ २१ ॥

वामहस्ते जरठेन खनित्रमवरोधयेत् । कनिष्ठिकायां रोधयेत् खनित्रम् । इति कृत्यम् । दक्षिणकरे कुट्टम्भकं धारयेत् भेदनार्थं दैवलक्षणानि रूपकर्मणि वेदयन्ते । इति भेदनविधिव्याख्यानम् ।

वाक्कायमनोमार्गेण चर्चाक्षेण मुनिश्रोतॄणामुपनिधानेन शैलभेदनभ्रस्कक्रम इति तृतीयप्रपाठकः ।

---

[16]तथा अङ्गानि केवलं रेखाचुम्बित अङ्गस्य तद्रेखा अवलम्बने तद् स्पर्शीतमिति । ङ ।

चतुर्थः प्रपाठकः

अङ्गप्रयोगः

अथ पिप्पलादः प्रहृष्टो होवाच – शिल्पजिज्ञासुत्रय, वाग्रूपाणि च तस्याङ्गज्ञानमाहुः[a]। पुरा ब्रह्मैकं सत्यमस्ति । तज्ज्ञानेन हृदयाकाशे तद् ब्रह्मैव ज्योतिः तस्य ज्ञानविज्ञानं विज्ञाय एवं यत्किञ्च वाचा तद्रूपेण विज्ञानवाचा प्रपन्नेनाचरन्ति । य एवं वेद । यत्र भावना शून्या तन्निर्गुणं गुणत्वभावनया सगुणं भवति । सगुणान् मनः स्थूलं भवति ।

प्रतीतात् प्रतीकः[b] ॥ १ ॥

प्रतीत-प्रतीक-प्रतिमा-क्रमेण त्रीणि मुख्यानि । यदा ज्योतिर्मण्डलानुभासे ब्रह्म उपलभ्यते तत् प्रतीतम्। यथा विज्ञानमयपुरुषः । यच्चक्षुषा न पश्यति येन चक्षूंषि पश्यन्तीति । यदुपमोपमेयक्रमेण अनुभवभावान् प्रदर्शयति तत् प्रतीकम् । "अङ्गुष्ठमात्रः पुरुष" इत्यादि-वाक्येन । या सपर्यायामानन्दं प्रददाति सा प्रतिमेति ।

अव्यक्त-व्यक्त-प्रकट-क्रमेण निर्गुण-सूक्ष्म-स्थूल भावेन जनानां दैवभावाहरणं कुर्वन्ती सा देवयजनविद्या। शतपथे छान्दोग्ये चोक्तः-एष क्रमः, एषा देवयजनविद्या। आत्मानन्देन यजनोपायेन त्रयस्त्रिंशद् देवताः तार्क्ष्ये ब्राह्मणे उक्ताः।

यथा अङ्गुष्ठमात्रपुरुषस्य भावः प्रभवति विकल्पेन अङ्गुष्ठमिति ज्योतिर्मात्रम्[1]। स यूपस्य दण्ड इव ।

रूपादङ्गानि सञ्जायन्ते ॥ २ ॥

तद्भावाद्रूपं रूपं प्रतिरूपं जायते । यथा पुरुषे । इति ज्ञानं ज्यायम्; यत्रान्यैर्द्विधा भवति तदितरज्ञानं निश्चितं भवति । एतदेव सत्यम् । तदितर इतरं जिघ्रति । तदितर इतरं पश्यति । तदितर इतरं श्रुणोति । तदितर इतरमभिवदति । तदितर इतरं मनुते । तदितर इतरं जानाति । यत्र इतराभावं यः पश्यति तत् केन कं विजानीयादिति[c] याज्ञवल्केन उक्तम् । य एवं वेद ।

अतो द्विधा ब्रह्म रूपवद् भवति ॥ ३ ॥

---

[1]ज्योतिः प्रतीकभावनाङ्गुष्ठम् ।

---

[a]आश्रु, ग, घ ।

[b]इत्यधिकपाठः, क ।

[c]एकेन एक विजानीयात्, ग । केन एक, क, ख । ज्ञातारं अपरे केन विजानीयादिति, ख, ङ ।

स्थापकाः सपर्यार्थं शैले रूपाणि चरन्ति[2] ।

रूपार्थं कोष्ठका मुख्याः ॥ ४ ॥

यथा शुल्वे तथा च शिल्पे । विना कोष्ठकं रूपस्य भावः सम्यङ् न भवति । सपर्यायां क्षुण्णता जायत इति । ऊर्ध्वग-पार्श्वग क्रमेण चूर्णेन रेखाविभाजनमिति कोष्ठविद्या ग्राभार्थम् ।

वर्गीकरणं मुख्यकृत्यम् ॥ ५ ॥

यज्ञार्थमिदं शुल्वं कारुकर्मार्थं शिल्पमिति ज्ञेयम् । इति सुलभक्रिया । एवं वेदे । रज्ज्वास्तावत् प्रसारणे वर्गीकरणमिति तस्य भावः । यावत् प्रमाणं क्षेत्रशैलं, तत्र रेखा अविकृतं प्रकुर्वन्ति मानदण्डैः शिल्पकाराः । तेन बृहद्वर्गा बहुधा भवन्ति क्षीणाकृतौ । एकः द्वौ द्वौ चत्वारः । चत्वारो द्विगुणितेन अष्टौ । एवं क्रमेण बहुधा कोष्ठका भवन्ति गुणवर्धनेनेति । यथा शुल्वविभाजने युग्मम् अयुग्मं यज्ञमेखलादीनर्धप्रमाणेन चिकीर्षाक्रमेण वर्द्धयन्ति तथा स्थापकाः ।

कोष्ठकान्तराले रूपस्यावयवो ध्येयः ॥ ६ ॥

स्थापकाः परिमिताङ्गावयवादि मानन्ति [मीयन्ते] । अयं तालनिर्यासो चिकीर्षाक्रमेण ।

परिमिताङ्गहाराद्[a] भावलक्षणानि जायन्ते ॥ ७ ॥

अपरिमिताङ्गानां तेषां भाववैलक्षण्यं भवति, इति दोषः । कुण्डस्य कोष्ठके व्यतिक्रान्ते होतारो मूका भवन्ति, तथा च मूर्त्याम् ।

कोष्ठके[b] व्यतिक्रान्ते रूपमवद्यं[c] भवति ॥ ८ ॥

स्थापकाः पैशाचत्वं लभन्ते[d] । अथ शुल्वविद्याशिल्पविद्ययोः को भेदः ? किं तस्य सन्धानमुपलभन्ते, किं पार्थक्यमिति वदन्तु धर्मपुरुषाः पिप्पलादाः ।

शुल्वं यज्ञस्य साधनं शिल्पं रूपस्य साधनम् ॥ ९ ॥

इति भेदः । शुल्वकारा दण्डरज्जुसहितं कुण्डस्थण्डिल-शाला-योनि-मेखला-यूपादि निर्णयन्ति ।

---

[2]तत्त्वज्ञानेन चित्तस्य विक्रियाऽभावावेशेन मनसः विक्रिया इति । तत्त्वबोधात् चित्तं स्थिरं भवति, भावप्रचोदने मनः तत्त्वबोधे प्रविलीयते, विसर्ग इव द्वयोः एका गतिः, अतो द्विधा एकत्वमिति परिणामः ।

---

[a]अङ्गरागात्, क ।
[b]रूपकोष्ठके, घ । कोष्ठमध्ये, ग ।
[c]अविद्य, क, ग ।
[d]शिल्पकाश्यपादि, ख अधिकपाठः ।

शिल्पकाराणां रूपशैले रूपशालादि ध्येयम् ॥ १० ॥

इति तेषां पार्थक्यं न मर्मणि भेदो जायते ।

यूपाद् रूपं रूपाद्[a] यूप इति स्वभावः ॥ ११ ॥

आहुः श्रोतारः केन रूपेण शुल्वकाराः कारुरीत्या यूपं निर्धारयन्ति यथा पूर्ववेदाचारेण ।

यूपस्य मानं ध्येयम् ॥ १२ ॥

शृणुत वास्तुकाराः । यजमानस्य त्रिमुष्टिकमानेन रेखामानय । तद्दैर्घ्येण सह द्विह्रस्वरेखया[b] वामगं त्रिहुतैकं चर, इति त्रिहुतीकरणम् । तत ऊर्ध्वे वामे च संकीर्णत्रिहुतं सृजयन्[c] लम्बमानेन चतुरस्रैकम् आचर, इति वर्गीकरणम् । तद् वर्गद्विखण्डेन विभाजितक्षीणैकभागो यूपस्योत्थानं ज्ञेयम् ।

षड्भागस्य[d] प्रयोगो ध्येयः ॥ १३ ॥

तत्र पार्श्वक्षेत्रे षड्पक्षेत्रलाभार्थमिदं विभाजनम्[3] । तद्षड्भागेभ्यो निम्नैकभाग पार्थिवाङ्गं प्रोत्थनार्थं, भूमिर्देवता । तदुत्तराद्विभागोऽधोऽङ्गं मेखलाबन्धनानन्तरं[e] न्यासार्थं[f] स मैथुनकाण्डः, रुद्रो देवता । तदुत्तरे द्वौ भागावुत्तमाङ्गं प्राणाऽऽवाहनार्थं प्रजापतिर्देवता । तदुत्तरैकभागस्तुङ्गाङ्गं ध्वजरोपणार्थं सविता देवता । एवं क्रमेण[g]–

पुरुषस्य रूपे[h]ऽङ्गचत्वारोऽष्टाङ्गक्रमेणोपजायन्ते ॥ १४ ॥

पार्थिवाङ्गं, कर्माङ्गं, अधोऽङ्गं, प्रजननाङ्गं, उत्तमाङ्गं, प्राणाङ्गं, तुङ्गाङ्गं, ज्योतिरङ्गं, क्रमेण पुरुषाकलेऽष्टाङ्गपुरुषस्य रूपम् ।

शिल्पकाश्यपधीराः पप्रच्छुः । प्रियधा किं रूपस्य तालम्, कस्तस्य भावो लक्षणञ्च सम्बन्धमिति । तदवगमाय उपज्ञाक्रमेण पिप्पलादो वव्रे ।

---

[3]यूपस्य ध्वजमानार्थं त्रिवृतकरणध्येयं मध्यनिर्धारणार्थं च निम्नोर्ध्वे लघुभागस्य मानसम्प्राप्त्यर्थमिदं मानमिति भावः ।

---

[a]रूपभावात्, ख ।
[b]द्विसमरेखेन, ख; द्विहर्षरेखया, ग ।
[c]सृजनेन, ख, ग ।
[d]षड्क्षेत्र, ख ।
[e]बन्धनार्थम्, ख ।
[f]न्यासक्षेत्रम्, ख ।
[g]मानुषाकृति, ग ।
[h]मानुष्यस्वरूप तथा, ङ ।

पालाशदण्डरज्जुसंयोगे[a] रेखामानय ॥ १५ ॥

शैले कोष्ठकानामुत्थितक्रमेण[b] रेखामाचरेत् । पयसा शोणशैलचूर्णसंयोगेन धीराः कोष्ठकान् प्रकुर्वन्ति । कोष्ठमध्ये पादाच्छिरोऽवधि रूपमुपलब्धव्यमिति ।

निम्नादूर्ध्वावधि सदा रेखादीनाचर ॥ १६ ॥

सा हि उत्थितक्रिया । स रुद्रपतिः पुरुष एवं वेदे ।

पुरुषस्तम्भ इव स्तम्भो वै यज्ञस्य रूपम् ॥ १७ ॥

दशयज्ञस्याधारः[4] स[5] वृषस्तम्भः पितृयज्ञार्थम्, रुद्रप्रीतये[c]। प्रजापतिरेव वास्तोष्पतिः स हि प्राणजागृतिरिति[d]।

यथा स्तम्भस्य दशाङ्गं तथा पुरुषस्य दशयज्ञप्रज्ञाश्च ॥ १८ ॥

निम्ने पादः, दर्भमेखला रज्जुन्यायेन निर्मिता । तदुत्तरे दण्डवत् पिप्पले उदुम्बरे वा तत्र मेखला वलयाकृतिः । तदुत्तरे स्तम्भस्य दण्डविलं[e] विष्णुर्देवता, तदुत्तरे स्तम्भस्य कटिरविशदशरावाकृतिः । तत्सम्मुखे मृगपादो यथा पङ्क्ते तथा नाभिः श्रुवस्य गर्भाकृतिः । तदुत्तरे सौम्यस्तम्भाकृतिः, अम्बालिका देवता । तदुत्तरे चतुरस्रकूटशाला, आवास इव स्तम्भस्य हृदयम् । तच्छालायाः रुद्रो देवता । शतकेशी शतशीर्षा वृषः[6], स ज्योतिः प्रणवरूपस्तारकः, तदुत्तरे स्तम्भस्य कण्ठः स शरावाकृतिः ।

---

[4]विंशो हि पुरुषो दश द्वादशाङ्गुल्यो दश यो ह्या इति शतपथे उक्तम् ।

दशेन्द्रियस्याधारः पुरुष इत्यर्थः । यथा पुरुषे दशाङ्गं तथा पिप्पलादीयपितृमेधेन स्तम्भाकृतियूपे दशाङ्गं कल्पयन्ति ऋषयः ।

[5]अष्टारयूपदेवता प्रतिष्ठायां वास्तुकर्मणि प्रयोजनं भवति । षोडशार यूप विष्णुमहायज्ञे प्रयोजनं भवति । वृषस्तम्भो मृताहे पितृयज्ञे वृषोत्सर्गे प्रयोजनमिथुनस्तम्भस्य प्रचलनं नास्ति । (उत्कलभाषायाम्) प्रथम द्वितीय पथररे करिब वृषस्तम्भं वट विल्व उदुम्बररे करिब ।

[6]रुद्र वृषरूपेण शुक्लयजुर्वेदे उक्तं 'च धर्मवृषभमिति "वृष वै धर्मः" पैप्पलादसंहितायां १ खण्डे "हिरण्यशृङ्गो वृषभो य समुद्रादुदाचरत्" । स वृष हि इन्द्र सखा शतवालो" इति अथर्ववेदे ३ उक्तम् । तद्वृष पितृरूपेण पितृयूपस्यावासे उपासयन्ति, पितृणां रुद्र, इति तस्य भावः ।

---

[a]प्रयोगे, ग ।

[b]०मुतिष्ठक्रमेण, ख ।

[c]मूर्तये, क ।

[d]स हि प्राणः जागृहीति, ग ।

[e]विलं, क । यूपस्य नाभिः, घ ।

स्वाहा देवता । तदुत्तरे स्तम्भस्य मूर्द्धमण्डलम्, सविता देवता, एवं क्रमेण दशयज्ञानुरूपं दशाङ्गस्तम्भं होतारः समुपदिशन्ति ।

स्थापकाचार्या स्तम्भाद्रूपं बोधयन्ति ॥ १९ ॥

पुरुषसमरीत्या दशाङ्गमेतदुच्चैः समदशकोष्ठके, आचरन्ति पुरुषाकलं यदेतद् वेदे ।

स्तम्भः कामचारिण[a]स्त्रिधामानयन्ति ॥ २० ॥

याज्ञिका यज्ञे विङ्वङ्गं प्रोथयन्ति ऐशान्ये पितृमेधे ।

दैवयज्ञार्थं यूपः ॥ २१ ॥

तथा हि अङ्गे शुल्वकारा मूर्द्धानं दण्डं च मानयन्ति । दण्डो भद्रो वा, अष्टांशो विश्वांशो वा यथाकाम्य इति, पार्थिवाः पशुमेधेन अरिमर्दनं कुर्वन्ति कृत्स्न[b]सिद्धिलाभार्थमाहुतयन्ति ।

तदा पितृमेधार्थं वृषस्तम्भं मिथुनस्तम्भं कामचारा होमे रोपयन्ति ॥ २२ ॥

प्रशस्तदण्डशिलायामूर्ध्वे शुकरमैथुनरूपम्, एतत्प्रयोगेण अरिः स्थाणुर्भवति स्तम्भ इव । पार्थिवाः पशुमेधिनः भोग्यप्रयोगमाचरन्ति । एवं वेदे प्रयोगे च, यत्किञ्चविजिज्ञास्यो यूपः, तद्रूपं केनैतत् पुरुषस्योद्भवं भवति रूपे । पिप्पलाद होवाच आथर्वणाङ्गिरस केन कोष्ठके पुरुषश्चाक्षुषो भवति ।

तद्बोधे[c] मानुषा रूपज्ञा भवन्ति ॥ २३ ॥

तं ह वक्ष्यामीति भगवान् पिप्पलादः सुप्रसन्नः तस्मै सौम्यपिप्पलाद होवाच ।

आहुः[d] शिल्पाचार्यास्तदेतत्सत्यम् । यथाऽऽदित्य उदयन् प्राच्या दिशः प्राणं सञ्चारयति तथा–

पुरुषस्य रूपाकले कोष्ठकस्याधो भावरूपं प्रसरति ॥ २४ ॥

[a]कामकामिनः, ख, घ ।
[b]कृच्छ्र, क ।
[c]तत्वबोधे, ख ।
[d]आसु, क ।

सा हि स्तम्भस्य दशाङ्गोदितक्रिया[a]। यथा दशयज्ञे दशकर्मणि कर्मोन्मेषो भवति[7]। यथा हि पुरुषः कर्ता, बोधा, रसयिता, मन्ता, स्रष्टा, श्रोता, द्रष्टा, ज्ञाता च विज्ञानात्मा ब्रह्म भवति तथा दशाङ्गे मनुष्या दशकर्माचरन्ति। एतद्भावे दशकोष्ठके पुरुषश्चाक्षुषो भवति। पादः, पादपर्वतः, दण्डः, दण्डगुल्फः, एतान्यङ्गान्यधोऽङ्गानीति। जानुकटिपर्वतान्तद्वयं मध्याङ्गमिति। उदरहृदयद्वयमुत्तमाङ्गमिति। कण्ठमूर्धद्वयं तुङ्गाङ्गमिति, एवं कल्पयन्ति रूपकाराः। इति पुरुषस्य दशाङ्गम्। पुरुषो दशाङ्गुलमिति भावः।

पूर्वं वेदेन उक्तम्। स हि ब्रह्मणो विकल्परूपेण प्रत्यक्षं भवति[b]। [8]

दशाङ्गरूपे रूपे इति तस्य भावः समानः ॥ २५ ॥

एतदर्थं कोष्ठकान् कल्पयन्ति[c] रूपकाराः।

ब्रह्मकीलाधारः, ब्रह्मकीलेन[9] सह क्षेत्रं विभाजय ॥ २६ ॥

ब्रह्मकीलमध्यगरेखया द्वैतांशे ब्रह्मकीलेन सह क्षेत्रं विभाजयन्ति। यथा धरायां मेरुकीलं, पशौ पृष्ठास्थि, वृक्षे सुषीरं, जीवे जीवात्मा[d], तथा रेखा हि सत्यम्। रेखा रूपस्य कारणम्। ततो रेखायां दशकोष्ठकान् विभाजय उत्तिष्ठक्रमेण, येन समोपक्षेत्राणि लभेरन्।

कति कति खण्डितानि भवन्ति। न्यूनातिरिक्तार्थं कारुज्ञा आद्यत्रिषण्णवक्षेत्राणि विभाजयन्ति। द्वौ द्वाविति क्रमेण दशकोष्ठकेषु चत्वारः खण्डिताः षडखण्डिताश्च। एवं दशकोष्ठका भुवनसंख्यका भवन्ति। यथा पिण्डे ब्रह्माण्डं कल्पयन्ति ऋषयः। यथाऽथर्ववेदिनां श्राद्धे[10] पितृयज्ञे पिण्डार्थं वज्रेण मण्डलमाचरन्ति।

वैश्वदेवे तथा दशकोष्ठकानाचरन्ति[11]। एवं क्रमेण पादः तदुत्तरे पादपर्वतेऽर्धांशः तदुत्तरे एकांशदण्डाः। तदुत्तरे गुल्फोऽर्धखण्डितांशः।

---

[7]पञ्च प्रयाजाः दैवपुंजने, आज्यभागः, प्रधानयागः, स्विष्टकृत्, प्राशित्रावदानम्, इड़ावदानम्, भागप्राशनम्, अन्वाहार्य-दक्षिणा, अनुयाजत्रयम्, ब्युहनम्, सूक्तवाक्, शंयुवाक्, पत्नीसंयाज इति दशकर्मभेदे दशयज्ञाङ्गसंयोगशीर्षरूपेण विष्णुक्रमः तस्य दशाङ्गस्य भावः।

[8]प्रत्यक्षदर्शनं सम्भवति।

[9]ब्रह्मकील इति मध्यरेखा, ग।

[10]अष्टकाश्राद्धे इन्द्रः विश्वेदेवाः प्रजापतिः, सप्तपुरुषार्थः पिप्पलादीयब्राह्मणाः।

[11]यथा मनुष्यगर्भान्तरे भ्रूणे कृमि-मज्जा-अस्थि-मांस-मेद-स्नायु-रक्त-केशात्मक-शिराच्छन्दे-चर्मादि दशास्तरणयुक्तं दशकोष्ठकं कल्पयन्ति शिशुवेदोपनिषदि आथर्वणीयाः (घ, ङ)।

---

[a]दशाङ्गे उदितक्रिया, ग।

[b]प्रकटो भवति, ग।

[c]एतद् दशकोष्ठमाचरन्ति, ख।

[d]जीवसत्ता, ग।

तदुत्तरे जानुद्व्यर्धांशसंयोगः । तदुत्तरे कटिरर्धांशखण्डितांशः । तदुत्तरे द्व्यर्धसंयोगे सम्मुखे मृणालमूलाकृतिर्विलाकारं नाभिः । तदुत्तरे उदरमेकार्धसंयोगे पीनाङ्गमिति । तदुत्तरेऽष्टावधि हृदयम् । तदुत्तरे कण्ठः अर्धखण्डितांशे ।

तदुत्तर एकार्धसंयोगे मूर्धेत्युत्तमाङ्गम् । इदं दशकोष्ठकेषु रूपं चाक्षुषं भवति ।

अङ्गादङ्गं सञ्जायते ॥ २७ ॥

इयं हि रचना । स हि न्यासः । अध ऊर्ध्वावधि गच्छन्ति दिव्यतां[a] क्रमेणोत्थितकरपादादयः प्रविधाङ्गानि ।

रेखासंयोगे तत्क्षेत्रेऽङ्गानि सौभगानि भवन्ति[12] ॥ २८ ॥

अग्निरेखायामुत्थिताङ्गानि । अप्पार्श्वगरेखायां स्थिराङ्गानि । मारुतरेखायां वेगप्रदर्शनाङ्गानि । एतन्निपातनेन रूपाणि मन आकर्षयन्ति । तदुत्तरम्–

क्षेत्रनेमिं रोधयेदिति[b] ॥ २९ ॥

रोधनरेखाचतसृणां मध्ये कोष्ठकानाचरन्ति स्थापकाः । एवं क्रमेण शिल्पकाश्यपाः रूपार्थं खिलपञ्जरं ध्येयमिति व्याख्यानं वास्तूद्गीथत्रयप्रबोधनार्थं भगवान् पिप्पलादो वव्रे ।

इति वाङ्कायमनोमार्गेण पिप्पलादीयवास्तुसूत्रे सम्प्रदानचर्चाक्षेण मुनिश्रोतारमुपनिधानेन अङ्गोत्तिष्ठादिमानबोधनमिति चतुर्थप्रपाठकः ।

---

[12] यथा शतपथे स्वर्णपुरुषरूपेण प्रजापतिरूपं कल्पयन्ति होतारः षष्ठाध्याये उक्तम् ।

---

[a] दिवं, क । दिव्यभावं, ख ।

[b] क्षेत्रनेमिरोधनार्थमिति पातनसूत्रचत्वारं ज्यायमिति । ख, ग ।

पञ्चमः प्रपाठकः

रूपभावनाबोधः

अथ हैनमाथर्वणाङ्गिरसशिल्पकाश्यपः पप्रच्छ यदि यज्ञार्थं शुल्वं[1] शिल्पार्थं शिल्पसूत्रञ्च रूपकर्मणि, इत्थं तदिदं ब्रूहीति[a]। पिप्पलादो होवाच। शिल्पमधीयानाः शिल्पोद्गातारः, शृणुत ।

भावस्यारोपणं रूपकर्मणि विधेयम् ॥ १ ॥

यज्ञशालास्थण्डिलार्थं शुल्वज्ञानं श्रेष्ठम् । तत्र श्रोणि[2] साधनमंशादि-पातनमिष्टकान्यासप्रयोगो भवतीति ध्येयम् । येन रूपेण[b]यथा रूपकर्मणि त्रिकोणिसाधनं कर्णाकर्षणं कर्णिकाकरणं लब्धक्षेत्रे मुख्यम् । एतदर्थं भाववोधनस्य प्रयोजनं भवति । शृणु, तस्य को भावः, कस्तेषां रूपस्य सन्धाः । देहः कर्माधार इति वदन्ति याज्ञिकाः ।

कर्म भावस्य प्रदायकम् ॥ २ ॥

भावं प्रददातीति ।

भावस्याऽऽधारो रसः ॥ ३ ॥

स रसः कर्मणश्चोदनेति देहे प्रस्कन्दयति वाङ्मनश्चक्षुः श्रोत्रकरपादादीनाम् उदयक्रमेण, देहलक्षणं भवति । भावविधानेन देहस्य रसाः प्रसरन्ति । रसात्-

मनसि वृत्तिर्बहुधा प्रजायते । तदा भिन्नभिन्नरसाद्रूपं नैकं भवति ॥ ४ ॥

नवधा रसः[c] ॥ ५ ॥

नवधा रसार्थं रेखापार्थक्यं जायते ।

[1]महर्षिकात्यायनस्य शुल्वं भगवतः पिप्पलादस्य शिल्पसूत्रमिति ।
[2]रेखाकृतिरिष्टकान्यास इति श्रोणिः । ज्योतिष्टोमे महावेधाः, श्रोणिरित्यादि ।

[a]This sentence follows after the Sūtra 1 in MSS क, ग.
[b]न रूपेण, ग ।
[c]Sūtra om. in ग ।

प्रथमरसः शृङ्गारः ॥ ६ ॥

यथा मोहात् पुरुषस्य नारीं प्रति मैथुनेच्छा प्रभवति तद् जीवमात्रस्य सत्यम् ।[a] यत्र मुदभावो विभाति सा शृङ्गारमूर्तिः[b] भवति । तथा द्वौ तनू देवदेव्योश्च क्रीडाङ्गगठनम् ।[c] युगलशरीरे क्रीडोपायेति, अक्षक्रीडादि मुदितविग्रहार्थम् ।

शृङ्गाररूपार्थमब्रेखा ग्राह्याः ॥ ७ ॥

प्रसन्नाननमिति तेषां लक्षणम् । कामनिवृत्तौ मन उल्लसितं भवति । हास्यं प्रददाति ।

स हासो[d] द्वितीयरसः ॥ ८ ॥

हास्यभावप्रदायकविग्रहा जनानां हृदये सुखं सञ्चारयन्ति । कारुप्रयोगे तेषामधर उन्मुक्तः, नेत्रं सौम्यमिति तेषां लक्षणम् ।

मुखलक्षणाद् रसं जानन्ति सर्वे ईक्षणेन ॥ ९ ॥

मनुष्यः मनोसुखार्थमुपासते । जनानां जले च रूपे उभय समानः ।[e] यदा दुःखं तदा सुखमिति सत्यं, रात्रिन्दिवमिव । सुखस्य परिणामो विषादः, विषादात् सर्वेन्द्रियाणि शिथिलानि भवन्ति ।

स तृतीयः करुणरस भाव इति ॥ १० ॥

नयनमर्धमुक्तं चेति तेषां लक्षणम् । करुणान् मनो निश्चेष्टं भवति । सोऽवसाद इति । अवसादात् पुनः विषादः सञ्जायते । ततः क्रोधो जायते ।

रौद्रः चतुर्थो रसः ॥ ११ ॥

स रौद्रभावः रूपे उग्र वदन्ति शिल्पकाराः ।[f] मुखं प्रशस्तं नेत्राणि स्फारितानि, हस्ते योधायुधमिति तेषां लक्षणम् ।

तिर्यग् रेखायां रूपाङ्गभावः प्रकटो भवति ॥ १२ ॥

इति विशेषः । रौद्रभावात् तनुषि विकारो जायते ।

---

[a] This sentence follows Sūtra 4 in क, ख and ग.

[b] ०रूप, ख, ङ ।

[c] Additional sentence in ख.

[d] हास्य, घ ।

[e] Two additional sentences in घ, ङ.

[f] Sentence om. in क.

स वीरभावः[a] पञ्चमः ॥ १३ ॥

तेष्वसमानि कायमुखनेत्राणीति लक्षणम् । कौणपलक्षणान्विता दृता पादरेखा समसरला देवराक्षसयोर्मध्ये घातकर्मैव । तेषां मुखे वैरभावस्तल्लक्षणं भवति भयङ्करतूर्वयाण इव ।

वैरभावे उत्कटे भयङ्करो[3] भवति । स वैलक्षणः षष्ठरसः ॥ १४ ॥

उभयपार्श्वे रूपस्याङ्गवैषम्यं ध्येयम् । ये वर्धितास्ते बीभत्सा ग्लानियुक्ताः ।

कुरूपाः क्षिप्ताङ्गाः मारुतरेखायामिति स सप्तमः ॥ १५ ॥

कामे निवृत्ते दैवभाव उपजायत इति शेषोपायः । अवगत्या विरतो भवतीति ।

शान्तभावः, सोऽष्टमो रसः ॥ १६ ॥

एवं जीवस्याष्टविकाररूपेणाष्टभावाः सम्पद्यन्ते[4] ।

भावानुगतरूपाणि चतुर्धा मुख्यानि ॥ १७ ॥

येषां शान्तास्ते सर्वेऽग्निरेखाश्रयिणः। येषां करुणास्ते सर्वेऽब्रेखा-श्रयिणः । आलस्यमूर्तिषु सर्वेऽबाश्रयिणः । येषां सर्वाङ्गानि कर्णरेखाश्रयाणि ते रौद्राः । रौद्रा मिश्रा वैरा मारुतरेखाया[b] आधारः । इहानुशासनं ध्येयम् ।

अथ शिल्पकाश्यपो होवाच । किमर्थं भावप्रबोधनार्थं रूपाणि ? कस्तस्य हेतुः ? भेदाद् दैवज्ञानमुपजायतेऽन्यच्च – भगवन्तः सत्यद्रष्टारो भावबोधार्थं ब्रुवन्तु ।

पिप्पलादो होवाच

लोके भावबोधस्य हेतुर्मनः ॥ १८ ॥

तद्भेदे भेद उपजायते देवयोन्यः, पितरः, सोमः, आशापालाः, विश्वेदेवाः, राक्षसाः, हि (ड़)ङ्गादयः । सर्वस्य वृत्तिरस्ति । सर्वे पृथक् कति मित्राणि कत्यरयः । अरिभावस्तेषां सन्धाः । होतारो देवान् यजन्ति ।

---

[3] अत्र भयङ्करे अद्भुतभावो विलीयते । शिल्पे अद्भुतभावः ऊहनीयः ।

[4] यद् प्रदर्शयन्ति तनुषि तद्भावः यदीक्षणेन हृदये सञ्चारयन्ति स रसः ।

---

[a] रसः, ग ।

[b] मारुतरेखाश्रयिण इति भवितुं युक्तम् ।

पिशाचमोक्षणार्थं तर्दादि[5] विमोचनार्थं यज्ञमाचरन्ति । एषा जैवसन्धा । यज्ञात् पिशाचा विनश्यन्ति । अरिसाधनार्थं ब्राह्मणाः पर्णमणिं धारयन्ति कवचे । ब्राह्मणा यज्ञबलेन, क्षत्रिया आयुधबलेन, वैश्या भूमिरसज्ञानेन, शूद्राः परिचर्यया दीप्ता[a] भवन्तीति वर्णभेदे क्रियाः । मोक्षार्थं यथा ब्राह्मणा यज्ञमाचरन्ति तथा त्रयो वर्णा रूपसपर्यायां मोक्षं लभन्ते । भावान्मुक्ता भवन्ति । एवमारोपणे रूपं ध्येयम् । एतदर्थं रूपध्याने[b] न बाधः ।

मनुष्याणां वृत्तिर्मुख्येति ॥ १९ ॥

वृत्तेर्निष्कल-सकल-भावा उपजायन्त इति मार्गः क्रियायाः परिणाम इति । तदर्थं शिल्पज्ञानाद्रूपं ध्यायन्ति, स्थापका ब्राह्मणा भवन्ति ।

सङ्कल्पाद् विकल्पः ॥ २० ॥

इति विशेषः । यथा सङ्कल्पाद् विकल्पः तथा भोगेच्छान्ते अरिमर्दनेच्छोपजायते । मर्दनान्तो भोगः । एतदिन्द्रियचक्रम् । विकल्पभावात्[c] श्रद्धा, श्रद्धायाः सत्ताभावः[d], सत्ताभावाद् भावयजनं प्रसरति । तद्भावेन रूपं रूपं प्रतिरूपाणि जायन्ते ।

एष भुवनकोषो[e] देहानुभूत्याः क्रमः ॥ २१ ॥

शृणु तत्क्रमं शिल्पश्रोतारः । ततः श्रोतारः पप्रच्छुः – भगवन् को भुवनकोषः? किं तत्स्वरूपम्? कस्तस्य क्रमभेदः? वदतु[f] धर्मपुरुष-पिप्पलादमहामतिः शिल्पकाश्यपाः पृच्छन्तीति । देहभुवनकोषस्य लक्षणं देहानुभूतिमिति ।

अथ भगवान् पिप्पलादः प्रवचनेन वव्रे । शिल्पकाराः सर्वकर्मणि शतकेशिवृषं प्रार्थयन्ते–

ॐ रुद्रशतकेशाय रुद्र एतद् नाशय भयं
रुद्र शतशीर्ष शमय भयं
वृषरूपाय शतकेशाय च धर्मरूपाय ते नमः ।

---

[5]तर्दः (खर्वत) – अथर्व० ६.५०.१ उक्तः, अन्नहानिकरः पतङ्गविशेषः ।

---

[a]तृप्ता, ग ।
[b]सपर्यायां, घ ।
[c]०ज्ञानात्, ख ।
[d]समभावः, ख ।
[e]एष भुवनस्य भावः, ग ।
[f]सर्वज्ञ, ङ ।

इति ब्रुवाणान्तरं पिप्पलाद उवाच । शृणुत[a], भुवना[6]स्तरणस्य सन्धाः। होतारो वैश्वानरे प्रजापत्यादिदेवान् यया वाचाऽऽजुह्वति स मन्त्रः[7] । स ध्वनिः, ध्वनेर्ब्राह्मणाऽऽत्मज्ञा भवन्ति, ते ध्वनेर्देवलक्षणानि कल्पयन्ति, ऋषीणां तल्लक्षणम्[8], तल्लक्षणं हि ऋतम्, तल्लक्षणाद्रूपं वृणुते मनुष्यलोके ।

यज्ञाद् ध्वनिः, ध्वनेर्लक्षणं, लक्षणाद्रूपं, रूपाद् भावः, भावाद् गुणः, गुणात् क्रिया, क्रियाया आचारः, आचारादुपायः, उपायाच्चेष्टा, चेष्टाया मार्गः, मार्गाद्रूपाणि, रूपात् प्रतिरूपाणि[9], रूपविद्याबोधाद् रूपक्रिया, एष सपर्याक्रमः वेदस्यायने भुवनकोषः ।

अरूपाद्रूपं तस्य फलम् ॥ २२ ॥

आदित्यो ह वै ब्रह्म, तदर्थं यज्ञः, दिशः पृथिव्याः सम्बन्ध इति मूलम्, आदित्यो ह वै ब्रह्मेति तस्य ध्वनिः । ध्वनेर्लक्षणं सूर्यस्य रश्मेर्या यत्र देवता पतिरेक आसीत् । तल्लक्षणम्[b]। रश्मिभि[c]र्द्विजा यजन्त्यमृतरथेनेति तस्य रूपम् । सूर्यो ज्योतिष्पतिरिति भावः, भावाद् गुण इति, स सूर्यस्तपति विश्वमिति तस्य गुणः, तद्गुणानुसृतौ ब्राह्मणा गायत्रीं जपन्ति, ये च इमे भूम्यामधियजन्ति दिवं प्रयान्तीति तत्क्रियाः, तारकामुपेत्य त उत्तिष्ठन्ते ब्राह्मणा इत्याचारः, त्रिकालेन कालसन्ध्यां प्रयोजयन्ति मन्त्रैः, प्रजायाः संरक्षणे ब्राह्मणा द्रविणं दधति, स उपायः । मन्त्रसंख्यासहितं प्रयोजयन्ति क्रियाः, सा चेष्टा, सा बहुधा श्रूयत इति मार्गः । एवं बहुमत्या दैवत्वे रूपं, रूपेणानेकत्वं जायते ।

तद्रूपं प्रतिरूपमिति, तज्ज्ञानं रूपविद्या, तच्छिल्पसूत्रमिति । वेदस्यायने रूपभुवनकोष इति, एतदर्थं रूपार्थं दिशः । अरूपाद्रूपं तस्य फलमिति पूर्वं वेदेनोक्तम्[10] ।

दिशानुसृतेर्दिशापालानुपासन्ते[11] ॥ २३ ॥

---

[6]चतुर्दशसंख्यक इत्यर्थः ।

[7]वाग् वै मन्त्रः शतपथब्राह्मणे उक्तम् । वाक्येन सह यद् प्रकटयन्ति ।

[8]यथा अथर्वसंहितायां लक्षणम्, ६.१४१.३: सहस्रपोषाय कृणुतं लक्ष्माश्विना । इति ।

[9]रूपं रूपं वयो वयः संरभ्यैनं परिष्वजे इत्युक्तम् अथर्व० १९.१.३ । ततः विष्णुरूपं, यदस्ति वचनेऽप्युक्तम्, पैप्पलादसंहितायां स्त्रीणां प्रतिरूपमुपासका तदर्थं प्रतिरूपाणि ।

[10]देवतायतनमिति, तानि न कम्पन्ते, दैवतप्रतिमा हसन्ति रुदन्ति नृत्यन्ति स्फुटन्ति सीदन्ति, उन्मीलन्ति निमीलन्ति, शतपथब्राह्मणे ७.१०. उक्तम् । ऐतरेयब्राह्मणे ४.५ रूपविद्या छन्दोमय दैवशिल्पम्, रूपेण उक्तम् । तथा शतपथब्राह्मणे ३.२ प्रतिरूपशिल्परूपेण उक्तम् । रूपं वै अर्चारूपं, प्रतिरूपाणि उपदेवतानि, अन्या मण्डनमिति ।

[11]यथा जैमिनीयब्राह्मणे (२.४) उक्तम् दिश उ एवं विश्वदेवाः दिशो वै प्राणः इति वाक्यम् ।

---

[a]शतपथिनः, ग adds ।

[b]लक्षणाद्रूपम्, ग ।

[c]सूर्यस्य इति अधिकः पाठः, ग ।

प्राच्यामादित्यः, दक्षिणे यमः, प्रतीच्यां वरुणः, उदीच्यां सोमः ध्रुवायामग्निः, एवमहल्लिकाः[12] वदन्ति, एवं पूर्वं वेदेनोक्तम्, तदा दशप्रचेतसः[13] आदित्या[a] आशापालाः[14] सन्ति, य एवं वेद ।

एवं दैवभेदान्मार्गभेदा जायन्ते ॥ २४ ॥

मार्गाद्रूपञ्च, अप्राकृतं नानृतं च । विष्णुदैवताद् वैष्णवाः[15], रुद्राद् रौद्राः[b], इडाया ऐड़ाः, अम्बाया अम्बिनः, सवितुः सौरा भवन्तीति ।

एतेन भेदेन ब्राह्मणाः प्रतिरूपाणि यजन्ति, य एतज्जानाति स रूपज्ञः[16], ये रूपशैले रूपमाचरन्ति ते रूपकाराः, ते रूपबोधे रूपाण्याचरन्ति । तद्रूपार्थं कामचारा यज्ञं कुर्वन्ति[17] कामनया य एवं वेद ।

इति वाङ्कायमनोमार्गेण पिप्पलादकल्पे सम्प्रदानं चर्चाक्षेण मुनिश्रोतॄणामुपनिधानेन रूपभावनाबोधाध्याय इति पञ्चमप्रपाठकः ॥

---

[12]अहल्लिका भाट इत्यर्थः कुन्तापीय रमणीविशेषः ।

[13]तारादि देवताः । द्यौश्च म इदं पृथिवी च प्रचेतसौ शुक्रो बृहन् दक्षिणया पिपर्तु । अथर्व० ६.५३.१ सूर्य इत्यर्थः ।

[14]आशानामाशापालेभ्यश्चतुर्भ्यो अमृतेभ्यः । अथर्ववेदे १.३१.१.

[15]विष्णुयाजकाः । पुरुषो ह नारायणोऽकामयत । यो वैष्णवो वामनः, शतपथे उक्तम् ।

[16]यथा ज्योतिष्येवं रूपं दधातीति शतपथे उक्तम् ।

[17]यथा पाकयज्ञे औपासने च प्रजापतिः, स्वीष्टकृत् अङ्गदेवता प्रातः सूर्यः प्रधानो भवति तथा विश्वदेवार्थं दैवयज्ञः ।

---

[a]दशाशापालाः, ग ।

[b]रुद्रियाः, ग ।

षष्ठः प्रपाठकः

सम्बन्धप्रबोधनम्

अथाथर्वणाङ्गिरसशिल्पकाश्यपादय उपेत्य पिप्पलादमाश्रमे पप्रच्छुः, भगवन्तः कुतो ह वा रूपे भेदः सञ्जायत इति श्रोष्यामः श्रेयः । तान् ह स पिप्पलादो होवाच, इयं-

न्यासधारणा श्रेष्ठा ॥ १ ॥

सा धारणा सृष्टिः । सौम्यपिप्पलादः सुप्रसन्न[a] इदं वव्रे, यथा प्रजाकामो वै प्रजापतिः स तपोऽतप्यत, स तपस्तप्त्वा मिथुनमुदपादयत्,[b] रयिञ्च प्राणञ्चेति, एतौ मे बहुधा प्रजाः करिष्यत इति पूर्वे प्रश्ने[c] मयोक्तम् । तथा कामचारिणः सुखं कामयन्ते । सुखमसीमं तत् सुखचक्रे[d]-

वृत्त्या दैवचिन्तने भेदः सञ्जायते ॥ २ ॥

स हि द्विधा, तद्भेदात्[e] प्रतिरूपाणि कल्पयन्तीति वादः । अथ हैनमाथर्वणाङ्गिरसादयस्त्रयः श्रोतारः पप्रच्छुः, भगवन्तः रूपाकले केनोपायेन ब्राह्मणा दैवेऽन्यसन्धामारोपयन्ति । कथं न्यसन्ति । ततः षोडशकलपिप्पलादपुरुषो[f] होवाच शृणुतामृतस्य पुत्राः ।

लक्षणप्रकाशार्थं शिल्पविद्या ॥ ३ ॥

शिल्पोद्गीथाः पुरोहिता क्रमेण बहुधा न्यासमाचरन्ति । स्थापकास्तथा च ।

न्यासोऽलङ्कारमुद्राऽऽयुधब्रह्मकक्ष[g] वाहनोपदेवारिस्तुवक क्रमेण रूपनवाङ्गमिति ध्येयम् ॥ ४ ॥

---

[a]सुप्रसन्नेन, ग, घ ।
[b]°मुपपादयेत्, ग, घ ।
[c]प्रश्नोपनिषदि, ख ।
[d]सुखार्थम्, ग ।
[e]तद् द्विधया दैवचिन्तने भेदः सञ्जायते, क ।
[f]वेत्थि होवाच, ग ।
[g]क omits कक्ष.

स रेखान्यासः, अलङ्करणम्, मुद्रा, (आयुधम्) बाध्रः, कक्षः, वाहनम्, उपदैवतम्, अरिणः, स्तुवका [इत्येवं] कल्पयन्ति । आशृणुत वत्सास्त्रयः, न्यासनवाङ्गानुशासनमिति[a] पिप्पलादो वव्रे ।

रेखां रूपाङ्गसौष्ठवप्राप्त्यर्थं शैले लिखन्ति प्राज्ञस्थापका । इति नवाङ्गं न मानुषे, दैवक्षेत्रे मुख्यम् ।

उष्णीषमस्तकाः कारुकाराः शैलक्षेत्रे दैवभावे रेखाः वज्रचूर्णेन लिखन्ति ।

तिस्रः रेखाः श्रेष्ठाः ॥ ५ ॥

ऊर्ध्वरेखा अग्निरेखाः यथा शिखा उत्थिता प्रज्वलति । पार्श्वगा रेखा अपच्छेदा यथा नदीनां प्रवाहः । कर्णक्षेत्रगा भेनकारेखा मारुतच्छेदा मारुतस्य तिर्यग्गतिरिव, उदाहृतरेखया शैलक्षेत्रे पञ्जराख्यं कोष्ठककर्माऽऽचरेत् । एष कोष्ठकः अग्न्यम्मारुतरेखासमष्ट्या संयोगेन सम्भवति ।

रूपक्षेत्रे कोष्ठकालिर्मुख्या ॥ ६ ॥

शैलगुहायां भित्तौ सूक्ष्मकोष्ठकरचने आकलान्युपलभ्यन्ते सुखेन । यथा षोडशकलो[1] वै पुरुषः षोडशांशैः पूर्णो भवति तथा –

षोडशकोष्ठकमध्ये रूपाणि प्रभवन्ति तद्रूपार्थं श्रेष्ठम् ॥ ७ ॥

वज्रचूर्णेन सह तत्क्षेत्रे शलघूर्णिकया वृत्तमेकं रचय मर्मलाभार्थम् । स नेमिः ब्रह्माभास इति । रूपे तद् विलं प्राणविलम् ।

[b]विलमिति मर्म, ब्रह्मेव ध्येयम् ॥ ८ ॥

तन्मर्मणाऽङ्गभावः प्रसरति ।

षोडशकोष्ठकप्रमाणविभागस्तु ब्राह्मदैवजैवोपदैव-याजकक्रमेण पञ्चधा ध्येयः ॥ ९ ॥

कोणचतुष्टयावलम्बनेन नेम्या सह कोणवर्गं कर्तय । कर्तितकोष्ठके, ऊर्ध्वदेशस्य क्षेत्रद्वये यक्षगन्धर्वानप्सरसादीन् खोदय । अधःस्थं तदनुपातय । क्षेत्रद्वयं स्तुवकक्षेत्रम् । उभयकोणे[c] मानवोपासकं रचय । अधोमध्यस्थले

---

[1]षोडशकलं वै ब्रह्म शतपथब्राह्मणे उक्तम् । "षोडशर्चेभ्यः स्वाहा" इति षोडशकला उक्ताः । अथर्व १९.२३.१३.

---

[a]रूपे नवाङ्गं स्मरन्ति ये विचक्षणाः । इत्यधिकः पाठः, ग ।
[b]तद्०, घ ।
[c]०पार्श्वे, ग ।

कोष्ठकौ द्वौ जीवक्षेत्रं दैववाहनार्थम् । मध्यस्थाश्चत्वारः कोष्ठकाः ब्रह्मक्षेत्रम् । तत्रार्चारूपस्याङ्गनिर्णयः । अधोर्ध्वावधि तुङ्गाङ्गपर्यन्तमापादशीर्षमाचर । ब्रह्मक्षेत्रस्य वामदक्षिणस्थं क्षेत्रचतुष्टयं जायाक्षेत्रम् ।

रूपाङ्गं चतुर्धेति विशेषः ॥ १० ॥

पार्थिवाङ्गं, जैवाङ्गं, प्राणाङ्गं, देवताङ्गमिति । पादान्ताद् गुल्फपर्यन्तं पार्थिवाङ्गम्[2] गुल्फान्नाभिपर्यन्तं जैवाङ्गम्[3], नाभेः कण्ठावधि प्राणाङ्गम्[4], कण्ठाद् ब्रह्मरन्ध्रपर्यन्तं द्योताङ्गम्[5] । तन्मूर्तितारकममूर्तितारकमिव[6] । यथापूर्वं वेदेनोक्तम् ।

ऊर्ध्वयुगभागयोः रूपस्याननालङ्कारैः सह दैवतेजोमण्डलम् । अण्डाकारं पिण्डाकारं वा स्यात् । तत्र शुक्लज्योती रसामृतं[7] विद्यते । एवं रूपेऽङ्गभेदाश्चत्वारः शिलादेवतार्थम् । वामे दक्षिणे क्षेत्रद्वये दिव्यक्षेत्रे देवशक्तिभिरुपदैवतानि तिष्ठन्तीति, उभयदिशि कोष्ठकाश्चत्वारः । एवं षोडशकोष्ठकानां सन्धा इति । महासूत्रं सर्वरूपक्षेत्रे विधेयम् । इति सौम्यः पिप्पलादो वव्रे ।

अथ शिल्पकाश्यपाङ्गिरसकोशलादयः पप्रच्छुः, भगवन्तो वास्तुकर्माङ्ग-अवतारषोडशकलपुरुषपिप्पलादाः । केनोपदेवता रूपे भावं प्रददाति । काः सन्धाः[a] श्रेष्ठा इति ।

वरदव्याख्यानकरसंयुतः स्वस्तिमुच्चार्य्य, सौम्यः पिप्पलादो होवाच । आशृणुत शिल्पर्षयो बिन्दुसन्धामादौ ।

बिन्दुर्ब्रह्मेव ब्रह्मध्रुवम् ॥ ११ ॥

रूपकोष्ठकान्तराले बिन्दुर्द्विधा । ब्रह्मबिन्दुर्मध्यबिन्दुर्ब्रह्मेव । ऊर्ध्वमध्यगः[b] सत्याख्यबिन्दुः द्वौ विशिष्टौ ।

ब्रह्म सत्यादौ ॥ १२ ॥

यथाऽऽदिपुरुषस्य नाभेः प्रजापतिः स्रष्टा सृजति प्रजाः । ब्रह्मजज्ञानं प्रथमं पुरस्तात् यथा जनन्या नाभितन्तोर्नालतन्त्ववधारणे मातृकोषे भ्रूण उपजायते लोकसृष्टौ, तथा रूपे ।

---

[2]यदङ्गं चरति धरायाम् ।

[3]नाभौ जीवसत्ता राजते प्रसरति च ।

[4]हृदये प्राणस्तिष्ठति ।

[5]ब्रह्मरन्ध्रे तेजो विभाति, आविर्भवति ।

[6]तत्तारकं द्विविधम्, मूर्तितारकममूर्तितारकञ्चेति । यदिन्द्रियान्तं तन्मूर्तिमत्, यद् भ्रूयुगातीतं तदमूर्तिमत् इति अद्वयतारके उक्तम् ।

[7]सर्वान्तरः स्वयंज्योतिः सर्वाधिपतिरस्म्यहम् इति स्वराट् योगतत्त्वोपनिषदि उक्तम् ।

---

[a]सम्बन्धः, ग ।

[b]ऊर्ध्वमण्डले, घ ।

ब्रह्मबिन्द्ववलम्बनेन रूपाङ्गानि सौभगानि भवन्ति ॥१३ ॥

तस्योर्ध्वबिन्दुः सत्यबिन्दुः । भ्रुवोर्मध्ये हिरण्मयेन[8] पात्रेण ब्रह्मरसो विद्यते । तद्रसाद् ज्ञानं प्रसरति जीवे । तथा रूपाकले तद् बिन्द्ववलम्बनेन रूपाङ्गवैभवं कल्पयन्ति स्थापका इति । पुरुषीरूपार्थं ब्रह्मकीलस्य त्रिभागानां[a] मध्ये मर्मार्थं बिन्दुं चिन्तयेत्, येनोपायेन रूपाणि सुभगानि भवन्ति, सिद्धिं प्रददति । लोकाः प्रहृष्टा भवन्तीति ।

अथ शृणुत श्रोतारः अलङ्करणन्यासम् ।

अलङ्करणं दैवभुषणमिति ॥१४ ॥

तद्भूषणात् प्रेक्षाभावः प्रसरति, याजका प्रहसन्ति[b] । बहुधा भूषणं ग्राह्यम् । उष्णीषम्[c], राज्ञां त्रिवलिकिरीटम्, केशग्रन्थिम्, ऋषीणां जटाम्, कर्णे नागकडारम्, लोलम्, प्रवर्तम्, वलयम्, पैण्डं[d] कुम्भं च रचय । कण्ठार्थं कुशच्छन्दः, स्वर्णनिस्पम्, रज्जुयुगलमिति, कट्यां मेखलाग्रन्थिम्,वस्त्रमाजानुलुलितम् । ऋषीणां कृष्णसारचर्मसूत्रम्, नारीणामङ्घ्रौ पञ्चवलयम्, करे व्यालच्छदः, करतले रेखादीन्, दैवपक्षे शङ्खपद्मादिनिधिलक्षणं निधेहि । इन्द्रार्थं वपूष्णीषम्, पशुपत्यर्थं विष्कचर्म, व्यालोत्तरीयादि दैवभूषणं रचयेति । अलङ्कारदर्शनान्मानुषाः सर्वे प्रमुदिता भवन्ति ।

प्रतिमुचः रतिः प्रसरति ॥१५ ॥

रत्यास्तद्दर्शनं भवति । स एष रूपप्रज्ञया[9] ब्रह्मसाक्षात्कार[10] आनन्दमिति, एवं वेदे ।

करमुद्रा रूपस्य भावं ज्ञापयति ॥१६ ॥

शृणु रूपबोधे मुद्राङ्गसन्धाः । यज्ञकर्मणि दैवाङ्गे च यथा यज्ञकृत्ये[e] होद्गीथाः करान् गाथाभिः सह प्रदर्शयन्ति प्रसारयन्ति सा मुद्रा । यज्ञस्य साधनमिति ।

---

[8]हिरण्मये परे कोषे विरजं ब्रह्म निष्कलमिति न्यायेन ।

[9]यथा नारदपरिव्राजकोपनिषदि उक्तम्–चक्षुषा रूपग्रहणं श्रोत्रे शब्दग्रहणमित्यादि । अथर्ववेदे–रूपं रूपं वयोवय इत्याद्युक्तम् ।

[10]तद् वै ब्रह्मणो रूपेऽमृतत्वं चैवामृतं च शतपथब्राह्मणे उक्तम् ।

---

[a]त्रिभागस्य, ग, घ ।

[b]प्रमुदन्ति; घ, ङ ।

[c]उष्णीषं वन्धने, ग ।

[d]पैण्डणिम्, ग, घ ।

[e]वृत्या, घ ।

रूपे तां योजयन्ति रूपकाराः रूपेऽत्र न भेदः, यत्क्रिया रूपाङ्गे प्रतिफलिता भवति। मुद्रापञ्चकं श्रेष्ठम् । तर्जनीवराभययोगव्याख्यानमिति । यथोद्गीथाः सदस्या उत्तरारण्यामवरारणिचालने[a] उदूखलप्रोक्षणे करौ प्रसारयन्ति । स्थण्डिलशोधने, कुशाण्डिके, पुरोडाशप्रोक्षणे च तन्मुद्रापञ्चकम् । तस्य प्रयोगं शृणु सौम्येति । अरणिमन्थने,—

ॐ अग्नये मथ्यमानायानुब्रूहीत्युच्चार्य[b] अध्वर्युर्मन्त्रेणाङ्गुलिं प्रदर्शयति सा तर्जनिका मुद्रा रूपे सौम्येति । यथा उदूखले हविर्वैतानप्रसारणार्थं करान् प्रसारयन्ति उदूखलोपरि सा ध्वजमुद्रा रूपे सौम्येति । स्थण्डिलवीक्षणे यज्ञगाथागायने—

ॐ यज्ञं ब्रूमो यजमानमृचः सामानि भेषजेति[c] वाक्यमुच्चार्य्य ब्राह्मणा यथा वैश्वानरं प्रार्थयन्ति करसम्पुटेन साऽऽवाहनीति वरमुद्रा रूपे सौम्येति। प्रवरकर्मणि कुशाण्डिकाकाले दर्भकङ्कणं करे धृत्वा यथाऽऽचार्या वैश्वानरमुत्थापयन्ति करप्रदर्शनेन सा रूपेऽभयमुद्रा रूपे सौम्येति । एवं च वराभयमुद्रायुग्मं[d] रूपस्य ब्रह्मक्षेत्रे ध्येयं, न जैवक्षेत्रे (प्रवण) आभाति सा कोष्ठके । पुरोडाशाच्छादने यजमानं प्रति, पुरोडाशवत्सा सुदुघा लोकेऽस्मा उपतिष्ठतीत्याद्युच्चार्य्य यथा सदस्या एषां करान् प्रदर्शयन्ति, हविष-इत्यादिवाक्येन पुरोडाशस्विष्टकृते यजन्ति सा योगमुद्रा रूपे, व्याख्यानमुद्रापि रूपे सौम्येति । इति मुद्रापञ्चकं रूपे ध्येयम् ।

अथ श्रृणुत शिल्पाध्येतारः शिल्पे[11] बाध्रसन्धाम् ।

बाध्रं बलं ज्ञापयति रूपे ॥ १७ ॥

बाध्रमित्यायुधम्[12]। सर्वं तनुवत् । कौणपान् प्रति देवाः क्षिपन्ति। तदाऽऽयुधस्य मन्त्रबीजानि[13] ध्येयानि । मन्त्रहीनायुधं लोष्ट्रं भवति । तथा खोदनेऽपि मन्त्रम्[14] उच्चारयन्ति स्थापकाः । तथाऽऽयुधस्य द्वादश बीजानि जानन्ति मन्त्रिणः । मन्त्रस्य सूक्ष्मनादो बीजमिति । तद्योगेन मन्त्रक्रिया प्रकटी भवति ।

इन्द्रस्यायुधं वज्रः । ॐ वं वज्राय, वंबीजेन प्रोक्षन्ति सा संहारशक्तिरिति[15] । मरुतस्यायुधं ध्वजः । ॐ धं ध्वजाय, धंबीजेन प्रोक्षन्ति ।

---

[11]कौषीतकिब्राह्मणे कलाविद्येत्युक्तम् । पिप्पलादसहिंतायाम् १ उक्तम् ।

[12]अथर्ववेदे (६.१३३.२) मेखलाबन्धनप्रसङ्गे उक्तम्–आहुतास्यभिहुत ऋषीणामस्यायुधम् इति । परामित्रान्दुन्दुभिना हरिणस्याजिनेन च । सर्वे देवा अतित्रसन्ये संग्रामस्येशते। अथर्व॰ ५.२१.७ (ग)

[13]आथर्वणीये आसुरीकल्पे बीजमन्त्रस्य प्रयोग उक्तः ।

[14]वाग् वै मन्त्र इति शतपथे उक्तम् । वाग् वै देवानां मन्त्र इति कौषीतकीये उक्तम् ।

[15]संहारण वं इति पूर्वपाठशब्दस्य शक्तिरित्यर्थः ।

---

[a]॰मन्थने, घ ।

[b]TS VI 3.5.3. ŚB III.4.1.22

[c]AVŚ XI.6.14

[d]॰युक्ते, ख ।

एषा धूनन[16]शक्तिरिति । यमस्यायुधं दण्डः । ॐ दुं दण्डाय, दुंबीजेन प्रोक्षन्ति । सा घातनशक्तिरिति । वरुणस्यायुधं पाशः । ॐ पं पाशाय, पंबीजेन प्रोक्षन्ति । साऽऽकर्षणी शक्तिरिति । ईशानस्यायुधं शूलम् । ॐ शुं शूलाय, शुंबीजेनप्रोक्षन्ति । सा भेदनशक्तिरिति । सोमस्यायुधं पात्रम्। ॐ पं पात्राय, पंबीजेन प्रोक्षन्ति । सा प्राणशक्तिरिति । वैश्वानरस्यायुधं स्रुक् । ॐ स्रुं स्रुवाय, स्रुंबीजेन प्रोक्षन्ति । सा त्यागशक्तिरिति । सूर्यस्यायुधं पद्मम्। ॐ पं पद्माय, पंबीजेन प्रोक्षन्ति । सा प्रल्हादिनी शक्तिरिति। अम्बाया आयुधं माला । ॐ मं मालायै, मंबीजेन प्रोक्षन्ति । सा ध्यानशक्तिरिति । विष्णोरायुधं चक्रम् । ॐ हुं चक्राय, हुंबीजेन प्रोक्षन्ति । सा माया[17]शक्तिरिति । कुवेरस्यायुधं कुम्भः । ॐ कं कुम्भाय, कंबीजेन प्रोक्षन्ति । सा निधिशक्तिरिति । गणदैवतस्यायुधमङ्कुशः । ॐ अं अङ्कुशाय, अंबीजेन प्रोक्षन्ति । सा संयमशक्तिरिति ।

रीत्या नादयुक्तं रचयन्ति कारुकारा आयुधानि । नाद इति मन्त्रस्य रसः[a]। स हि बीजमिति कृत्यं ज्ञेयम् । षोडशकोष्ठकेषु रूपस्य करसंयोगे नेमिस्पर्शनं ध्येयम् ।

अथ वास्तूद्गीथान् प्रति कक्षासन्धां सौम्याननो वव्रे (पिप्पलादः) ।

आसनषट्कं मुख्यम् ॥ १८ ॥

आसनं रूपस्य कृत्यं प्रकाशयति देहस्याकृतिः प्रकेतनमिति । उत्सर्गा चासीन[b]चेति भेदेन द्वे मुख्य इति । रूपाकले या उत्थितास्ता[18] उत्सर्गाः । रूपभेदे या आसीनास्ता आसिका इति ज्ञेयम् । यथा यज्ञे यज्ञकर्मणि तथा रूपप्रयोगे ग्राव्णि च ।

आसनं षड्धा । यथा यजमानाः स्वशालायां दर्भासने उपविशन्ति तत् सुखासनं रूपे । यथाऽरणिमन्थने अग्निध्रा रज्जुं चालयन्ति तद् विषमासनं रूपे ।

यथा वेद्युपरि आचार्या उपविशन्ति तत् स्वस्तिकासनं रूपे । यथा सूत्रायणकाले रक्षाविधाने पिशङ्गे सूत्रशृङ्खले तद्बन्धनकाले ब्राह्मणा वसन्ति तद् योगासनं रूपे । यथा सवित्राराधने द्विजा उपविशन्ति तत् कुक्कुटासनं रूपे । यथा होद्गीथा वाजसनेयसंहितोक्त[c] सन्ध्योपासनकाले करौ प्राचीं प्रति प्रसारयन्ति तत् सौम्यासनं रूपे, इति प्रयोग । इति आसनषट्कं रूपे यज्ञे[d] च ।

---

[16]कम्पनमित्यर्थः ।
[17]प्रज्ञा इत्यर्थः ।
[18]दण्डायमाना मूर्तिरित्यर्थः ।

---

[a]निर्यास, ख, घ, ङ ।
[b]चासिका, ग
[c]इत्याधिकपाठः ।
[d]कृत्ये, क ।

पप्रच्छुराङ्गिरस - शिल्पकाश्यपादिश्रोतारो भगवन्तः किमर्थमासने भेदा जायन्ते, कथमुपवेशनार्थमेतद् ध्येयमिति । इत्यगम्यरूपबोधार्थं तेषां काः सन्धा प्रवदन्तु श्रद्धया सौम्याः ।

आसनाद्रूपस्य[a] कृत्यभावं प्रचक्षते। सुखासनं रूपस्य शान्तभावं प्रददाति। विषमासनं वैरभावं क्षेपण- क्रियादि प्रकटयति । स्वस्तिकासनं प्राज्ञभावं प्रकट्यति, योगासनं ब्रह्मानुभूतिमात्मानुभूतिभावं च विज्ञापयति। कुक्कुटासनमुद्ग्रीवभावं प्रकाशयति । सौम्यासनं स्थैर्यं प्रददाति[b]। रूपाकलार्थमेतद् ध्येयम् । सर्वे शिल्पाचार्या ब्रह्मक्षेत्रे षोडशकोष्ठकान्तराले नेमिमध्ये रूपान्वये एतदाचरन्ति ।

शृणुत प्रियङ्करश्रोतारः, रूपाकले दैववाहनस्य[19] सन्धाः । वाहनानि रूपस्य गुणान् प्रकाशयन्ति विज्ञापयन्ति ।

गुणानुसृतं रूपत्रयम् ॥१९ ॥

सत्त्वात् सात्त्विकानि रजसो राजसानि तमसस्तामसानीति भेदाः । यानि रूपाणि सायुज्यं प्रददति तानि सात्त्विकरूपाणि । यानि कायसुखप्रदायकानि तानि राजसानि । यानि रूपाण्यरिं प्रति मृत्युप्रदानि तानि तामसानि ।[20]

गुणानुक्रमेण वास्तुवेदस्य रूपविद्या इति व्याख्यानम् । य एनां वेद । शृणु वाहनस्वरूपम्-

वाहनं रूपस्य प्रकृतिज्ञापकविशेषः ॥२० ॥[c]

यथा इन्द्रो[21] दिग्गजानाकर्षति[d]। पर्जन्यं वर्षयति । तथाऽऽकर्षणात्मकम् ऐरावतमारोहति । यथा यमो जीवस्य प्राणानाकर्षति[e], तथा घोरमहिषम्[22] आरोहति । यथा वैश्वानरो याज्ञिकैर्दीप्तो भवति, तथा मेषम्[23] आरोहति । यथा एकायने सविता भ्रमति सप्ततन्तुस्तथैकरथाङ्गाढ्यरथम्[24] आरोहति ।

---

[19]ऐतरेये यथोक्तवाहनरूपस्य रूपविशेष ।

[20]शतपथे छान्दोग्ये चोक्तः-एष क्रमः, एषा देवयजनविद्या । आत्मानन्देन यजनोपायेन त्रयस्त्रिंशद् देवताः तार्क्ष्ये ब्राह्मणे उक्ताः ।

[21]वृहद्धि जालं बृहतः शक्रस्य वाजिनीवत इति अथर्व० ८.८.६.

[22]प्राणो वै महिष इति शतपथे उक्तम् ।

[23]मेष इव वै सं च वि चोर्वच्यसे इति । अथर्व० ६.४९.२ ।

[24]सूर्यस्य वा एक रश्मिर्वृष्टिद इति शतपथे उक्तम् । स सविता रथेनेति ।

---

[a]देहस्य, ख, ग ।

[b]स्थैर्यभावं प्रकाशयति, ग ।

[c]Sūtra only found in the list of Sūtras in क.

[d]आकर्षयति, ख, ग ।

[e]आकर्षयति, ख, ग ।

यथा रुद्रो धर्मं सञ्चारयति तथा धर्मवृषभम्[25] आरोहति । 'यथा प्रजापतिर्ज्ञानेन प्रजा आकर्षति'[a] तथा हंसम्[26] आरोहति । यथा विष्णुर्मोक्षं प्रददाति तथा सुपर्णम्[27] आरोहति । यथाऽम्बा [रिपु]वर्गं[b] नाशयति तथा द्वीपिनम्[28] आरोहति ।

वाहनानि षोडशकोष्ठके जैवक्षेत्रे ध्येयानि । रूपे ब्रह्मक्षेत्रस्य निम्ने, अधोऽन्यच्च श्रेयः । आशृणु उपदेवतस्य[29] सन्धाः । सौम्य पिप्पलादो वव्रे ।

उपदैवतं प्रतिरूपमिति ॥ २१ ॥[c]

प्रजापतेरेते सर्वे देवा इमानि पञ्च महाभूतानि तद्गुणा[d] पृथिवी-वाय्वाकाशाब्ज्योतिरित्येतानि जायन्त इति । तद्भूत-ज्ञानात् स्वस्वगुणभावरूप इव प्रचक्षते । तद्भूत-ज्ञानादुपदैवतभावाः सन्ति ।

यथा वैश्वानर[30] इति ब्रह्म । स यज्ञः । यज्ञस्य[e] दाहिका[31]शक्तिः स्वाहा । पचनात्मिका स्वधा[32] । इत्थमुपदैवभावः प्रथितः[f] प्रसरति तत्सपर्यायामिन्द्रस्य प्रजननशक्तिरिन्द्राणी[33][g] । मारुतस्य वेगिनी शक्तिर्वायुनायी[h] सा दृता । यमस्य द्वौ गुणौ, पालिकाऽवनाशिकेति । तस्य पालिका शक्तिः आकूतिः[34], अवनाशिका मृत्युरिति[35] । वरुणस्य प्रवाहिका शक्तिर्वारुणी[36] । सोमस्य धारिका शक्तिरिलेति[37] । सूर्यस्य सवितुरवलम्बिनी शक्तिश्छाया[38] ।

---

[25]वृषभोऽसि स्वर्ग ऋषीनार्षेयान् गच्छ इति । अथर्व० ११.१.३५ ।

[26]हंसेति शब्दार्थः सर्वेषु देहेषु व्याप्तो वर्तते इति हंसोपनिषदि उक्तम् ।

[27]द्वा सुपर्णा सयुजा सखाया समानं वृक्षं परि षस्वजाते इति । ऋ०.१.१६४.२०; अथर्व० ९.९.२० ।

[28]एना व्याघ्रं परिषस्वजानाः सिंहं हिन्वन्ति महते सौभगाय इति । अथर्व० ४.८.७ ।

[29]वास्तुवेदे इदमुपदैवतं प्रतिरूपमित्यर्थः । प्रतिरूपं शतपथब्राह्मणे एकादशकाण्डे उक्तम् । तेषां चर्य्या जैमिनीयब्राह्मणे–प्रत्यङ्ङ् ह्येष सर्वाणि रूपाणि य आदित्यः स प्रतिरूपमित्युक्तः ।

[30]वैश्वानरो वै सर्वेऽग्नय इति शतपथे उक्तम् ।

[31]असौ वैश्वानरो योऽसौ तपति (पचति) इति शतपथे ।

[32]पुरुषे येनेदमन्नं पच्यते इति शतपथे उक्तम् ।

[33]सेन्द्रस्य पत्नीति गोभिलगृह्यसूत्रे उक्तम् ।

[34]जीवस्याऽवयवात्मिका ।

[35]अग्निर्वै मृत्युरिति कौषीतकि ब्राह्मणे, मृत्युर्वै तस्य शतपथे च ।

[36]ऐतरेये वारुणी रात्रिरिति उक्तम् ।

[37]इला वै अन्नमिति अथर्ववेदे उक्तम् ।

[38]तमश्छाया ।

---

[a]आकर्षयति ख, ग । प्रजापतिः प्राणान् सञ्चारयति, ग ।

[b]अपवर्गं, क, ख, ग, ङ ।

[c]Sūtra only found in the list of sūtras in क

[d]अधिकपाठः, क ।

[e]अग्नेरिति युक्तम् ।

[f]ग्रथितः ।

[g]इन्द्रायणी, क, ख, ग, घ ।

[h]Possibly it has the influence of अग्नायी.

साऽऽवेशिनी शक्तिरुषा[39] ।

विष्णोर्मुक्तिप्रदा श्रीशक्तिः[40] हिरण्यवर्णा हरिणी धारिणी शक्तिः पृथिवी[41] । शेषस्य सहना शक्तिः धृतिर्व्यापिनी शक्तिः विधृतिः[a] यथा क्षमाऽन्नधृतिरिति। विधृतिः सौख्यमिति । हिरण्यगर्भस्य कालात्मिका[b] शक्तिः । गायत्री[42] ज्ञानरूपा, सावित्री[43] मेधारूपा, सरस्वती[44] प्रज्ञारूपा देवी विशिष्टा त्रिकालरूपा च ।

राष्ट्रया[45] रुद्रेति[c]। तस्य प्रजननशक्तिरम्बा[46]ऽम्बालिका[47] चेति द्वे । दुर्गाया रक्षणशक्तिः सुन्दरी मोहिनी चेति द्वे आकर्षणरूपे । एतत्क्रमे दैवगुणस्यानुक्रमे उपदैवतानि जायाभावेन जायन्ते । तदेतल्लक्षणानि ।

अथ प्रतिकीर्णमाथर्वणाङ्गिरसशिल्पकाश्यप-कुवित्स-कोशलादयः प्रणम्य पप्रच्छुः, भगवन्तः पिप्पलादा दिव्यपुरुषाः कथं का हेतय इत्यबोध्यमिति विशदेन ब्रुवन्तु सौम्याः । दिव्यपुरुषपिप्पलादो वव्रे । शिल्पोद्गीथाः शृणुत वक्ष्यामो विस्तरेण अपसार्थममुथ उपरूपाकलस्यानुशासनं पूर्वं वेदेन यथोक्तम् ।

प्रजापतिरसृजत् कालम् । दक्षिणोत्तरौ द्वौ । उत्तराद्देवा दक्षिणात् पितरः । उत्तरात्सविता दक्षिणाच्चन्द्रमाः । प्रतिकाममृषयो दक्षिणं प्रतिपादयन्ति। तत् पितृयानं रात्रिरिति । ब्रह्मचारिणो मोक्षकामा उत्तरं प्रतिपादयन्ति। तद्धि देवयानं दिवम् । दक्षिणादर्यमलोकाः पञ्चपादपितरः[48] । उत्तराद्द्वादशाकृतिदिवमाहुः । एतन्न्याये गुणेनैकं ब्रह्म द्वादशधा भवति। तथा हि सूर्यो ज्योतिषां पतिरिति गुणानुसृतेर्देवस्तल्लक्षणानुसृते रूपाणि, ततः प्रतिरूपाणि जायन्ते । एतत्सत्यम् ।

यथा यज्ञात् त्याग[49] इति मुख्यम् । दैवभावे तत्स्वाहा[50] । त्यागवृत्तिरिति

[39]उषा देवी वाचा संविदाना वाग्देव्युषसा संविदाना इति अथर्ववेदे उक्तम् ।

[40]द्यौरित्यर्थः । भूतभविष्यदभीष्टवीर्या लक्ष्मीर्वलमिति अथर्ववेदे उक्तम् ।

[41]सेयं देवानां पत्नीति शतपथे उक्तम् ।

[42]तेजसा वै गायत्री प्रथममिति ताण्ड्यब्राह्मणे ।

[43]वाक् सावित्रीति गोपथब्राह्मणे उक्तम् ।

[44]सारस्वतरूपम् ऐतरेये उक्तम् ।

[45]सविता राष्ट्रं राष्ट्रपतिरिति शतपथे च ११.४.३.१४ ।

[46]अम्बा अथर्ववेदे उक्ता ।

[47]भेषजरूपा अम्बालिकेति वाजसनेये उक्ता ।

[48] "देवाः पितरः पितरो देवा । यो अस्मि सो अस्मि", अथर्व० ६.१२३.३ काण्डे । स विश्वेदेवा तथा पितर उपदेवा वसुपितर रुद्रपितामह आदित्य प्रपितामह इति पितृयूप प्रोत्थानमन्त्राणि २४ सूक्तोक्तं च ।

[49]मुञ्चतांहसोअंहस इति वदन्ति । अथर्व० १.३१.२ । ये दक्षिणतो जुह्वति जातवेदो दक्षिणाया दिशोऽभिदासन्त्यस्मान् इति त्यागः । अथर्व० ४.४०.२ । इन्द्रासोमा तपतं रक्ष इति वदन्ति । अथर्व० ८.४.१ । विषेण भङ्गुरावतः प्रति स्म रक्षसो जहि इति भोगः अथर्व० ८.३.२३ ।

[50]स्वाहा वै सत्यसम्भूता ब्रह्मणो दुहितेति । शतपथे उक्तम् ।

[a]धात्री व्यापिनीशक्तिः विधात्री, ख, ग, घ ।

[b]कलात्मका, ग ।

[c]सवितुमिति, क ।

स्वाहा । भोग्यमिति स्वधा, इदं पितृभावः ।

यथा विष्णुर्मोक्षं ददाति । मोक्ष इति श्रीः । भोग्यरूपेण पृथिवी[a] भोग्या[51] । यथा रुद्रस्य मोक्षगुणादम्बा, भोगवृत्त्याऽम्बालिकेति द्वे । यथेन्द्रस्य त्यागवृत्त्या यज्ञाः, भोगवृत्त्येन्द्राणीति । यदा गुणा बहुधा उपवृत्त्या (तदा) बहुधा प्रतिरूपाणि भवन्तीति परिपश्यन्ति धीराः ।

यथा वैश्वानरस्य सप्त वृत्तय[b] उत्थानाद् विलयान्तं प्रवदन्ते । क्रमेण ताः स्निग्धा, धूम्रा, तप्ता, उत्तप्ता, दाहिका, भस्मा, निर्वाणेति । एतत्क्रमेणाग्निस्तपति। तद्गुणात् सप्त जिह्वा जायन्ते । जिह्वायाः प्रतिरूपाणि कल्पयन्ति। (पूर्वक्रमेण) काली, कराली, मनोजवा, सुलोहिता, सुधूम्रवर्णा, स्फुलिङ्गिनी, विश्वरुची इत्येताः सर्वाः स्त्रीरूपाः रूपभावे ग्राह्याः ।

यथा श्रुतिरिति महती । सा मेधारूपेण भारती सम्भवति । मेधाया यथा वाणी प्रभवति तथा श्रुतेर्महती महीयसी सरस्वती[52] जायते पराविद्याया रूपा । तत्तदाकारात्मिकाः पुष्टिभावेन लक्ष्मीदेवहूत्यादयः । एताः सर्वाः षोडशक्षेत्रस्य द्विपार्श्वे दैवक्षेत्रे तत्तद्रूपस्य जायाभावेनोपदैवतानीति सत्यं ध्येयम् – रूपकारा वास्तूद्गीथाः ।

उपदैवताद्रूपज्ञानं प्रसरति ॥ २२ ॥

सपर्यया भूतविद्याः[53] प्रशम्यन्ति ।

अरिसन्धा ध्येया ॥ २३ ॥

रूपधाराया वृत्तिरिति श्रेष्ठा ॥ २४ ॥

अथ रूपधारायाः शृणु वृत्तिभेदान् । यथा वृत्त्याः परिणामः । प्राजापत्य-प्रथम-वृत्तिर्मनः[54] । मनसो वृत्तिः प्राणः[55] । प्राणस्य वृत्तिः क्रिया। क्रिया[c] हि विद्या[56] । सा द्विविधा कथयन्ति ऋषयः । सदसद्विद्येयम्। या ऋतस्य धारा सा दैवक्रिया । सा परा विद्या । या अनृता सा अक्रिया । सा अदैवा अपरेति । तदपराज्ञानादसुराः । अहर्देवा आश्रयन्ते रात्रिमसुराः[57] ।

---

[51]एतेन विष्णोः श्रीदेवी भूदेवीति वृत्तिद्वयं सूचितम् ।

[52]सरस्वतीं देवयन्तो हवन्ते सरस्वतीमध्वरे तायमाने । सरस्वतीं सुकृतो हवन्ते सरस्वती दाशुषे वार्यं दात् ॥ अथर्व० १८.४.४५ ।

[53]लौकिक सिद्धयर्थे या विद्या सा भूतविद्या, घ ।

[54]मन इव हि प्रजापतिः तैत्तिरीयब्राह्मणे उक्तम् । (२.२.१.२)

[55]प्राणो वै हरिः स हि हरतीति । कौषीतकिब्राह्मणम् (१७.१) ।

[56]यद्यामं चक्रुर्निखनन्तो अग्रे कार्षीवणा अन्नविदो न विद्यया। (अथर्व० ६.११६.१) ।

[57]गोभिलगृह्यसूत्रे उक्तम् ।

---

[a]वसुन्धरा, ग, घ ।

[b]गुणाः, ग ।

[c]क्रिया विविधा इति, ग ।

येषां भयशोकाः सन्ति, यथा निकन्दिनः[a], कण्वजम्भाः, यातुधानाः, पृश्निपर्ण्यादयोऽवयोनयो गुणानुभेदेनैते सर्वेऽन्यार्थघातकाः सर्वेऽरिणो देवे च लोके यज्ञं घातयन्ति । एते सर्वे शलभक्षका बीभत्सरूपाः कोकमुखा रुक्षग्रीवाः शिमिजाः[58] । सर्वे वैराज्यकिम्पुरुषाः क्रुधा देवघातकाः । एतानरीन् षोडशकोष्ठकरूपक्षेत्रे मर्दितरूपेण जैवक्षेत्रे आचरन्ति प्रतिरूपचर्यायाम् । एते शलभक्षिणो देवानां भयदा भवन्ति । एतैस्तेषां दुःखम् । यज्ञात् तरन्ति । एतदर्थं केचिद्वा ऋषीन् ध्यायन्ति देवाः । देवयजनान्मुनयो मनस्विनो भवन्ति । दैवभावेन देवार्थं होतारोऽन्नसमिधः क्षिपन्ति वैश्वानरे । ऋषयः स्तोतारो भवन्ति ।

स्तोतॄणां[b] रूपे सुभगविशेषः[59] ॥ २५ ॥

गाथाः[60] पठन्ति । जना यजन्ति बहुधा रूपं सर्वक्रियाधारः मनुष्यलोके रूपविद्या । नादः सत्यमिति ध्येयम् । रूपं चरन्ति वास्तुवेदिनः स्थापका वास्तूद्गीथाः । स्तोतॄणां बहुधा पैला नालन्दिनोऽप्सरसो देवान् मोदयन्ति मोदकाः ।

कायमनोवाक्येन गायन्ति ते स्तुवका भ्राजिनः । यक्षा गायन्ति गाथाः । गन्धर्वा[61] देवानन्दार्थं नृत्यन्ति । सर्वे मिश्रयोनयः षोडशकोष्ठकक्षेत्रे ऊर्ध्व[c]कोणगतक्षेत्रे निधेयाः उपदैवक्षेत्रे ।

ये नरा दैवभावपरायणास्ते याजका । ध्याने तेषां सत्ता दिव्येव विभाति । तान् जैवक्षेत्रस्य पार्श्वगतक्षेत्रे अधःक्षेत्रद्वये न्यसेत् । एवं दैवरूपं षोडशकोष्ठकं ध्येयम् । ते तु धन्या ये क्रतूँश्च यज्ञानाचरन्ति उपासन्ते रूपाणि । रूपज्ञानाद् प्रज्ञा[d] प्रभवति लोके ।

प्रज्ञार्थमेतद् वास्तूपाख्यानम् ॥ २६ ॥

एतदर्थं प्रज्ञां व्याख्यापयाम इति । वास्तुसूत्रोपनिषद् भगवतः पिप्पलादस्य भव्यं व्याख्यानम् । यो जानाति स रूपाचार्यो भवतीति वास्तूद्गाता इति ध्येयम् । ये ध्यायन्ति ते मुक्ताः । परमऋषिभ्यो नमः ।

---

[58]शिमि-कर्म, तज्जाताः ।

[59]स्तोतुर्यो वचः शृणवद्धवं च मे इति ॥ (अथर्व० ६.२.१)

[60]कुन्तापसूक्तादयः खिलपाठाः । यथा शुनःशेपस्य शतगाथा इति ।

[61]योषित्कामा गन्धर्वा गन्धेन वै रूपेण चरन्तीति शतपथे उक्तम् ।

---

[a]निकन्दाः, ग ।

[b]स्तावकः, घ ।

[c]तिर्यक, ग ।

[d]यज्ञः, क ।

[e]Om. in ख, ग, घ ।

स्तुता मया वरदा वेदमाता

प्र चोदयन्तां पावमानी द्विजानाम् ।

आयुः प्राणं प्रजां पशुं कीर्तिं[62] द्रविणं ब्रह्मवर्चसम् ।

मह्यं दत्त्वा व्रजत ब्रह्मलोकम् ॥

(अथर्व० १९.७१.१)

इति ॐ नमो विश्वकर्मणे ।

ॐ विश्वकर्मा मा सप्तऋषिभिरुदीच्या दिशः पातु तस्मिन् क्रमे

तस्मिंछ्रये तां पुरं प्रैमि ।

स मा रक्षतु स मा गोपायतु तस्मा आत्मानं परि ददे स्वाहा ॥

इति

(अथर्व० १९.१७.७)

इति षष्ठप्रपाठकः समाप्तः ।

परमऋषिभ्यो नमः । परमऋषिभ्यो नमः ।

सम्पूर्णेयं वास्तुकर्मावतारपिप्पलादस्य आथर्वणीय-वास्तुसूत्रोपनिषत् ।
उड्रदेशिकेन आथर्वणोद्गात्रा सोमभट्टेन कृता परिशुद्धिटिप्पणी समाप्ता ।

[62] प्रासादविग्रहादिषु ।

COLOPHON क

इदम् आथर्वणीय वास्तुसूत्रोपनिषद् अथर्वणाचार्यसोमभट्टेन कृत विषयबोधिनिटिप्पणी समेत लिखितं मया बांकी कुरुमचइनि ग्रामवासिना वास्तुशास्त्रि क़ामदेव उद्गाथा श्री रामचन्द्रदेव भूपालस्य पञ्चदशाङ्के राजा हरिचन्दन नृपार्थ । ॐ नमो महादेव्यै ॥

सूत्रपाठः

प्रथमप्रपाठकस्य सूत्राणि

1. वास्तोष्पतिर्ज्ञेय इति ।
2. षट्शिल्पाङ्गप्रयोगेण प्रजनयन्ति रूपाणि ।
3. यूप इदं ज्योतिः ।
4. वृत्तज्ञानं रेखाज्ञानं च यो जानाति स स्थापकः ।
5. शिल्पात् प्रतिमा जायन्ते ।
6. स प्रवह्णः शिल्पसूत्राध्यायं स्थापकविद्यां चावदत् ।
7. शरीरमूर्तिरहिते मन आवेश्य विशेषेण विकल्पिदोषयुक्तं भवति ।
8. वास्तु षडङ्गमिति श्रेष्ठम् ।
9. षड्धा शैलं ज्ञेयम् ।
10. शैलादङ्गरागज्ञानं प्रसरति ।

द्वितीयप्रपाठकस्य सूत्राणि

1. निर्दिष्टार्थकप्रतिमा ग्राह्या ।
2. पातनं प्रथमा क्रिया ।
3. मर्दनं द्वितीया क्रिया ।
4. विलमिति मर्म ज्ञेयम् ।
5. न कृत्यरूपार्थं रेखाकरणं कर्त्तव्यम् ।
6. आदौ वृत्तम् वृत्त मिति विश्वम् ।
7. एकैकस्य संयोगे एकीभवति इति तस्य भावः । वृत्तं हि पूर्णम् ।
8. रेखान्वये सर्वाङ्गानि न्यासय ।
9. तेजांसि सरलरेखाः ।
10. नाभौ रूपकर्म प्रारभ्यते ।
11. प्राजापत्यरीत्या वृत्तं हि तेजस्तदाऽपांभासे चतुरस्रम् ।
12. कर्णद्वयं मरुद्भावेन आचरन्ति ।
13. धरेव कर्णिकक्षेत्रमाकर्षयन्ति स्थापकाः ।
14. लब्धबिन्दुः रसायाः प्राणः ।
15. त्रिहुताग्निः स्मर्यतेऽपि च लोके ।
16. निम्नगास्त्रिहुता आप इति ।
17. षट्कोणको हि आकर्षणीविद्याविशेषः ।
18. यथा रूपे तथा यूपेऽनुच्छेदान्ता ग्राह्याः ।

19. खनित्रप्रकारो ध्येयः ।
20. सूत्रायने रेखाः सुभगा भवन्ति ।
21. खिलपञ्जरज्ञानं श्रेष्ठम् ।
22. उत्थितरेखा अग्निरूपाः पार्श्वगा अबरूपाः तिर्यग्रेखा मरुद्रूपा इति ।
23. रूपसौभगाद् ध्यानभावो जायते ।
24. अग्निरेखायामुत्तुङ्गरूपाणि जायन्ते ।
25. अब्रेखायामुत्सुकरूपाणि जायन्ते ।
26. मारुतरेखायां तैजसरूपाणि ।
27. रेखाज्ञानं सर्वमिति ज्ञेयम् ।

तृतीयप्रपाठकस्य सूत्राणि

1. रूपस्य भावो मुख्यः ।
2. भावानुसारतो रेखाविधानमिति ज्ञेयम् ।
3. तेषां बहुधा कृत्यं श्रेयः ।
4. न्यासार्थं कालबोधो ध्येय इति ।
5. तद्भेदनेऽभिमन्त्रेयन्ति खनित्राणि ।
6. खनित्रपञ्चकं श्रेष्ठम् ।
7. रूपप्रकर्षार्थं रूपाङ्गं स्निग्धमिति ।
8. शिल्पकाराः प्रलेपयन्ति द्रावकरसम् ।
9. एषा हेतिविद्या श्रेष्ठा ।
10. रक्षार्थं पर्णमणिः परिधेयः ।
11. भेदनादङ्गसौभगं प्रभवति ।
12. रेखानुपातेनाङ्गानि निधेयानीति श्रेष्ठकृत्यम् ।
13. गाथानुप्रासे लक्षणं व्यक्तं भवति ।
14. ध्यानप्रयोगे रूपसौष्ठवं स्पष्टं भवति ।
15. यथा प्रकृतिस्तथा रूपलक्षणम् ।
16. अङ्गानि अर्धाकले सुषमं ध्येयानि ।
17. हर्सावधि उभयदिशि चोर्ध्वे न वर्धयेत् ।
18. रक्षाविधानेन विघ्नघातयः ।
19. रेखाक्रमेण भेदनं चतुर्धा ज्ञेयम् ।
20. नेम्योत्तरे रूपाङ्गं न वर्धयेत् ।
21. खनित्रचालनविधिर्ध्येयविशेषः ।

चतुर्थप्रपाठकस्य सूत्राणि

1. प्रतीतात् प्रतीकः ।
2. रूपादङ्गानि सञ्जायन्ते ।
3. अतो द्विधा ब्रह्म रूपवद् भवति ।
4. रूपार्थं कोष्ठका मुख्याः ।
5. वर्गीकरणं मुख्यकृत्यम् ।
6. कोष्ठकान्तराले रूपस्यावयवो ध्येयः ।
7. परिमिताङ्गहाराद् भावलक्षणानि जायन्ते ।
8. कोष्ठके व्यतिक्रान्ते रूपमवद्यं भवति ।
9. शुल्वं यज्ञस्य साधनं शिल्पं रूपस्य साधनम् ।
10. शिल्पकाराणां रूपशैले रूपशालादि ध्येयम् ।
11. यूपाद्रूपं रूपाद् यूप इति स्वभावः ।
12. यूपस्य मानं ध्येयम् ।
13. षड्भागस्य प्रयोगो ध्येयः ।
14. पुरुषस्य रूपेऽङ्गचत्वारोऽष्टाङ्गक्रमेणोपजायन्ते ।
15. पालाशदण्डरज्जुसंयोगे रेखामानय ।
16. निम्नादूर्ध्वावधि सदा रेखादीनाचर ।
17. पुरुषस्तम्भ इव स्तम्भो वै यज्ञस्य रूपम् ।
18. यथा स्तम्भस्य दशाङ्गं तथा पुरुषस्य दशयज्ञप्रज्ञाश्च ।
19. स्थापकाचार्या स्तम्भाद्रूपं बोधयन्ति ।
20. स्तम्भः कामचारिणस्त्रिधामानयन्ति ।
21. दैवयज्ञार्थं यूपः ।
22. तदा पितृमेधार्थं वृषस्तम्भं मिथुनस्तम्भं कामचारा होमे रोपयन्ति ।
23. तद्बोधे मानुषा रूपज्ञा भवन्ति ।
24. पुरुषस्य रूपाकले कोष्ठकस्याधो भावरूपं प्रसरति ।
25. दशाङ्गयूपे रूपे इति तस्य भावः समानः ।
26. ब्रह्मकीलाधारः, ब्रह्मकीलेन सह क्षेत्रं विभाजय ।
27. अङ्गादङ्गं सञ्जायते ।
28. रेखासंयोगे तत्क्षेत्रेऽङ्गानि सौभगानि भवन्ति ।
29. क्षेत्रनेमिं रोधयेदिति ।

पञ्चमप्रपाठकस्य सूत्राणि

1. भावस्यारोपणं रूपकर्मणि विधेयम् ।
2. कर्म भावस्य प्रदायकम् ।
3. भावस्याऽऽधारो रसः ।
4. मनसि वृत्तिर्बहुधा प्रजायते । तदा भिन्नभिन्नरसाद्रूपं नैकं भवति ।
5. नवधा रसः ।
6. प्रथमरसः शृङ्गारः ।
7. शृङ्गाररूपार्थमब्रेखा ग्राह्याः ।
8. स हासो द्वितीयरसः ।
9. मुखलक्षणाद् रसं जानन्ति सर्वे ईक्षणेन ।
10. स तृतीयः करुणरस भाव इति ।
11. रौद्रः चतुर्थो रसः ।
12. तिर्यग्रेखायां रूपाङ्गभावः प्रकटो भवति ।
13. स वीरभावः पञ्चमः ।
14. वैरभावे उत्कटे भयङ्करो भवति । स वैलक्षणः षष्ठरसः ।
15. कुरूपाः क्षिप्ताङ्गाः मारुतरेखायामिति स सप्तमः ।
16. शान्तभावः, सोऽष्टमो रसः ।
17. भावानुगतरूपाणि चतुर्धा मुख्यानि ।
18. लोके भावबोधस्य हेतुर्मनः ।
19. मनुष्याणां वृत्तिर्मुख्येति ।
20. सङ्कल्पाद् विकल्पः ।
21. एष भुवनकोषो देहानुभूत्याः क्रमः ।
22. अरूपाद्रूपं तस्य फलम् ।
23. दिशानुसृतेर्दिशापालानुपासन्ते ।
24. एवं दैवभेदान्मार्गभेदा जायन्ते ।

षष्ठः प्रपाठकस्य सूत्राणि

1. न्यासधारणा श्रेष्ठा ।
2. वृत्त्या दैवचिन्तने भेदः सञ्जायते ।
3. लक्षणप्रकाशार्थं शिल्पविद्या ।
4. न्यासोऽलङ्कारमुद्रायुधबाध्रकक्षवाहनोपदेवारिस्तुवकक्रमेण रूपनवाङ्गमिति ध्येयम् ।
5. तिस्रः रेखाः श्रेष्ठाः ।
6. रूपक्षेत्रे कोष्ठकालिर्मुख्या ।
7. षोडशकोष्ठकमध्ये रूपाणि प्रभवन्ति तद्रूपार्थं श्रेष्ठम् ।
8. विलमिति मर्म, ब्रह्मेव निधेयम् ।
9. षोडशकोष्ठकप्रमाणविभागस्तु ब्रह्मदैवजैवोपदैवयाजकक्रमेण पञ्चधा ध्येयः ।
10. रूपाङ्गं चतुर्धेति विशेषः ।
11. बिन्दुर्ब्रह्मेव ब्रह्मध्रुवम् ।
12. ब्रह्म सत्यादौ ।
13. ब्रह्मबिन्द्ववलम्बनेन रूपाङ्गानि सौभगानि भवन्ति ।
14. अलङ्करणं दैवभुषणमिति ।
15. प्रतिमुचः रतिः प्रसरति ।
16. करमुद्रा रूपस्य भावं ज्ञापयति ।
17. बाध्रं बलं ज्ञापयति रूपे ।
18. आसनषट्कं मुख्यम् ।
19. गुणानुसृतं रूपत्रयम् ।
20. वाहनं रूपस्य प्रकृतिज्ञापकविशेषः ।
21. उपदैवतं प्रतिरूपमिति ।
22. उपदैवताद्रूपज्ञानं प्रसरति ।
23. अरिसन्धा ध्येया ।
24. रूपधाराया वृत्तिरिति श्रेष्ठा ।
25. स्तोतॄणां रूपे सुभगविशेषः।
26. प्रज्ञार्थमेतद् वास्तूपाख्यानम् ।

GLOSSARY

abhaya-mudrā: handpose bestowing fearlessness or safety.

abhijit: name of a constellation.

abrekhā: "water-line", horizontal.

adhvaryu: officiating priest who recites the verses of the Yajurveda.

Agni: sacrificial Fire, Vedic divinity of Fire, symbolised by an upright triangle.

agnirekhā: "fire-line", vertical.

āhuti: sacrificial offering.

akāmya: worship or sacrifice done without desire for worldly ends such as sons, wealth etc., hence spiritual worship.

ākarṣaṇī-vidyā: science of attraction, the hexagram as a means of attracting the gods and also the devotees.

alaṅkaraṇa: ornaments, decoration.

aṅga: both the body and the limbs; in the text it is not always clear to which of the two it refers.

aṅgaprayoga: the arrangement of the limbs (or body) of the figure(s) in the panel, following the lines of the *pañjara*.

Āṅgirasa: descendent of Aṅgiras, one of the seven Ṛṣis, seer of hymns of the ṚV and AV; one of the disciples of Pippalāda.

ardhākala: half-relief.

āsana: posture; seat.

āśāpālāḥ: the guardians of the quarters (*dikpāla*), deities presiding over the space-directions.

Ātharvaṇāṅgirasa: descending from Atharvan and Aṅgiras, a designation of the AV; in the VSU a name of a Ṛṣi, disciple of Pippalāda (the same as Āṅgirasa).

bhayaṅkara: the terrifying mood, one of the nine *rasas*.

bībhatsa: disgust, one of the nine *rasas*.

bīja: seed (of the mantra), mystical letter or syllable.

bindu: drop, dot, point; crossing-point of the lines of the *pañjara*.

brahmabindu: the central point (*marman*).

brahmamaṇḍala: the central circle of the *pañjara*.

brahmakīla: the vertical middle line.

brahmakṣetra: the four central compartments of the grid for the main figure.

brahmarandhra: opening in the crown of the head, yogic centre.

brahmāṇḍa: "the egg of Brahman", the cosmos.

caturasra: a quadrangle, rectangle or square.

dairghyarekhā: vertical line.

darbha: sacred grass.

dhāraṇā: the act of holding firmly, mental concentration, firm understanding, clear conception.

dharmapuruṣa: "holy man", honorific title.

dhātupuṭitā: a kind of stone with metal lines, considered unfit for sculpture.

dhvaja: flag.

dhvaja-mudrā: handpose with extended hands.

dhvani: sound, the suggested meaning of a word or poetry.

dhyāna: inner vision, meditation, visualization of a particular aspect of the divinity, which is described in a *śloka* and represented iconographically.

dhyānarūpa: an image for meditation (in contrast to an image for worship or *arcāmūrti*), or any divine image which is conform to the *dhyāna*.

daivakṣetra: "divine field", the two upper central compartments of the sixteenfold grid for the head or aureole of the main figure; or the two central side-fields for the Śaktis (VI.21).

drāvakarasa: liquid to assist the fusion of metals, or to soften the stone; distilled mineral acids.

dvimukhī: two-pointed instrument for measuring equal distances.

dyotāṅga: light-part of the figure or Yūpa, from the throat to the top of the head.

ekāśrayi: a principle of composition, where the body or main limb of the image is placed along one straight line.

gāthā: sacred songs or verses of non-Vedic origin.

Gāyatrī: the most sacred mantra of the ṚV (III.62.10), addressed to Savitṛ, the Sun, recited by all twice-born morning and evening.

ghūrṇikā: points of the compass, consisting of a wooden stick with iron point, connected with a rope to a ɪ eg.

grābhakāra: sculptor, influence of the vernacular, probably derived from Skt. *grāvan*, stone.

gṛdhradanti: type of chisel with teeth.

guṇa: quality, constituent, esp. the three constituents of primordial nature (*prakṛti*): *sattva, rajas, tamas*; also the divine quality or attribute (*saguṇa*).

harsa: border-line of the panel, boundary (derivation not clear).

hāsa: laughter.

hāsya: humour, one of the nine basic sentiments.

heti: instrument, implement.

hetividyā: science of the implements, method of using the instruments.

hiraṇyarekhikā: a type of stone with yellow (golden) lines.

hotṛ: Vedic priest who offers oblations and recites verses of the ṚV.

iṅgida: probably the same as *iṅguda*, the medicinal tree *terminalia catappa* whose oil is used.

jaivāṅga: the vital part of the body of the figure, from knee to navel.

jaivakṣetra: the field of the living beings or animal-field: the two central lowest compartments of the sixteenfold grid of the panel (below the *brahmakṣetra*) in which the *vāhanas* etc. are represented.

jaṅgiḍa: an amulet for protection.

jaṭā: matted hair of ascetics, and of Śiva.

jaṭāveda: a particular way of recitation of Vedic texts.

kakṣā: recess, interior, niche.

kalpanā: fashioning, creating, imagination.

kāmacārin: lit. the one who moves at will, who acts freely, according to his desire; here applied to the artist.

karamudrā: handpose.

karṇarekhā: corner-line, diagonal.

karṇikakṣetra: corner-field, rhombus.

karuṇa: the sentiment of compassion, sorrow, one of the nine *rasas*.

kāruśālā: sculptor's hall, workshop.

khādira: wood of the tree *acacia catechu*.

khaṇḍāśrayi: compositional principle, when only a part of a limb of the figure follows a line.

khanitra: instrument used for carving, chisel.

khanana: digging, carving.

khilapañjara: compositional diagram, lit. cage of the *khila* (open field, empty surface).

khilavidyā: supplementary knowledge, supplements to the Veda; in the VSU also the knowledge of the compositional diagram.

kila: wooden peg; line.

kīrttyāvāsa: "abode of glory", the image-panel.

koṣṭhaka: grid, net-work of vertical and horizontal lines for dividing the panel, consisting of sixteen fields.

kṛtya-rūpa (*kṛtya-mūrti*): image made of clay, for temporary use.

kukkuṭāsana: crouching posture.

kumbha: water-pot, symbol of fullness.

Kumbhīka: demon or evil spirit.

kuṇḍa: pit for the sacrificial fire, of various shapes, the enclosure is made of bricks.

kuśa: sacred grass.

kuṣṭharasa: the extract (juice) of the plant *costus speciosus* or *arabicus*.

kuṭumbhaka: mallet for chiselling, hammer.

Kuvitsa: name of one of the disciples of Pippalāda.

lakṣaṇa: characteristic, feature, attribute of a god or image.

lāṅgalī: a type of chisel (like a plough).

lāñjī: a type of chisel.

līlāvigraha: illustrative panels, representing mythological stories (the myths or legends being understood as *līlā*, the play of the gods), not intended for worship.

madhyaprastha: horizontal middle line.

madhyarekhā: vertical middle line.

mahīlukā: name of the sacred cow in the AV.

mānadaṇḍa: measuring rod.

maṇḍala: circle; symbolic diagram used in the ritual.

mardanam: rubbing, polishing of the stone.

marman: core, central point of the panel, centre of the circle.

māruta: derived from Marut, the wind, "wind-line", diagonal.

Maya: name of an Asura, the architect of the *daityas*, author of the Mayamata.

mekhalā: girdle, belt; the layers around an altar (*kuṇḍa*).

Meru: mythical mountain, the centre of the earth, *axis mundi*.

mithunacchandas: "metre of union", the hexagram.

mithunastambha: pillar with the representation of a pair of boars, used for fertility rites and for protection.

mudrā: hand gesture, with symbolical significance.

mukhyapratimā: main image for worship.

mūlarekhā: fundamental line; there are eight: the four border-lines, the central vertical and horizontal and the two diagonals.

muṣṭi: measure, from the elbow to the clenched hand.

nemi: circumference of the circle.

nyāsa: lit. placing, fixing, laying down; the harmonious setting of the constituent parts of the image-panel: composition.

pālāśa: wood of the tree *buta frondosa*.

pañjara: lit. a cage or a skeleton; compositional diagram.

Parjanya: the rain-god, personification of the rain-cloud, invoked for fertility.

pārthivāṅga: earth-part, lowest part of the figure or Yūpa, from the feet to the knee.

pāṭhāṃūlikā: root of the plant *clypea hernandifolia*, which has medicinal properties and is used for magical purposes (AV).

piṇḍa: ball or globe; rice-ball offered to the ancestors; the body as microcosm.

pitṛvila: hole on top of the Yūpa for the offering to the forefathers, in which the flag is fixed.

Prakṛti: nature, primordial nature (fem.), one of the two fundamental principles in Sāṃkhya (cf. Puruṣa).

prāṇa: breath, life-breath, vital energy.

prāṇāṅga: part of the life-breath of the figure or Yūpa, from the navel to the throat.

prastharekhā: horizontal line.

pratīka: symbol.

pratimā: image, icon.

pratimāśālā: image-hall, cave-temple.

pratirūpa: image, likeness, representation, imitation of an original form; in the narrow sense secondary image (such as the attendant figures, etc.).

pūrṇākala: free-standing sculpture, figure in the round.

Puruṣa: Man, Person, the archetypal Man, the supreme Being, the spiritual principle in man.

rajas: principle of energy, activity, one of the three qualities of *prakṛti* (*guṇa*).

rajju: rope, used for measuring.

rasa: lit. juice, essence, flavour; the (eight or nine) basic sentiments of the aesthetic experience.

raudra: the violent or fierce mood, one of the nine *rasas*.

rekhā: line.

rekhānvaya: (limbs) following the lines of the *pañjara*.

rekhāvāsa: lit. abode made of lines, the compositional diagram which houses the image.

rūpa: form, archetype or original form; image.

rūpāṅganyāsa: composition (placing) of the limbs or parts of the figure.

saikatālikā: sandstone.

śailabhedana: stone-carving.

śakti: female energy, consort of the god.

samarekhā: straight line.

samavarṇā: stone of one colour, e.g. granite.

śaṅkhadrāva: a solvent for dissolving shells.

śānta: peace, the last of the nine *rasas*.

śatakeśī vṛṣa: the hundred-haired Bull, a symbol of the Sun (with innumerable rays) and of Rudra.

ṣaṭkoṇaka: hexagram, consisting of two intersecting triangles.

ṣaṭśilpāṅga: "six limbs of the body of Śilpa", six disciplines of Art (cf. I.8).

sattva: purity, goodness, one of the three qualities of *prakṛti* (*guṇa*).

satya-bindu: central point in the upper part of the panel, corresponding to the *ājñā cakra*.

saumya: peaceful, gentle, graceful; one type of image representing the graceful aspect of the god (cf. *ugra*).

saumya-yūpa: plain round Yūpa.

siddhi: power, extraordinary faculty, perfection.

Śilpa: arts and crafts, here mainly sculpture.

śilpakāra, śilpī: artisan, sculptor, artist.

śilpakarman: work of Art, sculpture.

Śilpakāśyapa: Vedic teacher mentioned in the Bṛhad. Up. VI.5.3, one of the disciples of Pippalāda; the Kāśyapa Śilpa (Śāstra) is attributed to him.

skambha: pillar, the central post of the universe, *axis mundi*.

sparśī: compositional principle when a limb of the image is only touching a line of the *pañjara*.

śrāddha: ancestor-worship, ceremony for the dead.

śṛṅgāra: love, the erotic sentiment, one of the nine *rasas*.

śroṇi: arrangement of the bricks of the Vedic altar.

stambha: pillar (also *skambha*).

sthaṇḍila: sacrificial ground.

sthāpaka: one who establishes or erects an image or a temple: architect and/or sculptor, chief architect.

sthāpakavidyā: science of the architect and/or sculptor, architecture.

sūcīmukhā: a type of chisel with sharp point.

Śulva: the Vedic science of making altars, platforms etc., laid down in the Śulvasūtras, ancient Indian geometry.

svāhā: ritual exclamation (hail!), the oblation personified as a goddess.

tāla-niryāsa: law of measurement and proportion.

tamas: darkness, inertia, one of the three qualities of *prakṛti* (*guṇa*).

tāmrā: very hard stone.

Tāpinī: last part of the name of several Upaniṣads belonging to the AV.

tiryagrekhā: oblique line.

trihuta: lit. threefold offered; a triangle.

udumbara: the tree *ficus glomerata* and its wood.

udgītha: Sāmavedic chant; the syllable OM; here used as a title for a priest related to the Sāmaveda and AV.

ugra: powerful, violent, fierce; one type of image representing the terrible aspect of the god (cf. *saumya*).

vāhana: vehicle, animal serving as vehicle to the god.

Vaiśravaṇa: a teacher of Śilpa, author of the Vaiśrāvaṇa Śilpācāra.

vaiśvadeva: offering to all the gods.

Vaiśvānara: "belonging to all men", an aspect of Agni, the sacrificial Fire.

vajra: thunderbolt, Indra's weapon; a hard instrument; white stone powder for drawing lines.

vajrā: a type of chisel.

vajralabdhā: type of stone with layers of mineral.

varamudrā: the boon-bestowing hand gesture.

Vāstoṣpati: the Lord of the house, protecting deity of the house, identified with Viśvakarman.

Vāstu: site, building, house: architecture, here also sculpture.

vāstusthāpakavidyā: the science of architecture (and sculpture).

vikalpa: differentiation, imagination, variety, diversity.

vila: hole, centre of the panel.

vīra: heroism, one of the nine basic sentiments (*rasa*).

Viśvakarman: "the all-maker", divine architect, prototype of the human architect.

Vṛṣastambha: bull-pillar, wooden post with a bull on its top, used in *śrāddha* ceremonies.

vṛtta: circle.

Yātudhāna: a kind of demon or evil spirit (AV).

yugalāśrayi: compositional principle where two limbs of the image are set on corresponding lines.

Yūpa: sacrificial post for tying the victim (in the animal sacrifice), pillar.

INDEX